W9-AVY-769

THE AMERICA

The Story of the World's Most Famous Yacht

THE AMERICA

The Story of the World's Most Famous Yacht

by CHARLES BOSWELL

DAVID McKAY COMPANY, INC.
New York

THE AMERICA

The Story of the World's

Most Famous Yacht

Library of Congress Catalog Card Number: 68-10959

MANUFACTURED IN THE UNITED STATES OF AMERICA

VAN REES PRESS • NEW YORK

For

Pat,
John, Anne,
and
Thomas

Contents

Acknowledgments

THE library of the New York Yacht Club houses a fine and extensive collection of books, periodicals, news clippings and documents related to yachts and yachting. I thank Admiral Joseph J. Clark, USN (Ret.), for graciously acting as my host at the Club; Robert H. Wessmann, Chairman of the Library Committee, for access to the collection; and Sohei Hohri, the Club's knowledgeable librarian, for placing before me a wealth of material pertinent to the yacht *America*'s long and eventful career.

Other librarians in this country who have generously participated in my quest for information include:

Elizabeth Alexander, Librarian, P. K. Yonge Library of Florida History, University of Florida, Gainesville.

Margaret Butterfield Andrews, Assistant Librarian in Charge of Special Collections, University of Rochester Library, Rochester, N.Y.

Audrey Broward, General Services Division, Jacksonville Public Library, Jacksonville, Fla.

Ida M. Cohen, Reference Librarian, New York State Library, Albany.

Charles W. Davis, Assistant to the President and Director of Library Development, G. W. Blunt White Library, Marine Historical Association, Inc., Mystic Seaport, Mystic, Conn.

John L. Lochhead, Librarian, The Mariners Museum, Newport News, Va.

James W. Patton, Director, Southern Historical Collection,

The University of North Carolina Library, Chapel Hill, N.C.
Virginia Rugheimer, Librarian, Charleston Library Society, Charleston, S.C.

Samuel C. Williams, Curator of Special Collections, Library, Stevens Institute of Technology, Hoboken, N.J.

In addition, in England, my researches have been abetted through the kind efforts of M. W. B. Sanderson, Librarian, and D. Goddard, Assistant Librarian, National Maritime Museum, Greenwich; and N. Stanton, Research Section, Illustrated Newspaper Group, London.

Also in England, Martin C. Carroll, Jr., Cultural Attaché, American Embassy, London, provided me with guidance to potential sources of British material; T. W. B. Shaw, Captain, RN (Ret.), Her Majesty's Secretary, Royal Western Yacht Club of England, Plymouth, did his utmost to help; P. Sullivan, Deputy Registrar, General Register and Record Office of Shipping and Seamen, Board of Trade, Cardiff, Wales, supplied needed information; and the Reverend Claude D. T. Sparshott, Vicar Emeritus at Napton-on-the-Hill, Southam, Warwickshire, proved himself both tireless and ingenious in running down clues.

I offer my special thanks to Alexander A. Lawrence of Savannah, Ga., lawyer and historian, whose sophisticated exertions located material essential to the saga of the *America* during her Confederate interlude; to Thomas R. Neblett, Ph.D., of Wayne State University, Detroit, who generously shared with me certain facts about the yacht and her succession of owners that he had collected over the years; and to Frederick Stevens Hicks, Naval History Division, Office of the Chief of Naval Operations, Department of the Navy, Washington, who supplied me with detailed data concerning the many naval officers involved with the *America* throughout the decades—one, his great-grandfather, Thomas Holdup Stevens, retired as a Rear Admiral in 1881.

I am further appreciative of inquiries made on my behalf in Washington by William A. Albaugh, III, of Falls Church,

Va., an authority on Confederate arms; and in Jacksonville, Fla., by Frederick Williams, a stockbroker interested in local history; Dena Snodgrass, a member of the Jacksonville Historical Society; Dorothy G. Schlobohm, of the Jacksonville Area Chamber of Commerce; and Jessie-Lynne Kerr, of the *Florida Times Union,* who employed her talents as a present-day newspaperwoman to cover the *America's* visits to Jacksonville more than a century ago.

For information concerning the last years and the destruction of the yacht *America,* I thank Marjorie Rigg, an antiques dealer of Holly Beach Farm, Annapolis, Md., whose husband, H. K. Rigg, edits *The Skipper,* a nautical magazine; Jack A. Garrow, Lieutenant, USN, formerly Public Information Officer at the Naval Academy; and Jack M. White, Lieutenant Commander, USN, the Academy's Public Affairs Officer at present.

CHARLES BOSWELL
Woodstock, New York

ONE

"A Violation of Naval Architecture"

THREE MEN share the primary credit, in amounts by no means equal, for building the yacht *America*. The three were George Steers, William H. Brown, and John Cox Stevens.

George Steers formed a mental image of the yacht, drawing on his experience with other swift vessels he had designed in the past. Then he carved her model, shaped her lines on a mold-loft floor, and for several months supervised every detail of her construction.

William H. Brown owned a shipyard in New York City at 12th Street and the East River. Brown realized that while his yard, geared for the building of commercial craft, had never before produced a yacht, there had to be a first time for everything. Moreover, Brown knew George Steers and so respected his talents that he was willing to provide the facilities, materials, and skilled labor needed for his friend's risky project.

John Cox Stevens, Commodore of the New York Yacht Club since its inception, had sailed other craft designed by George Steers. He interested in this new vessel five additional members of the Club, and together they formed a syndicate. They contracted ahead of the yacht's building to buy her for a stipulated sum, provided she was finished and ready to sail by a specified date and met certain difficult conditions of seaworthiness and speed.

The *America* contributed enormously, both in this country and abroad, to the sport of yachting. She lasted in substance for nearly a century, and during this amazingly long life for a yacht she faithfully served not merely her original owners, but a succession of others: titled Britishers, the Confederate States Navy, the United States Navy, and a Massachusetts politician famous more for his venalities than for his virtues. And while the *America* lasted long in substance, she lasted even longer in spirit, for her spirit is alive today, embodied in the first cup she captured. Known at the outset as the 100-Guinea Cup, that trophy was soon named anew the America's Cup, as well it should have been. It remains a perpetual challenge trophy and a symbol of the best in aquatic sportsmanship.

The narrative to follow, however, is only peripherally the story of the America's Cup. Rather, it is the story of the *America* herself and the men concerned with building, buying and sailing her. Since no story worth the telling should begin at the beginning, this one will abide by the rule and start a bit further along, although the *America* even then was lacking a name.

Early in 1851, Sir Henry Bulwer, the British Ambassador to the United States, inspected a schooner yacht under construction in New York and was impressed with her radical and yet graceful lines. A few weeks later, while on a mission home to England, he spoke of the vessel to friends, and as a result the Earl of Wilton, Commodore of the Royal Yacht Squadron, addressed the following letter to Commodore Stevens of the New York Yacht Club:

7 Grosvenor Square, London
22nd February, 1851

Sir:

Understanding from Sir H. Bulwer that a few members of the New York Yacht Club are building a schooner which it is their intention to bring over to England this summer, I have taken the liberty of writing to you, in your capacity of Commodore, to request you to convey to them and to any friends that may accompany them on board the yacht, an invitation on the part of myself and the members of the Royal Yacht Squadron to become visitors of the Club-House at Cowes during their stay in England.

For myself, I may be permitted to say that I shall have great pleasure in extending to your countrymen any civility that lies in my power, and shall be very glad to avail myself of any improvements in shipbuilding that the industry and skill of your nation have enabled you to elaborate. I remain, Sir,

Your servant,
Wilton,
Commodore, R.Y.S.

It is apparent from this letter that Lord Wilton was as much a diplomat as Sir Henry Bulwer. While he struck gracious notes of cordiality and hospitality, his tune gave no promise that should the New Yorkers put in an appearance at Cowes, Isle of Wight—the yacht-racing capital of Britain—they would find some vessel or vessels willing to give their yacht a run for her money. His Lordship, in other words, skillfully avoided committing any craft flying the Royal Yacht Squadron pennant to a contest with a sight-unseen opponent.

In replying, John Cox Stevens used his pen with equal fluency and even greater subtlety. He pretended to have read in Lord Wilton's letter passages it did not contain, and he spoke glowingly of the seafaring skills of Royal Yacht Squadron members. At the same time, he deprecated his own abilities in this direction, as well as those of the members of the club he headed. Should the exchange of letters appear in the press, he knew that he could, if he wished, force Lord Wilton's hand. And yet if in his judgment it would not be to the best interest of the New York Yacht Club to race against some patently superior British vessel, he had an easy out. This is the letter Stevens wrote:

New York, March 26, 1851

My Lord:

I regret that an accident prevented the reception of your letter until after the packet of the 12th had sailed. I take the earliest opportunity offered to convey to the gentlemen of the Royal Yacht Squadron, and to yourself, the expression of our warmest thanks for your invitation to visit the Club House at Cowes. Some four or five friends and myself have a yacht on the stocks which we hope to launch in the course of two or three weeks.

Should she answer the sanguine expectations of her builder, and fulfill the stipulations he has made, we propose to avail ourselves of your friendly bidding and take with good grace the sound thrashing we are likely to get by venturing our longshore craft on your rough waters.

I fear the energy and experience of your persevering yachtsmen will prove an overmatch for the industry and skill of their aspiring competitors. Should the schooner fail to meet the expectations of her builder, not the least of our regrets will be to have lost the opportunity of personally thanking the gentlemen of the Royal Yacht Squadron and yourself for your considerate kindness.

With the hope that we may have the pleasure of reciprocating a favor so frankly bestowed, I remain your lordship's most obedient servant,

John C. Stevens
Commodore New York Yacht Club

The first picture of the yacht *America* appeared, not in a journal indigenous to the land of her birth, but in England. A blotchy woodcut showing the yacht building on the stocks occupied a generous portion of the first page of *The Illustrated London News* for Saturday, March 15, 1851, a date in between the letters exchanged by Commodores Wilton and Stevens. *The Illustrated London News* was then a highly popular weekly with an international circulation, and it remains so today. There is cause to suspect that, because of its widespread readership, the yacht's likeness and an accompanying story were planted in it either by Sir Henry Bulwer or by the Commercial Attaché of his Washington legation—perhaps by royal command. On May 1, the Great International Exhibition, or Industrial World's Fair, was scheduled to open in a building covering twenty acres in Hyde Park, London, and to last until mid-October. Queen Victoria's consort, her beloved Prince Albert, had taken on the directorship of the Exhibition, and to insure its success every device imaginable was used to lure to England visitors of all interests and breeds, yachtsmen and yachting buffs included.

The story supporting the picture of the vessel on the stocks bore the simple heading "New American Yacht," and this is the essential portion of what it said:

> The yacht of which we have engraved a sketch is now building at New York, to compete with the English yachts next summer at Cowes.
>
> The builder, Mr. W. H. Brown, is to receive about one-third more than her value (say £24 a ton) if she succeeds in outsailing any competitors of the same tonnage in England. Her construction is on a novel principle: drawing 10 ft. aft, she tapers away forward to about half that draught, and is totally without any gripe. Aft, her keel is about 30 inches deep; diminishing in depth forward, and gradually ascending in a graceful curve into cutwater and stem. Her tonnage, 175 tons; length 94 feet; extreme breadth, 23 ft. 6 in.; depth of hold 9 ft. . . . The intelligent foreman, Mr. Steers, as well as the American gentlemen who are to own her if she succeeds, are very sanguine of success.
>
> This is an original and spirited undertaking, and will, if successful, completely alter the present system of yacht architecture. We do not, however, think she can compete with the sharp and deep English yachts. Whatever the result may be, it cannot fail of being extremely interesting, and valuable to both countries. As a model, she is artistic, although rather a violation of the old established ideas of naval architecture.

While somewhat faulty in describing the embryonic yacht and grievously faulty in prophesying that she would not fare very well in foreign competition, the story was otherwise reasonably sound. Sound, that is, except for the author's delineation of the roles played in the production of the vessel by George Steers and William H. Brown.

In terms of formal education, it is doubtful whether George Steers advanced further than grade school. And yet even in his youth he became acquainted, through trial and observation, with those laws of physics and mathematics applicable to water and wind and the shape that solid objects should assume the better to float lightly on the one and move swiftly and evenly along, propelled by the other.

George was the son of Henry Steer, an English shipwright, who immigrated to the United States in 1819 and obtained employment in the Washington Navy Yards. Henry brought with him his wife and their two daughters and two sons, James R. and Henry T., and soon afterwards balanced the family's surname by affixing an ultimate "s," making it Steers. The next child was George, born in Washington on July 20, 1820, and soon there was a fourth son, Philip, and eventually seven more children.

To support his wife and their increasing brood, Henry Steers stirred himself with greater physical and mental alacrity than the average shipwright. One of his assignments in Washington involved assisting in the building of a marine railway which, through the use of a wheeled carriage, would haul from the water vessels of considerable size with substantially less effort than the system of chucks and greased skids formerly employed. While Steers did not design the original device, he contributed to it so many practical improvements that soon he obtained a modicum of fame.

This recognition led to an invitation from a group of capitalists to build a marine railway in New York, and he and his family moved there in the mid-1820s. On successfully completing the job, he immediately tackled another, wholly his idea, which involved the installation of a string of semaphore signals between Sandy Hook, at the entrance to New York Bay, and the city itself many miles distant, thus greatly accelerating maritime communication.

Whatever savings Henry Steers accumulated from these two practical projects he eventually spent in part supporting his family while engaged in a third venture of a visionary sort. This involved the raising of the British frigate *Hussar,* sunk off New York in the turbulent waters of Hell Gate, at the confluence of the Harlem and East Rivers, during the Revolutionary War. For legend said that the *Hussar* had carried in a strongroom, in the aft section of her hold, paychests for the British army, and that these chests had contained—and still contained—$20,000,000 in gold.

The sponsors of the project promised Henry Steers 12½ percent of the take, in return for months of difficult work. In an era devoid of diving bells or even proper diving helmets, he succeeded in sawing the *Hussar* in half and in raising her stern. He broke open her strongroom, but it contained neither paychests nor a single piece of gold.

Legends, however, are as difficult to destroy as flies in summer. And it should be added here parenthetically that as late as January 1966, a New York City newspaper quoted a municipal official on the subject of the *Hussar.* Some enterprising citizen should raise her, the official said (seemingly unaware of the fruitless gamble of more than a century before), and for his efforts be permitted to keep 20 percent of her booty. "The remaining gold must go to the deserving needy and poor of our city," the official added generously.

Regardless of what the *Hussar* fiasco cost Henry Steers in lost earnings, he suffered no defeat of spirit. He had accomplished what he had set out to do, and this very fact so enhanced his reputation that in 1831 he was approached by a second group of financiers, interested in salvaging the valuable cargo of a ship wrecked off the coast of Mexico. Henry agreed to take on the job provided he was assisted by his son James R. (then 23) and provided, too, that they receive not merely shares of the expected booty, but in addition, wages and expenses while employed.

Henry and James R. were off on the Mexican junket until

1834, roughly three years. Today, nothing is known of where they worked on the coast of Mexico, what ship they raised, or the nature of her cargo, but it is known that they were successful and that they returned to New York with enough money for Henry Steers to build his own shipyard.

He chose a site at 10th Street and the East River, a couple of blocks from the yard of William H. Brown. The two became friendly, as did the various members of their respective families. All of which turned out to be of good portent, for many years later this continuing friendship facilitated arrangements for the building of the yacht *America*.

George Steers was 14 in 1834, and he grew to maturity in his father's shipyard. At 14, he put together his first vessel on his own—a scow—which his older brothers, James R. and Henry T., did him the favor of breaking up, knowing the leaky, makeshift craft to be woefully unsafe. But George soon learned the closely related arts of ship design and construction, and at 19 he turned out a neat and speedy little sailboat—17 feet overall—which he named after the political figure then midway through his term as President of the United States, Martin Van Buren.

George raced the *Martin Van Buren* on the Hudson River, notably in a contest covering a course of 24 miles, for which a prize was offered by John Cox Stevens. George's entry performed brilliantly and came in 3 miles ahead of the runner-up, *Gladiator,* a vessel hitherto considered the champion in her class. On accepting the prize from John Cox Stevens, George first met the man who would wield such an enormous influence in shaping his career.

Stevens, born in 1785, was 54 at the time of this meeting. He was the eldest of the six sons of the late Colonel John Stevens, an officer in the Continental Army during the Revolution and later Treasurer of New Jersey. Although born and reared in New York, Colonel Stevens as a young man moved to New Jersey, where he bought a large tract of land. The tract, lying between Hoboken and Weehawken, occupied a peninsula which jutted out into the Hudson River directly across from New York City. On the river side the land lay flat, but on the shore side it rose freakishly into a miniature mountain, at the top of which the Colonel built a huge battlemented residence of stone he called "The Castle," and the peninsula itself soon took the name "Castle Point."

Colonel Stevens developed widespread business interests, among them steam locomotion both on water and on land. As for water, he is credited with the invention of the first practical screw propeller, which he employed successfully in the river steamer *Phoenix* as early as 1809, and a few years later he operated the first steam ferry across the Hudson between New York and Hoboken. As for movement on land, the Colonel has been called the founder of the Pennsylvania Railroad, since he initiated lines that eventually formed the nucleus of that great system.

Colonel Stevens died in 1838, leaving his already rich sons all the richer. But aside from wealth, he endowed them additionally with his interest in invention as applied to transportation. In three—Robert L., Edwin A., and John Cox—this heritage matured to a marked degree.

Robert L. imported from England the famous steam locomotive "John Bull" and improved on various features of its mechanism. But today railroad men have greater cause to thank him for inventing the T-rail, the hook-headed spike, and the fishplate rail joint—all trackage devices still in universal use.

Although the youngest of the Stevens brothers, Edwin A. had such a sound head for business that his father made him trustee of his estate. But Edwin was inventive as well and at an early age patented a plow and a dump wagon, and he later devised a novel means of forced draft for steam boilers. The *Naugatuck*, an ironclad vessel of his design, termed "impractical" by the Navy Department, lay for years unused until the Civil War encounter of the *Monitor* with the *Merrimack*, after which she was quickly commissioned. Following Edwin's death in 1868, a dream he had shared with his father became reality. He left a large part of his wealth toward the founding, in 1870, of the Stevens Institute of Technology, at Hoboken, a school which today boasts an enrollment of some 2,500 potential inventors.

John Cox Stevens contributed numerous ideas of a scientific nature to his younger brothers, but took out no patents of his own. He increased his wealth through canny investments in banks and insurance companies, and in addition he was for a time active in the operation of a line of steamers, begun in 1827, plying the waters of the Hudson between New York and Albany. It seems apparent, however, that his principal interest was sport. During the horse-racing season he was often to be found at the tracks around New York, where he was known as a heavy, but shrewd, bettor. He had friends in abundance, and yet like many men of equal prominence he also had enemies.

His enemies found opportunity to criticize him when he introduced cricket into this country, claiming that his attitudes were more British than American. He countered by laying out a baseball diamond on a level portion of the Stevens property at Castle Point, which was already the site of a wooded park, open to the public. The park had acquired the name "Elysian Fields" and had become a favorite haunt of holiday picnickers.

The wealth of John Cox Stevens was matched by that of the woman he married, Maria Livingston, a famous belle from an old and socially prominent New York family. The pair traveled extensively and possessed all that could be desired in terms of worldly goods, including a mansion on Washington Square in New York City and a large country estate up the Hudson in Dutchess County. But their life together of thirty years remained destitute of what many couples yearn for the most, a child.

It might be thought that, because of this void, the interest Stevens took in young George Steers was at least in part paternal. Such, however, seems not to have been the case, for Stevens, in his business dealings with George, drove as stringent a bargain as was his custom—a fact vividly reflected in after years when it came to the matter of drawing up a contract for the building of the yacht *America.*

But this contract was far in the future when George and his *Martin Van Buren* won the prize Stevens offered. Seemingly, the winning of the prize encouraged George to attempt the building of a larger vessel, and by 1841 he had launched the 27-ton *Manhattan,* 44 feet 6 inches in length, with a 14-foot-8-inch beam, originally rigged as a sloop, but afterward as a schooner, at which time she was used for yachting with her name changed to *La Coquille.* Later in 1841, George demonstrated his versatility by designing and constructing a racing shell for oarsmen. Although it was 30 feet long, the fragile craft weighed only 140 pounds, and with her crew aboard she drew a mere 4 inches of water. Obviously George was not averse to cultivating the interest of John Cox Stevens, for he named his racing shell after that gentleman.

George turned 21 in 1841, and during the year his father, Henry, died at the age of 62. Not long afterward, Henry's shipyard was sold, probably to facilitate the division of his estate among the members of his large family. But George experienced no difficulty in securing another operational base, for already his talents had achieved recognition all along the waterfront. He moved his models and instruments to the shipyard of Smith & Dimond, at 4th Street and the East River, where he made use of their tools, hoisting and launching devices, artisans and materials, sharing with them a percentage of his profits. George was accompanied in this move by his brother James R., and the two worked together in a fluid form of collaboration until 1845 when James R. was appointed Inspector of Customs for the Port of New York by the newly inaugurated President of the United States, James K. Polk.

While at 4th Street, George designed and built the 53-foot schooner *Cygnet,* his first vessel of any considerable size embodying from the outset the creature-comfort facilities of a yacht, and sold her to William Edgar, who became a charter member of the New York Yacht Club a couple of years later.

John Cox Stevens inspected the *Cygnet,* and although he admired much of what he saw, she was not wholly to his liking. He discussed with George Steers the several features he felt should be incorporated in a yacht, and while George argued vehemently against some, he nevertheless ended up designing a schooner exactly in accord with his mentor's wishes. But he did not build her. Stevens awarded the contract to the shipyard of William Capes, at Hoboken, and on her launching in June 1844, she was christened *Gimcrack,* a word meaning, according to Webster, "a showy, useless trifle."

Actually, the *Gimcrack* was neither showy nor useless. In length 51 feet and in depth only 5 feet 2 inches (plus a fin keel of iron extending an additional 2 feet 4 inches), she displaced a mere 25 tons and was therefore small compared with many yachts of that era. Further, her usefulness is a matter of recorded importance in maritime history, for aboard her the New York Yacht Club came into being.

The first attempt to found a yacht club in America occurred in 1811, but the enfeebled organization died the next year. Three additional cases of infant mortality among yacht clubs took place during the three decades following, and not until 1844 did a healthy fledgling of this complexion, capable of longevity, come into being. An obstetrical record of the incident is still extant and reads as follows:

Minutes of the New York Yacht Club

On Board of the *Gimcrack*, off the Battery,

New York Harbor, July 30, 1844, 5:30 P.M.

According to previous notice, the following gentlemen assembled for the purpose of organizing a yacht club, viz: John C. Stevens, Hamilton Wilkes, William Edgar, John C. Jay, George L. Schuyler, Louis A. Depau, George B. Rollins, James M. Waterbury, James Rogers, and on motion it was resolved to form a yacht club. On motion it was resolved that the title of the club be the New York Yacht Club. On motion it was resolved that the gentlemen present be the original members of the club. On motion it was resolved that John C. Stevens be the Commodore of the club. On motion it was resolved that a committee of five be appointed by the Commodore to report rules and regulations for the government of the club. The following gentlemen were appointed, viz. John C. Stevens, George L. Schuyler, John C. Jay, Hamilton Wilkes and Captain Rogers. On motion it was resolved that the club make a cruise to Newport, Rhode Island, under command of the Commodore.

The following yachts were represented at this meeting, viz. *Gimcrack*, John C. Stevens; *Spray*, Hamilton Wilkes; *Cygnet*, William Edgar; *La Coquille*, John C. Jay; *Dream*, George L. Schuyler; *Mist*, Louis A. Depau; *Minna*, George B. Rollins; *Adda*, Captain Rogers. After appointing Friday, August 2, at 9 A.M., the time for sailing on the cruise, the meeting adjourned.

John C. Jay, Recording Secretary.

Of the eight yachts listed, George Steers had designed, or designed and built, three. During the cruise to Newport, the yachts comprising the fleet of the newly formed Club fell in with the yachts of certain prominent Bostonians, and these gentlemen—David Sears, Captain R. B. Forbes, and Colonel W. P. Winchester—became the first non-New Yorkers to join the Club. During the summer of the following year, 1845, the Club built its first residence—a modest abode occupying a waterfront site a bit up the Hudson from the Stevens family's Elysian Fields property across the river from New York—and held its first regatta. The winner was *Cygnet*, the schooner yacht of 45 tons George Steers had designed and built for William Edgar.

Also in 1845, George left Smith & Dimond and with a partner formed the shipbuilding firm of Hathorne & Steers, for which a yard was acquired in the Williamsburg section of Brooklyn, across the East River from George's former location. Here, during the next four years, George designed and built several commercial schooners for the Great Lakes, two yachts, and three pilot boats for New York Harbor. The yachts were the schooner *Cornelia*, 74 feet in length, and the *Una*, a fast centerboard sloop of 64 feet with a beam of 17 feet 10 inches, which lasted for fifty years. George sold the *Una* to James M. Waterbury, a charter member of the New York Yacht Club, who once sailed her to Boston in a mere 32 hours.

George's first two pilot boats followed prevailing fashion in such vessels, which was what their owners ordered. But George built the third for Captain Richard "Old Dick" Brown, and this most seasoned and knowledgeable of New York Harbor pilots had enough faith in the young designer to give him his head and let him model and construct what he wanted. The result was the *Mary Taylor,* a pilot boat as daring in her innovations as the popular music-hall performer for whom she was named. For it had been the flesh-and-blood Mary Taylor who first publicly danced the "scandalous polka" in America, at Niblo's Gardens in June 1844, and who had continued shocking increasingly large and appreciative audiences during the several years following.

George built the pilot boat *Mary Taylor* in 1849. She had a lean and clean bow which entered the water easily and slid through it much in the fashion of a ski passing through snow. Hers was other than the bluff "apple cheek" look usual to the bows of pilot boats, and her after-body, too, was long and clean. George had a friend his own age, William Ross Wallace, a lawyer turned poet (famous for the lines "The hand that rocks the cradle/Is the hand that rules the world"), who once said of the *Mary Taylor* and her builder:

> Undoubtedly the chief feature of George Steers' mind is originality.... His system of marine architecture is based upon the assumption that for a vessel to sail steadily and rapidly, the displacement of water must be nearly uniform along her lines.... When George Steers laid the keel of the pilot boat *Mary Taylor,* he engaged in advance to make a faster and steadier craft than had ever left the port of New York, and he succeeded exactly according to expectation. Previous to this achievement, a vessel had never been built where the center of displacement had not been forward of the beam. Fears were generally entertained

that this new form would prove a failure. Some predicted that the vessel would plunge under water; others thought that in rough weather no one could live on deck; all of which prophecies are certainly contradicted by fact. For encountering less resistance from the narrow bows, the vessel went faster, experienced no corresponding strain, and suffered no more in the storm than in the breeze. The advantages of George Steers' system may be thus summed up:—First, greater speed with the same tonnage and canvas. Second, greater stability in the vessel —that is, an increased hold on the water. Third, greater evenness and equality of motion resulting from an equalized leverage—since the masts, as levers, work more uniformly upon the fulcrum of the ship.

William Ross Wallace was also a friend of Edgar Allan Poe, and it is probable that George Steers knew Poe, for at one point during the 1840s the two lived around the corner from each other in New York, George on Cannon Street and Poe on East Broadway. During this same decade, a crime disturbing to John Cox Stevens and his brothers came to light on their Hoboken property. Mary Cecelia Rogers, a girl famous for her beauty, who clerked in the shop of a New York tobacconist, disappeared over a weekend and days later was found across the Hudson, lying murdered amid the shrubbery of the Elysian Fields picnic grounds. While the crime was never solved in fact, Poe gave it fictional solution in "The Mystery of Marie Roget," one of the world's first detective stories. Poe transferred the locale of the murder to Paris, called the Hudson the Seine, and nominated as the murderer a naval officer who had transported his victim across the river aboard a sailing vessel. Near the murder scene the vessel lost her rudder, and when an investigator found and traced the rudder the murderer was caught.

But Poe, in writing the story, obviously had in mind no vessel produced by George Steers, for his were too well built to lose so important a component as a rudder. This was particularly true of the pilot boat *Mary Taylor,* a craft of such stability and speed that soon her novel features were widely imitated.

Aside from the *Gimcrack,* John Cox Stevens owned a huge centerboard sloop, *Maria,* designed by his brother Robert L., and built by the builder of the *Gimcrack,* William Capes of Hoboken. When launched, she measured 92 feet on deck, 26½ feet in beam, and with her centerboard up she drew only 5 feet 2 inches of water. That centerboard was large and heavy; unlike most, it was not pivoted, but was raised and lowered by means of coiled springs and counterbalancing weights. Her mast, boom, gaff, and bowsprit were so long that they would have made her topheavy had they not been hollowed out and then trussed inside with cross-braces to renew their strength. The *Maria,* named after her owner's wife, was built solely for racing and to this end carried nearly 8,000 square feet of canvas in her mainsail and jib. A few years after she was built, she figured prominently in the trials of the *America.*

In 1849, following the appearance of the *Mary Taylor,* John Cox Stevens paid George Steers the compliment of having his *Maria* rebuilt forward in imitation of the fast and yet sturdy pilot boat. The *Maria*'s comparatively blunt bow was sharpened and lengthened until she measured 110 feet on deck and 107 feet 9 inches at the waterline. Withal, she remained a vessel fit only for smooth water, and rarely did she venture outside New York Harbor unless the seas ran to her liking and a steady barometer gave her permission.

Later in 1849, the partnership of Hathorne & Steers broke up, and George Steers found himself at loose ends. What caused the rupture is today unknown and can be dealt with only speculatively. James K. Polk concluded his term as President of the United States, and Zachary Taylor, his successor, did not reappoint James R. Steers as Inspector of Customs for the Port of New York. Perhaps George insisted on taking his brother (of whom he was extremely fond) into the firm of Hathorne & Steers, and Hathorne objected, or there may have been some other reason. Seemingly, however, Hathorne ended up by buying George out, possibly with the proviso that George, under his own name, would not again enter the shipbuilding business for a specified period. So much, at least, would account for the fact that in 1850, when Commodore John Cox Stevens and five of his fellow members in the New York Yacht Club began dickering for the building of the yacht *America*, the name of the builder chosen never appeared in writing as George Steers. Rather, it was William H. Brown. Obviously George had made a deal with his and his late father's old friend. George would use Brown's shipyard, his force of skilled artisans, his materials and other facilities, and therefore it was always Brown who signed the various letters of agreement prepared by Commodore Stevens and his friends.

Along with the Commodore, those who became co-owners of the yacht *America* were the following:

Edwin A. Stevens, the Commodore's brother. He was 55 in 1850 and a widower, with a motherless daughter, Mary, aged 9. But eventually he would remarry and have eight more children. He served as Vice-Commodore of the New York Yacht Club for the period 1855–58, and as Commodore from 1859 until 1865.

Hamilton Wilkes, a gentleman of leisure. He was the first Vice-Commodore of the New York Yacht Club, serving for eight years. He resided at Hyde Park, in Dutchess County, New York, where John Cox Stevens and his wife also owned an estate. Wilkes was physically a big man, who prided himself on his horsemanship, his great physical strength, and his glowing good health. But surely he overestimated the last. During the winter of 1850–51 he daily sat about the yard of William H. Brown, interestedly watching the building of the *America*, and eventually the exposure laid him low with some pulmonary malady from which he died in 1852.

John K. Beekman Finlay, another gentleman of leisure. He resided on an estate near the resort town of Saratoga, New York, left him by an uncle for whom he was named, and other bequests made him independently wealthy. He knew little of yachting and cared less, but he did enjoy the society of New York Yacht Club members.

Colonel James Alexander Hamilton, son of the Secretary of the Treasury in George Washington's Cabinet who is better known to many for his fatal pistols-at-ten-paces encounter with Aaron Burr. Colonel Hamilton came by his rank honestly as an officer in the U.S. Army during the War of 1812. He attended Columbia with John Cox Stevens, afterwards studied and practiced law, and in 1829 President Andrew Jackson appointed him U.S. Attorney for the Southern District of New York. Colonel Hamilton, whose mansion at Dobbs Ferry, New York, overlooked the Hudson, both made and married money; his means permitted him to travel widely; and he lived to be ninety. Aficionados of yachting history are indebted to him for his *Reminiscences,* published in 1869.

George L. Schuyler, a native of Rhinebeck, a village on the Hudson in Dutchess County. A grandson of General Philip Schuyler of the Continental Army, George Schuyler's chief recreation, next to yachting, was collecting material concerning the American Revolution. Schuyler married two of Colonel Hamilton's daughters, for when the first died he followed an Old Testament injunction and took to wife her sister. While perhaps he would have been happier as a professional historian, fate placed him in the shipping business, and he accepted the challenge by making a great success. Born in 1811, he was thus 39 in 1850 and therefore the youngest of the syndicate of six responsible for the building of the yacht *America.*

Possibly because of the maritime nature of Schuyler's work and the energy springing from his comparative youth, the other five in the syndicate made him the representative of all in their dealings with George Steers through the intermediacy of William H. Brown. At least, it is to be hoped that that was the cause. For certainly it is not to be hoped that the choice of Schuyler rested on the belief that he would draw up letters of contract unfair to George Steers. However, the letters of contract themselves best speak their aim, and the first, written in Schuyler's hand and addressed to himself, but actually signed by William H. Brown, read as follows:

New York, Nov. 15, 1850

George L. Schuyler, Esq.
Dear Sir,

I propose to build for you a yacht of not less than 140 tons custom house measurement on the following terms—

The yacht to be built in the best manner, coppered, rigged, equipped with joiner's work, cabin and kitchen furniture, table furniture, water closets, etc., etc. ready for sea—you are to designate the plan of the interior of the vessel and select the furniture.

The model, plan and rig of the vessel to be entirely at my discretion, it being understood however that she is to be a strong seagoing vessel, and rigged for ocean sailing.

For the vessel complete and ready for sea you are to pay me $30,000 upon the following conditions—

When the vessel is ready, she is to be placed at the disposal of Hamilton Wilkes Esq. as umpire, who after making such trials as are satisfactory to him for the space of twenty days, shall decide whether or not she is faster than any vessel in the United States brought to compete with her.

The expenses of these trials to be borne by you.

If it is decided by the umpire that she is not faster than every vessel brought against her, it shall not be binding upon you to accept her and pay for her at all.

In addition to this, if the umpire decides that she is faster than any vessel in the United States, you are to have the right, instead of accepting her at that time, to send her to England, match her against anything of her size built there, and if beaten still to reject her altogether.

The expense of the voyage out and home to be borne by you.

The test of speed in England to be decided by any mode acceptable to you and consented to by you in writing.

Respectfully yours,
W H Brown

It is doubtful that George Steers or Brown, before Brown affixed his signature to the letter, obtained legal advice. For had this been done, a lawyer might have pointed out that on the syndicate's side the document seemed heavily weighted, notably with respect to the appointment of Hamilton Wilkes, a member of the syndicate, as umpire. The situation looked, in fact, somewhat like a boxing match with a backer of one of the fighters acting as referee.

In reply to the letter he had written for Brown to sign, Schuyler, on the same day—and possibly at the same sitting—wrote this one over his own signature:

W. H. Brown, Esq.
Dear Sir,

Your proposal to build for me a yacht of not less than 140 tons custom house measurement for $30,000, payable on certain conditions detailed in your letter of the 15th inst., has been submitted by me to some of my friends interested in the subject.

The price is high, but in consideration of the liberal and sportsmanlike character of the whole offer, test of speed, etc., we have concluded that such a proposal must not be declined.

I therefore accept the proposal, and you will please go ahead without loss of time. I only stipulate as a condition on my part that the yacht must be ready for trial on the first day of April next.

Very truly yours,
George L. Schuyler

New York, Nov. 15, 1850

The difference in the complimentary closings of the two letters should interest social scientists. While the first ends "Respectfully yours," the second, with its "Very truly yours," is not in the least subservient. Whether or not the distinction was committed consciously, it is true that George L. Schuyler, the wearer of a frock coat and starched linen, looked upon himself and his fellows in the syndicate as belonging to a higher order of humanity than men who went about their daily duties less elegantly clad. Although George Steers and William H.

Brown were themselves bosses of a sort, they felt it not at all beneath them to pitch in frequently and work with their hands. Commodore Stevens and Colonel Hamilton shared Schuyler's upstage attitude, as their behavior indicated once the *America* was built and sent to England.

In November 1850, that day was a long while away. In designing the yacht, George Steers worked slowly, principally by means of his accustomed trial-and-error method. The protractor, the compass, and the T-square were drafting instruments he employed only rarely, as was the drawing board with its "stretch" of rag paper. Instead, he carved a model, and if the first turned out not to his liking, he went on to another and perhaps still others. His was the method of an artist, and thus removed from that of an engineer. When finally he had what was right, he knew it in the main intuitively and not so much as a result of calculation.

From the model, he lifted the lines, multiplied their dimensions according to scale, and laid them out in battens of full size on a mold-loft floor. Then in accord with the battens, he cut the gracefully curving timbers forming the frame of a vessel's hull. In a general way, the hull of the *America* resembled that of the *Mary Taylor,* although the yacht's hull was larger, of greater refinement than that of her prototype, and more radical in her departure from the usual.

As may have been surmised by the fatal character of the malady Hamilton Wilkes contracted as he sat about Brown's shipyard watching the building of the *America,* the winter of 1850–51 proved severe. Since there was no overall shed to shelter the workmen, the cold and the inclemency of the weather hindered their progress. Consequently the arrival of the first of April found the yacht not merely far from ready for her trials, but not as yet ready for launching.

Acting for himself and his syndicate associates, George L. Schuyler took advantage of the agreement thus abrogated by driving an even tougher bargain with George Steers. Its strictures were spelled out in this letter:

W. H. Brown, Esqr.
Dear Sir,

I have this morning laid before the gentlemen associated with me your proposal to renew the contract between us for building a yacht, the time for delivery to be fixed on the 1st of May next.

The delay has been one of more consequence to the convenience of some of these gentlemen than I had supposed. One of them is obliged to sail for Europe on the first of May, and consequently will lose all the trials, and another who is ready to sail at that time is obliged to change all his plans.

I propose to continue the contract between us, which expired April 1st, to May 1st, 1851, as the time for the delivery of the vessel, all other conditions to remain as before, providing you consent to the following alterations in your letter of Nov. 15th, 1850:

On the first page, after the words, "The expense of these trials to be borne by you," you agree to insert the words, "The vessel to be at my risk as regards loss, or damage from any source." The last clause of your letter to read as follows: "In addition to this, if the umpire decides that she is faster than any vessel in the United States, you are to have the right, instead of accepting her at that time, to send her to England, match her against anything built there, which in your judgment gives her a fair chance in a trial of speed, and, if beaten, reject her altogether; the expense of the voyage out and home to be borne by you, and the vessel to be at your risk. The test of speed in England above referred to shall be decided by the result of any one or more trials acceptable to you, and to which you, or some person authorized by you, shall have consented in writing."

Please answer immediately whether you accept these changes, and if you do, go ahead without loss of time.

Yours truly,
George L. Schuyler

New York, April 2d, 1851

George Steers, with his back against the wall, directed Brown to bow assent to the amended conditions, and Brown did so. But surely George Steers must have wondered why his delay in completing the yacht should have made him responsible for her loss or any damage she might sustain while undergoing, in local waters, trials managed by her prospective purchasers. And he must have wondered, too, why the stakes had been so radically changed in the middle of the game that now, should the yacht be tested in England, such tests might involve any number of competing vessels, including perhaps some of much greater size.

The first of May arrived, with the yacht still not ready for her buyers, or even for launching. On May 3, however, her launching took place, apparently without any christening ceremony, and just who suggested—or when it was first suggested—that she be called *America* is today unknown. No other name, nonetheless, could have been half so appropriate in the light of her sturdy beauty, her grace of movement, her longevity, and above all her many achievements, especially in the realm of speed.

Curiously, the *America*'s capacity for fast sailing either went unrecognized at the outset or, if recognized, was not fully and fairly reported by the whole of the New York press, dependent as most of the papers were for information on that supplied by the yacht's syndicate of buyers. On Tuesday, May 13, George Steers handed over the *America* to the syndicate for trials in local waters. Hamilton Wilkes, the umpire named in the letters of contract, did not serve as such, possibly because of some early manifestation of the illness that would result in his death a year later. In his stead, George L. Schuyler, of all people, sailed aboard the *America* as umpire, although in so doing he might have laid himself open to a charge of conflict of interest, since he continued as chief negotiator for the vessel's purchase.

The yacht the *America* found herself tried against was the huge sloop *Maria,* with her owner, Commodore John Cox Stevens, proudly aboard. He and his crew knew how best to sail the *Maria* over the waters of New York Harbor and the seas immediately outside, for they had been doing just that, scores upon scores of times, since her launching in 1845. During those six years, in her building and rebuilding, a reputed $100,000 had been spent on *Maria,* and the canvas she carried exceeded by more than 2,500 square feet the sail-spread of the *America.*

On the other hand, the new yacht had not been in the water long enough for her seams to swell thoroughly or for her crew to acquaint themselves with her workings. Further, regardless of how much they were taken up, her shrouds slacked and continued to do so, as new shrouds always will when first introduced to strain. Also, those aboard the *America* discovered belatedly that she was sadly wanting in ballast by an estimated 8 tons and was consequently topheavy for failure to sit as deep as she should in the water.

In spite of these drawbacks, the *America* outsailed *Maria* on the first two days of the trials—or so reported one New York newspaper, the *Courier and Enquirer.* This paper said that on Wednesday, May 14, in a 2-hour beat to windward and return, the *America* whisked back to her allotted anchorage far ahead of *Maria,* and that on the following day, Thursday, May 15, the *America* again drew ahead of *Maria* as though the sloop were standing still. Only on Friday, May 15, the third day of the trials, reported the *Courier and Enquirer,* did the *America* lose to *Maria,* and that loss was the result of an accident. Through mishandling, she sprung the head of her foremast and carried away her main gaff.

In a letter dated Saturday, May 17, Commodore Stevens answered the *Courier and Enquirer* claims. Interestingly, he did not send his answer to that paper, but to another, the *Herald,* owned by James Gordon Bennett, a fellow yachtsman. It was the contention of Commodore Stevens that in the Wednesday trial *America* came in ahead only because *Maria* ran aground, and that in the Thursday trial *America* made so fine a showing because a guest aboard the *Maria* had unwittingly altered the position of her centerboard, thus reducing her draft.

Toward the end of his letter, Commodore Stevens wrote, "No one of the gentlemen interested in the success of the *America* would more sincerely rejoice at the proofs of her good sailing than myself. But as I do not believe that it will serve the interests of her builder, . . . to sanction an account so wide of the truth, I send you this statement."

Three days later, on May 20, George L. Schuyler wrote the *Courier and Enquirer* directly. After acknowledging that he had been umpire, he backed up Commodore Stevens by saying, "As far as the trials went, the *Maria* proved herself faster than the *America;* but so nearly are they matched that the builders of the *America* feel confident that with new spars . . . a different result may be anticipated. . . . Commodore Stevens, with his usual courtesy, has informed us that the *Maria* is again at our service when we are ready for any trials in smooth or rough water, in heavy or light weather. In about ten days, the question between these two will be determined by another trial."

Schuyler's talk of the *Maria*'s ability to race in rough water during heavy weather seems extravagant, for never had she participated in such a contest. If the *Maria* had been fit for conditions of that sort, the likelihood is that she, rather than a keel yacht of the *America*'s sturdiness, would have been chosen by the syndicate to cross the Atlantic and take on the British yachting fleet over their notoriously turbulent racing courses. Proof of the *Maria*'s heavy-weather deficiencies is to be found in her subsequent history. Some time after the death of John Cox Stevens, her name was changed to *Maud* and she was sold into the fruit-carrying trade. In October 1870, while on a voyage from Honduras to New York carrying a cargo of coconuts, she was lost with all hands in an Atlantic storm.

Indeed, the extravagance of Schuyler's talk is indicated further by the fact that *Maria* was never again tried against the *America.* On May 24—four days after assuring the *Courier and Enquirer* that within ten days there would be such a trial—Schuyler wrote this letter:

W. H. Brown, Esqr.
Dear Sir,

So much more time has elapsed than was anticipated by you in completing the yacht *America* that I fear, if delayed much longer by further trials, the proper season for sending her to England will have passed. The gentlemen interested with me in the contract I have with you have consented that I should make an offer for the vessel as she is, releasing her from further trials and despatching her forthwith. I will give you $20,000 in cash for the yacht, finished as per contract, equipped and ready for sea, to be delivered to me on or before the second of June next. All expenses of trials, etc., heretofore incurred by you to be paid by you.

Yours truly,
George L. Schuyler

New York, May 24th, 1851

If George Steers was at all capable of strong emotion, this letter must have infuriated him. He had invested six months of his time and much of his capital building the *America,* and in addition he was considerably indebted to William H. Brown for the use of his shipyard. In the event another customer for the yacht had come along, surely Steers would have sold her out from under the syndicate—and taken human delight in doing so. But no such customer appeared. For while $20,000 was only two thirds of $30,000, it was still a lot of money in 1851, when a dollar was worth many times its multiple today and men of wealth interested in yachting were not nearly so plentiful.

So George Steers stifled his disappointment and his anger and sold the *America* for the amount offered. But in the doing he was probably motivated by influences beyond those of an economic character. Just as an artist wants his paintings exhibited or a writer his books published, so did George Steers want the racing yacht he had built to participate in the sort of competitions for which he had designed her.

On June 17 the *America* received her certificate of registry at the New York custom house, where she was found to measure, according to U.S. standards, 170 and 50/95 tons. On the following day she was turned over to her syndicate of purchasers.

The syndicate engaged a crew for her and were fortunate in employing as captain Richard "Old Dick" Brown, the owner of her prototype, the pilot boat *Mary Taylor*, who consequently knew just how to handle her and who bore the reputation of being the most skillful sailor ever produced by the Port of New York. Her first mate, Horatio Nelson "Nelse" Comstock, came from Connecticut, as did three of her seamen. In addition there were a second mate named Howes, a cook and a boy helper, and three more seamen, one of whom doubled as carpenter.

At one point, George L. Schuyler and certain other syndicate members intended crossing the Atlantic aboard the yacht. But business pressures prevented Schuyler from going, and the lack of his comparatively youthful company discouraged his older associates from a voyage so adventurous. While Commodore John Cox Stevens, his brother Edwin A., and Colonel James A. Hamilton did not abandon the junket altogether, they decided to cross instead by a steam packet, which would put them on the other side considerably ahead of the yacht. This left empty berths aboard the *America* which, in a gesture of magnanimity, Schuyler invited George Steers and some of his relatives to fill. Steers accepted, taking with him his older brother, James R., and the latter's two sons, George, 2nd, and Henry, aged respectively seventeen and fifteen. For the voyage, the *America* was heavily provisioned with both edibles and potables. The Steers brothers and the yacht's officers and crew brought aboard their own liquid refreshments, and in addition the Stevens brothers and Colonel Hamilton, with a view toward entertaining guests abroad, had stowed away in lockers a large quantity of the best that American distillers and vintners could provide. The *America*'s working sails for the voyage were a spare set belonging to the *Mary Taylor*, and she carried her own new racing sails, made by R. H. Wilson (then located in

New York, but afterward in Port Jefferson, Long Island), folded in the lazarette beneath her cockpit.

As the yacht stood ready for sea, she bore only undercoats of gray paint of a high lead content, for it was the purpose of her owners to have her top-coated afresh, with black for her hull and a glistening white for other areas, once she had crossed the Atlantic. On this account, rather than have her proceed directly to a British port, it was planned that she should enter the English Channel at its southernmost extremity and when in the longitude of the Isle of Wight—her eventual destination—she should swing to the southeast and make for Le Havre, France. There the Stevens brothers and Colonel Hamilton would await her, and there she would be put in final shape to sail over and "test conclusions" with the British yachting fleet.

So far, no detailed description of the *America* had appeared in print. In 1851, on neither side of the Atlantic was there a periodical devoted exclusively to yachting, although *Hunt's Yachting Magazine,* a monthly, began publication in England the following year. But in both London and New York there were journals devoted to sports generally which carried some yachting news, *Bell's Life* in the former city and *Spirit of the Times* in the latter. William Trotter Porter, the towering 6-foot-6-inch proprietor and editor of *Spirit of the Times,* was a close friend of Commodore Stevens, and in his issue for June 22, 1851—the day after the *America* sailed—he gave the departed yacht quite a bit of play.

The story, dated the day before and headlined THE NEW YACHT AMERICA, occupied a long column. Its essential portions, together with a few corrections and amplifications, are presented here:

> This superior piece of naval architecture takes her departure from this port this morning, to test her sailing qualities with the choice yachts of Great Britain.... As the result will be watched with much lively interest on both sides of the Atlantic, it being a trial for superiority in the sailing powers, beauty of model, and symmetry of construction, between the vessels of

England and the United States, a description of the *America* cannot be otherwise than interesting to our readers. . . .

She is 95 feet on deck [correctly 101 feet], from stem to stern; 80 feet keel; and 23 feet [breadth] amidships. She draws 11 feet of water in sailing trim. Her spars are respectively 79½ and 81 feet long, with 2⅞ inches rake to the foot. Her main gaff is 26 feet long, and main boom 58 feet. She carries a lug foresail, with fore gaff 24 feet long. Length of bowsprit 32 feet [17 feet hollow outboard]. The frame is composed of five different species of wood, namely:—white oak, locust, cedar, chestnut and hackmatack; and is supported by diagonal iron braces, equidistant from each other four feet. From stem to midships the curve is scarcely perceptible, her gunwales being nearly straight lines, and forming with each other an angle of about 25 [correctly 34] degrees. The cutwater is a prolongation of the vessel herself, there being no addition of false wood as is usual in most of the sharpest bowed craft.

Her after cabin is a spacious and elegantly fitted up apartment, 21 feet by 18 feet in the clear, on each side of which are six neat lockers and China rooms. It [is surmounted on deck by a gabled skylight 8 feet by 3 feet and] contains six commodious berths. Joining the cabin are two large state rooms, each eight feet square, with wardrobes and water closets attached. Between these and the fore cabin there are two other state rooms, a wash room and pantry, [and a galley, flanked by water tanks, 21 feet by 9 feet]. The fore cabin is ventilated by a circular skylight of about 12 feet circumference, and it contains fifteen berths. A gangway connects the fore and after cabins. Directly under the cockpit, which is 30 feet in circumference, there is a tastefully fitted up bathroom. [A companionway, entered through a hatch with double doors, leads from the cockpit to the area below.]

The *America* has a plain raking stern, adorned with a large gilt eagle resting upon two folded white banners garnished with beautifully carved flowers of green color. Her sides are planked with white oak three inches thick, the deck with yellow pine two and a half inches thick. Three streaks of the clamps are of yellow pine three inches thick. The deck beams are also of yellow pine. All the coamings are of the finest description of mahogany. The rails [bulwarks], which are composed of white oak, are fourteen inches high, six inches wide, and three inches thick. She is copper fastened throughout, and copper sheathed from the keel to six inches above the water line, making eleven and a half feet in all.

It is impossible for the pen of the most graphic describer to convey anything like an accurate conception of the beauty and perfection of the *America*. She can only be seen to advantage when viewed at a distance, from different points, by the natural and living eye. Under such circumstances, only, can her symmetrical and swan-like model be appreciated....

Mr. George Steers, the modeller and builder of the *America*, takes passage in her, for the main purpose of being able to judge, by practical observation, where rests the material difference between the model and construction of English and American built yachts; and also to see which nation will win the palm of superiority in point of sailing qualities. Whether the *America* shall come off victorious is yet a problem; but be the result as it may, she cannot but be an object of deep interest and admiration on the other side of the water; and the elegant appearance which she will make in gliding up to meet her competitors, must call forth applause on Mr. Steers, her builder and fashioner.

TWO

"A Challenge Fastened on Her Beams"

THE *America* was the first yacht to cross the Atlantic for racing. She carried 45 tons of ballast, tanks of fresh water, and her lockers crowded with provisions for the long voyage. Consequently she rode a bit deeper than her builder intended. Her working canvas consisted of the *Mary Taylor's* mainsail, foresail, jib, and a mainmast topsail, and in addition she spread at times a large square sail rigged to a cross-arm spar, for use on the foremast when driving before an ocean wind.

The log kept by "Old Dick" Brown, the captain, consisted largely of notations concerning weather and position. James R. Steers, on the other hand, wrote regularly and at length in his private journal, and in the doing proved himself a nautical Samuel Pepys keen in observation and wry in humor. The survival of copies of this journal permits graphic insight into what went on aboard the *America* as she sailed over the 3,200 miles of deep water separating New York and Le Havre, and later anchored at Cowes. While during the ocean crossing there were no recorded flare-ups of temper among the fifteen men and boys comprising the ship's company, this pacific condition did not always prevail after the yacht reached her final destination and Colonel Hamilton and the Stevens brothers were often aboard.

The *America* cast off her hawsers and slipped away from the dock at Brown's shipyard at 8 A.M. on Saturday, June 21, 1851.

There was little wind, and for the next three hours a tug towed her out of the East River and across the placid waters of New York Harbor, finally leaving her on her own. At 1 o'clock, the *Pacific*, an ocean packet, passed her, and the officers and crew of this steamer, knowing "Old Dick" Brown and the Steers brothers, gave the yacht nine cheers and fired two guns. During this ceremony Captain Nye of the *Pacific* stood atop his wheelhouse with his hat in his hands, and those aboard the yacht returned the salute "with as good a heart," wrote James Steers, "as it was given."

The wind picked up, and at 3 o'clock the *America* crossed Sandy Hook bar going 11 knots. Outside the bar, fog closed in and the sea grew increasingly rough. Howes, the second mate, fell victim to seasickness and "turned in rather squeamish," but others aboard warded off the malady by each taking a slug of brandy—"about ten drops," James Steers confided to his journal, no doubt chuckling over his minimal estimate. At midnight the yacht was making 8 knots, but by morning her speed had fallen off to 5½.

For midday dinner on Sunday, June 22, the cook provided "roast turkey and green peas, boiled beef and pork with a bread pudding to top off with." A sounding taken read on the line 22 fathoms. Since the second mate continued seasick and the others feared his illness might prove contagious, they all downed some more brandy at four in the afternoon and gave toasts "to our friends at home." Then, because it was Sunday, they ate a second dinner that evening consisting of "veal potpie and Indian fritters with sauce." Until midnight the winds continued light, and the distance run for the preceding 24 hours was no more than an "old man might walk," a mere 69 miles.

On Monday, June 23, however, conditions changed. On a course ESE, through rain driven by a strong wind S by E, the yacht ran a low of 10 knots and a high of 13½. She crowded on all her canvas, including the square sail, "or 'Big Ben,' as the Captain called it," but an hour later "took him in as he would not stand, the wind hauling." In 24 hours, the *America* logged

284 miles, her record for the voyage. Also she sighted her first ship on the broad Atlantic, an English brig.

Throughout Tuesday, June 24, the rain persisted in harassing squalls, and for the bulk of the time the yacht skipped along under a double-reefed mainsail surmounted by a gaff topsail. Even so, she logged for the day 240 miles, and at 6 P.M. "passed a ship going the same way, supposed to be the *Lady Franklin.*"

Toward midday on June 25 the *America* overhauled a ship "with a large cross in her fore topsail," but was not near enough to speak her. James Steers marveled at the speed of the yacht his brother had built, writing, "The way we passed everything we saw was enough to surprise everybody on board." But he balanced this intra-family compliment with another for the cook: "Had for dinner today a beautiful piece of roast beef and green peas, rice pudding for dessert."

The yacht ran 254 miles on Thursday, June 26, through a haze in the morning which had cleared away by afternoon. She spoke an English brig from Falmouth and then encountered a fleet of fishermen hauling in cod. "But we could not stop to fish, having a fair wind," the journal-keeper lamented, and then told of dining on both turkey and chicken. "Had some good brandy to top off with," he added, and for the first time during the voyage gave the yacht's position. By observation at noon she was at latitude 44° 20′, longitude 50°.

The crew of the *America* coppered her forward starboard bulwark on Friday, June 27, for there had been chafing from the rigging. Young George Steers, the son of James, felt sick, and his father gave him "castor oil which physicked him only once." Then James himself took a dose of calomel, which, regardless of whatever other effect it may have produced, diminished his appetite not in the least. He had chicken fricassee and apple sauce for midday dinner and hot cakes for supper. "Wind very light," James Steers commented. "All sail set we can give her. She is the best sea boat that ever went out of the Hook. The way we have passed everything we have seen must be witnessed to be believed. Run for this day 144 miles. Course E. by S. Wind S."

The light breezes continued on Saturday, June 28. Those members of the yacht's crew not busy sailing her fell to work holystoning her deck and cockpit. "At 3 P.M.," James Steers wrote, "we passed and spoke the British bark *Clyde* of Liverpool, 15 days from New York, bound to Liverpool. We saw her about 10 o'clock right ahead and at 6 P.M. she was out of sight astern. The captain said [of the yacht]: 'She sails like the wind.' Also saw the British bark *Sophie,* from New Brunswick for Liverpool, 13 days out." But impressed as he was with the *America*'s speed, James Steers could not forget her cuisine, and he ended his comments with: "Had for dinner today stewed chicken, with apple pie for dessert. Plenty of good brandy and water. Sea smooth as oil. Thus endeth this day."

On the day following—Sunday, June 29—the tranquil sea "breezed up" and gave the *America* a bit of a tossing. She pitched, but withstood it well enough, while her crew reefed her mainsail and took off the bonnets of her foresail and jib. "I don't think it ever rained harder since Noah floated his ark," James Steers observed. "In taking in the gaff topsail, it caught and split from end to end. Had for dinner today roast chicken and beef. Apple pie for dessert. Little George feeling a little better."

The rain continued throughout Monday, June 30, as did the wind, and at one point the *America* was driving ahead "bowsprit under." James Steers complained to his journal, "Bucketfuls of water came down and ran over the cabin. All my clothes are wet. Should I live to get home this will be my last sea trip." Not only was "Little George" seasick now, but so was his uncle, "Brother George." And yet James Steers, complacently and with good appetite, ate for dinner "fried ham and eggs, boiled corn-beef, mashed potatoes and rice pudding." He noted the yacht's position as longitude 40° 45′, latitude 47° 11′.

The morning of Tuesday, July 1, found the crew of the *America* hanging out their clothes in an attempt to dry them.

"This is the first day the sun has shone," James Steers noted, "but it will rain before night. At noon saw something at a point on our lee bow and we ran down to see what it was. We found it to be a dead whale, the largest anybody on board had ever seen. The fat was at least a foot thick. Had for dinner today boiled ham and plum pudding. Longitude 38° 7′, Latitude 47°."

A strong wind sent the yacht bounding forward for much of Wednesday, July 2. "Unbent the large jib," James Steers recorded, "and bent the small one. It looks like a shirt on a bean pole. Repaired the gaff topsail and set it. At 10 this morning passed a clipper brig bound the same way and we passed her faster than she was going ahead. At noon had to get the yard five or six feet outside the rigging to help support the foremast. There was a heavy head sea and she was making the water fly some. Little George a little better. Brother George sick. I am making him some gruel. Our cook is not a very good caterer. He can boil a piece of beef or pork, or roast a piece of beef or turkey, but the puddings are heavy and the crusts of his pies are as tough as a leather apron. He made some wheat fritters and you wanted better teeth than I have to chew them fine enough to digest. But here we are 1,300 miles from Havre, and if this wind will only last six days we will be snug in harbor, barring any accident. Brother George sick of his cruise and I expect will leave as soon as he arrives, or soon after. Distance run this day 209 miles."

The wind blew "stiff" on Thursday, July 3, and the yacht ran with her sails reefed. Portions of her rigging broke loose, and a man climbed the mainmast to seize them. "He did so, after a fashion," James Steers observed, "but she shook him so I could hardly think he could hold on, and we made sail again. We had for dinner today veal stew with bread pudding for dessert. Gave Brother George an emetic and he feels better. Distance run this day 212 miles. Longitude 30° 5′, Latitude 48° 46′."

While the morning following was thick and foggy, a breeze sprang up and the fog cleared before noon. "It's a beautiful day," James Steers informed his journal, "this being the 4th of

July, the greatest of all days to all true-hearted Americans, and the Wonder of the World. The Captain would not let anybody work any more than was absolutely necessary. He gave them a bottle of gin and you would laugh to hear the toasts given at dinner. Then the wind died away and it was as still as a mill pond. Brother George is a little better, but he has not gained as fast as you would think he ought to. His appetite is poor. If we have three days good wind we will make the land. Distance run this day 179 miles. Longitude 25° 36′, Latitude 49° 11′."

The calm continued throughout July 5, 6, and 7, and during those three days the yacht ran a total of only 147 miles. "We were in hopes of making the passage in 14 days," wrote James Steers, "but if we have so little wind we may be a week more. Here we are tumbling about and not making any headway." James Steers now diagnosed his brother's trouble as more homesickness than seasickness. In an effort to effect a cure, he gave George a shower bath by throwing buckets of water over him in the cockpit, and that made everybody laugh, George included. The captain set the crew to work "making a capstan cover, yoke ropes, gangway ropes and such like," and James Steers, watching, once more tilted a glass. "I drink to those I love and respect," he wrote. "Amen."

There were light breezes from the north on the morning of Tuesday, July 8, and as they freshened in the afternoon James Steers noted with delight the *America*'s reaction: "She commenced stepping along pretty lively, which I tell you was very gratifying to all on board, after four days rolling about and not wind enough to keep her steady. At 2 P.M. set the squaresail, or 'Big Ben,' or 'Broad Mouth,' as the Captain now calls it. We have three vessels in sight. One is a large ship with everything set, and she can go. We passed them like leaving a dock. We would like to have been close enough to find out what her name was." But these jubilant entries were followed by another of dire lament: "Our liquor is all but gone." Now the yacht's position was longitude 17° 56′, latitude 49° 26′.

With the favorable winds continuing, the *America* sailed rapidly throughout Wednesday, July 9. "All hands well," James Steers noted. "Busy pointing ropes and cleaning up. Expect to sight land tomorrow. Exchanged signals with a large American ship bound west, supposed to be one of the Liverpool packets. We are having a glorious run and calculate at noon that we are about 480 miles from Havre. We had for dinner today beautiful pieces of beef and pork, also flapjacks. We also had to break open one of the boxes marked 'Rum' [belonging to Colonel Hamilton and the Stevens brothers], as all of our own stock was consumed and we were not going to starve in a Market Place. So we took out four bottles and think it will last us. Distance run 272 miles. Longitude 11° 48′, Latitude 49° 12′."

During Thursday, July 10, the speed of the *America* averaged 10½ knots. Throughout the morning she chased and gained on three square-rigged ships with all sails set until they veered off her course. "I hope we will be in Havre tomorrow," James Steers wrote, and then with reference to one of the purloined bottles of rum he added, "I need something to keep me up. We have been out nineteen days today. Distance run today 250 miles. Longitude 5° 43′, Latitude 49° 31′."

At 1:30 in the morning of Friday, July 11, the lookout aboard the *America* saw a dark mass ahead and knew he sighted land. It was the Scilly Isles off the extreme southwest coast of Cornwall, England. The yacht ran toward the Isles and soon encountered what she was after, a pilot boat carrying pilots familiar with the English Channel. "This Channel beats everything and all conception that I had of its extent and magnitude," wrote James Steers. "The pilot boats beggar all description. They are about 40 feet long, sloop rigged, or cutter, as they call them. Most of them carry only two pilots and these two as dirty as chimney sweeps. The first thing they ask is, 'Do you want a pilot?' If answered in the affirmative, they ship over the side a small boat and board you. The pilot steps aft and is introduced to the Captain. They make a bargain as to the amount.

He next asked, 'Have you a bottle of spirits aboard for the boat?' I will give the words that passed between our Captain and the pilot. In answer to the first question the Captain said no. 'Have you any pork or beef?' The Captain told the cook to get some of each kind and give it to the boat. 'Could you spare some tea and coffee? Have you any bread to spare? We have been out this trip three weeks last Tuesday.' Here the Captain filled away and the boat had to leave."

A strong wind from the northwest carried the yacht flying across the Channel on a course almost due east. Off the Dorset landmark called Portland Bill she veered to the southeast, skirted Pointe de Barfleur, France, and with but slight alteration of direction drove on for Le Havre. "We have every sail set," wrote James Steers, "and the way she slides along 'knocks' the pilot. He wanted to heave the lead himself, so we gratified him. He could not believe that she was going twelve knots, because she made so little fuss."

The *America* dropped anchor off Le Havre at 9 that night, and James Steers noted in his journal: "We have made the run from the foot of Twelfth Street to Havre in twenty days and six hours, and you will observe that we were becalmed, in all, five days and four hours, or 124 hours out of this time. The *Zurich* packet beat us one day and left six days before us. Lay to all night off Havre. At 4 A.M. squared away and got in about 10 A.M., Saturday, July 12, 1851."

Like any famous vessel, the *America* has been the victim of numerous spurious stories. One, contributed by G. W. Sheldon to the July 1882 issue of *Harper's New Monthly Magazine,* contained this bit of imaginative writing:

> One of the most brilliant successes of the clipper era was the yacht *America*. . . . After a sail of twenty-two days and four hours, during five days of which she was so becalmed as to make only six miles a day, she reached the neighborhood of Havre, her port of destination, and was met by a Channel pilot-boat, which at once showed the French flag, and was supposed, of course, to carry a French pilot. As soon as the pilot stepped

on board, James R. Steers said to his own pilot, Richard Brown, who had brought the yacht from New York, "Dick, that fellow is no Frenchman." Immediately Dick walked up to the stranger, and shouted, in most emphatic tones: "I tell you what, my friend, if you let this yacht scrape bottom, I'll throw you overboard." Dick kept hold of the tiller himself, and would not give it up. As the yacht approached the lights of Havre, the pilot confessed his inability to take her in. He left her, and hurried in his own boat to Cowes, with the news that "the Yankee is the fastest vessel going."...

So it came to pass that when the Steers brothers and the rest of the party crossed the Channel, and offered to back their yacht with wagers, they discovered that they had been betrayed. There was nobody to take their bets. So confident of success were they that they had brought $4,000 each to invest in that way, while Dick Brown had manifested his faith by mortgaging his own pilot-boat in New York to John C. Stevens for $2,000, every cent of which he intended to stake upon the race. But the "French" pilot, who had been employed by somebody to get on board the *America* and learn her sailing qualities, had destroyed their chance of winning a dollar....

While it is true that soon after the arrival of the *America* abroad an event took place which demonstrated her speed and caused owners of certain rival yachts to regard her warily, the event had nothing to do with an English spy posing as a French pilot. This particular fabrication, among the many contained in the G. W. Sheldon story, could be dismissed as ludicrous, but for the reflection cast on the honor of the British yachtsmen of that era, an upright body. The actual incident disclosing the *America's* superiority took place not off Le Havre, but some days afterwards in the vicinity of Cowes, and was the fault—if fault it could be called—of the Americans aboard her. The facts will be told at their proper place, a bit later on in this narrative.

Captain Brown and the Steers brothers found Le Havre picturesque. "This is a very romantic place," James Steers wrote, "but art has done more than nature. The harbor is a continuation of a canal with gates about every 500 feet. The tide rises and falls about 24 feet. The piers are all of hewn stone beautifully fitted together, and paved streets join the canals. At about every 200 feet are swinging bridges. The streets are paved with square blocks of stone."

Through crossing the Atlantic by steamer, the Stevens brothers and Colonel and Mrs. Hamilton had reached France ahead of the *America,* and they waited in Paris for word of the yacht's arrival at Le Havre. Concerning this sojourn and the *America*'s prospects, Colonel Hamilton wrote for his subsequently published *Reminiscences* the following:

> Such was the want of confidence of our countrymen in our success, that I was earnestly urged by Mr. William C. Rives, the American Minister [to France], and Mr. Sears, of Boston [David Sears, a member of the New York Yacht Club], not to take the vessel over [to England], as we were sure to be defeated. My friend, Mr. H. Greeley [Horace Greeley, editor and publisher of the *New York Tribune*], who had been at the Exhibition at London, meeting me in Paris, was most urgent against our going. He went so far as to say: "The eyes of the world are on you; you will be beaten, and the country will be abused, as it has been in connection with the Exhibition." I replied, "We are in for it, and must go." He replied, "Well, if you do go, and are beaten, you had better not return to your country." This awakened me to the deep and extended interest our enterprise had excited, and the responsibility we had assumed. It did not, however, induce us to hesitate. I remembered that our packet ships had outrun theirs, and why should not this schooner, built upon the best model?

Eventually news came that the *America* had arrived safely at Le Havre. Commodore Stevens and his brother proceeded there immediately, and after a bit more than a fortnight Colonel and Mrs. Hamilton left Paris for Cowes. At Le Havre the Messrs. Stevens, through connections with the French naval authorities, arranged for the yacht to be placed in a government dry dock, where the copper encasing her bottom was scraped and polished, the gripe at her forefoot was minutely reduced, a sliver was planed from her rudder, and she was painted afresh nearly all over.

She emerged from this treatment with gleaming white upper works and a hull of glistening black decorated with gold trail-boards forward, a gold stripe along her sides, and the eagle on her transom awarded new feathers of gold. Finally, her own sails were bent to her spars, and she was ready to enter the Channel again and to race against any and all yachts belonging to that breed of people for whom the Channel was named.

Following the basic portions of the refitting, George and James Steers and the two teen-aged sons of the latter left for a few days to see the sights of Paris and London. But by Wednesday, July 30, they reached the Isle of Wight, and on finding that the *America* had not yet arrived there, they secured accommodations overlooking the waters separating the Isle from the Hampshire coast.

From here they could keep watch for the appearance of the *America*. In this vigil they were not alone, for a yachting correspondent for *Bell's Life* also did sentinel duty. In a dispatch to the sporting periodical dated Cowes, Thursday, July 31, the correspondent wrote:

> Wednesday morning an intimation reached this place by the Havre steamer, which left the day previous, that the yacht had departed for Cowes, and, consequently, everyone interested in her arrival was on the *qui vive*. Calms, however, retarded her progress. At nine P.M. the intelligence was confirmed by the arrival of the U.S. Steamer *Humboldt* in the roads, from on board which Colonel Hamilton and his lady disembarked to await her coming. This morning, about six o'clock, a suspicious-looking craft was observed working down with light winds, owing to which and the flood tide she shortly afterwards brought up in mid-channel. The schooner had a red ensign forward, the American swallowtail burgee at the main, and the American ensign at the peak. Throughout the forenoon a perfect calm prevailed. At noon the ebb tide made to the westward, and a light westerly breeze also sprang up. The *Lavrock*

cutter got under way to meet the *America,* which shortly after followed her example, and both yachts worked up to our rendezvous in company, witnessed by several of our celebrated yacht skippers and *cognoscenti.* A slight opportunity was afforded them to watch the schooner's progress through the water with one of our cutters; however it would be premature to offer an opinion of the merits of either. The *Lavrock* had her boat towing astern; she is supposed to be one of our fastest cutters and she held her own. About one the *America* anchored in the roads abreast the castle, and has since been inspected by several visitors....

While the correspondent for *Bell's Life* did not openly admit that the *America* had beat the *Lavrock* in this scrub race, nor indeed that any contest had occurred, so much is implied by his assertion that the cutter had "held her own" and that she would have made a better showing but for the drag of her dinghy.

The Steers brothers also witnessed the event. On sighting the *America* lying motionless offshore, they vainly signaled that they wished to board her and a bit later noticed her sails filling. "The cutter *Lavrock* got under way to try her," James Steers noted in his journal. "In sailing 4 miles, we beat her ½ mile. This cutter is about 80 tons, new, built by Mr. White of Cowes. She is styled here 'White's Improvement'."

Commodore Stevens told the story of the *Lavrock* much later, following his return to New York. On October 2, 1851, he and his brother and Colonel Hamilton were guests of honor at a dinner given at the Astor House, and when called upon to speak, the Commodore explored the incident in detail:

Gentlemen, you may, perhaps, have observed that my hair is somewhat grayer than it was when I last met you. I'll tell you how it happened. In coming from Havre, we were obliged, by the darkness of the night and a thick fog, to anchor some five or six miles from Cowes. In the morning, early, the tide was against us, and it was dead calm. Later a gentle breeze sprang up, and with it came gliding down the *Lavrock,* one of the newest and fastest cutters of her class. The news spread like lightning that the Yankee clipper had arrived, and that the *Lavrock* had gone down to show her the way up.

The yachts and vessels in the harbor, the wharfs, and windows of all the houses bordering on them, were filled with thousands of spectators, watching with eager eyes the eventful trial they saw we could not escape; for the *Lavrock* stuck to us, sometimes laying to, and sometimes tacking, evidently showing she had no intention of quitting us.

We were loaded with extra sails, with beef and pork, and bread, enough for an East India voyage, and were somewhere between four and five inches too deep in the water. We got up our sails with heavy hearts—the wind had increased to a five or six knot breeze; and after waiting until we were ashamed to wait longer, we let her get about two hundred yards ahead and then started in her wake.

I have seen and been engaged in many exciting trials at sea and on shore. I made the match with Eclipse against Sir Henry [a horse race], and had heavy sums, both for myself and for my friends, depending upon the result. I saw Eclipse lose the first heat and four-fifths of the second without feeling one-hundredth part of the responsibility, and without suffering one-hundredth part of the trepidation I felt at the thought of being beaten by the *Lavrock* in this eventful trial.

During the first five minutes not a sound was heard, save, perhaps, the beating of our anxious hearts, or the slight ripple of the water upon her sword-like stem. The captain was crouched down upon the floor of the cockpit, his seemingly unconscious hand upon the tiller, with his stern, unaltering gaze upon the vessel ahead. The men were motionless as statues, with their eager eyes fastened upon the *Lavrock* with a fixedness and intensity that seemed almost supernatural. The pencil of an artist might perhaps convey the expression, but no words can describe it.

It could not, nor did not, last long. We worked quickly and surely to windward of her wake. The crisis was passed; and some dozen of deep-drawn sighs proved that the agony was over. We came to anchor a quarter, or, perhaps a third of a mile ahead, and, twenty minutes after our anchor was down, the Earl of Wilton was on board to welcome and introduce us to his friends.

To the Earl and his family, to the Marquis of Anglesey and his son, Lord Alfred Paget, to Sir Bellingham Graham, and a host of other noblemen and gentlemen, were we indebted for a reception as hospitable and frank as ever was given to prince or peasant. From the Queen herself we received a mark of attention rarely accorded even to the highest among her own subjects; and I was given to understand that it was not only intended as a courtesy extended to myself and friends, but also as a proof of the estimation in which she held our country; thereby giving a significance to the compliment infinitely more acceptable and valuable.

But none of these welcomings, early in the sojourn of the *America* at the Isle of Wight, were so hospitable as to include an invitation to the Stevens brothers and Colonel Hamilton that they race their yacht against some native opponent. With reference to the *Lavrock* incident, Colonel Hamilton, in his *Reminiscences,* wrote:

I mention this because it had a most important bearing on subsequent events. The *Lavrock* being a cutter, although of less tonnage than the *America,* was ranked by the Club [the Royal Yacht Squadron] as a match for a schooner not larger than the *America.* She having been so much beaten in so short a distance, induced an estimate of the *America's* sailing qualities, which much impaired the confidence of the Club in the superiority of their yachts.

Commodore Stevens waited a polite couple of days and then countered the silence on the part of his British hosts in a manner typically American. Perhaps sessions at a poker table had taught him that when holding what looked to be winning cards it was advisable to open, lest the hand be passed out. In an envelope endorsed "Yacht *America,* August 2, 1851—Commodore Stevens presents his respects to Lord Wilton, and begs to present for his consideration the enclosed proposition," he sent this note:

The New York Yacht Club, in order to test the relative merits of the different models of the schooners of the old and new world, propose through Commodore Stevens, to the Royal Yacht Squadron, to run the yacht *America* against any number of schooners belonging to any of the Yacht Squadrons of the Kingdom, to be selected by the Commodore of the Royal Yacht Squadron, the course to be over some part of the English Channel outside the Isle of Wight, with at least a six-knot breeze. This trial of speed to be made at an early day to be selected by the Commodore of the Royal Yacht Squadron. And if on that day there shall not be at least a six-knot breeze, then, on the first day thereafter that such a breeze shall blow.

On behalf of the New York Yacht Club,
John C. Stevens, Commodore

Cowes, August 2, 1851

After dispatching the note, Commodore Stevens, together with his brother Edwin and Colonel and Mrs. Hamilton, visited London. Before going, the Commodore told the Steers brothers of his challenge and requested that, if a reply were received within an expected few days, he should be notified immediately. But none came while he was away.

During the Commodore's absence, James Steers made these entries in his journal:

On Sunday we went to church, about 4 miles off. The name of the place is Wappingham [Whippingham]. This is a little parish church. We were invited to go, that is George and myself, so, according to previous agreement, we went to see the Queen, Prince Albert and the young animals. We had a delightful sight of them. The Queen is of small stature, say about 4 feet 10 inches, rather stout, not anyway good looking, dressed very plain. Prince Albert is a fine looking fellow, and so is his son, the Prince of Wales, about ten years old, I believe. The Queen has two ladies of honor to wait on her, two every month, that is, to give them a change. . . . On Monday these two ladies came on board of our boat. When I told them I had the pleasure of seeing them before, the prettiest one said: "Yes, Sir, I believe I saw you at church on last Sabbath." I replied in the affirmative. She conversed quite freely and was much pleased with the boat. She said she had been on board of every yacht but was never on board of such a one, not excepting the Queen's. She gave us an invitation to go through the Osborne palace [Osborne House, a summer residence of Queen Victoria on the Isle of Wight near Cowes].... We are run down with [visited aboard the *America* by] gentlemen and ladies all day long, one day after another. I have a half bushel of cards, all requesting us to call.... Yesterday there was a yacht race off Southampton for a hundred guinea prize. Six started in the first class, eight in the second. About one o'clock, the Marquis of Angleville [Anglesey] came on board and gave us an invitation to sail in his cutter *Pearl* of 130 tons. We saw the whole race and I believe candidly we could have beaten the whole fleet under our mainsail and jib....

In 1851 the Marquis of Anglesey (born Henry William Paget) was 83 years old, but in spite of his age and his physical disabilities an extremely active yachtsman. For decades he had served in the British Army and had ended up retired as a field marshal, minus a leg. This had been blown off at Waterloo, allegedly by the last cannon fired by Napoleon. Legend also depicted him as reporting to his commander, Wellington, "By God, Sir, I have lost my leg!" and Wellington replying complacently, "Why, so you have, my good fellow, so you have."

Twice married, the Marquis was the father of eight sons and ten daughters. A founder in 1812 of what was then called simply the Yacht Club at Cowes (a name which underwent various alterations until finally by royal warrant it became the Royal Yacht Squadron in 1833), the Marquis ordered built for himself the cutter *Pearl* in 1815. Aboard her, his favorite son, Lord Alfred Paget, was christened that same year, with the father holding the infant by a leg and dipping him head first into the sea. It was no wonder, then, that Lord Alfred grew up to become Clerk Marshal to Queen Victoria, an office embracing many duties of trust, one being the supervision of the Queen's two steam yachts, the 225-foot *Victoria and Albert* and the smaller *Fairy*.

In 1851 the Marquis of Anglesey resided in and served as governor of Cowes Castle, an ancient structure dating back to the reign of Henry VIII, and the Royal Yacht Squadron had its clubhouse in a building on the Parade at West Cowes, across the Medina River from the Castle. Three years later, following the death of the Marquis, the Squadron took over the Castle, and its former clubhouse became the Gloucester Hotel.

While, at the time of the *America*'s visit, the Marquis and his son wielded enormous influence in the affairs of the Royal Yacht Squadron, the Earl of Wilton, as Commodore—and as an extremely popular Commodore, at that—wielded perhaps more. He was a skilled politician and a man of great tact and diplomacy, traits he had exhibited since an early age. Born in 1799, he was thus 52 in 1851. He was the second son of Robert Grosvenor, the Marquis of Westminster, and of Grosvenor's wife, the former Eleanor Egerton, daughter of Thomas Egerton, then the Earl Wilton. Aware at an early age that as a second son he would not be likely, by the laws of primogeniture, to inherit either his father's title or estates, he took the name of his maternal grandfather, and at the death of the latter became the Earl of Wilton by royal license.

The Earl owned the huge topsail schooner *Xarifa,* reputedly once a slave-ship, captured and condemned and rebuilt into a yacht. He was a sportsman in areas beyond yachting, in coach and flat racing and as a gentleman rider in steeplechases. An accomplished musician, he regularly played the organ on Sundays during London's winter season at the Chapel Royal, Savoy, off the Strand, an edifice that had served in medieval times as a recognized sanctuary for fugitive lawbreakers. This bit of doggerel concerning Earl Wilton once appeared in a magazine:

> His character, how difficult to know—
> A compound of psalm tunes and tally-ho;
> An amorous lover with a saintly twist,
> And now a jockey, now an organist.

The Stevens brothers and Colonel and Mrs. Hamilton remained in London only a few days, barely long enough to take in the Great International Exhibition at Hyde Park. They returned to the Isle of Wight eagerly anticipating an early answer from Commodore Wilton to Commodore Stevens's challenge sent on August 2, only to discover that none had as yet arrived. While they waited, they employed Robert Underwood, a seasoned British pilot familiar with local waters found for them by the U.S. consul at Southampton, together with a couple of equally trustworthy British seamen, to assist in working the yacht if a race could be arranged.

These additions to the crew, plus the stream of visitors coming constantly aboard, crowded the *America*'s accommodations. This factor and another soon resulted in a rupture of the hitherto friendly relations between the owners of the vessel and George and James Steers and the latter's two sons. Since the four members of the Steers family were not employees of the owners, they considered themselves guests, and yet now that they had assisted in bringing the yacht safely across the Atlantic and putting her in shape for racing they complained of not being treated as such.

In journal entries for Friday and Saturday, August 8 and 9, James Steers wrote:

> I am much dissatisfied with "Old Stevens." He is a damned old hog, bristles and all. I will tell you. On Friday night, Henry went on board to go to bed, when lo and behold the stateroom door was locked. On Saturday morning, Henry told me and George of it, and George felt bad. We have had to sleep on shore ever since we have been here. So George went up to "Johnny" and told him we were going to leave. He wanted to know the reason. Then I spoke and told him what I thought of him. He saw George at the hotel and said he did not mean anything by it, he had some things in it [the stateroom], and the door being left open he was afraid some of the men would take them. He has not even asked us to take a drink since he came on board, but we take about two bottles every day. At night,

he sits down on the cabin floor in his shirt tail and counts them all over. When he finds any missing he calls the steward and says: "Where the hell does my liquor go to?" He [the steward] says: "I don't know, sir. The Messrs. Steers take some when they want any." "How do they get it when I carry the key?" The steward told him we had a key to the wine locker. He has not said anything to either of us yet, and if he does he will get hell or something worse.

Friday, August 8, was a day unsatisfactory to John Cox Stevens for another reason, which may have accounted for his temper. On that day he finally received a reply to his challenge of August 2, and the delays it voiced were no doubt irritating to a man of his temperament. The reply read:

The Commodore of the Royal Yacht Squadron has the honor to acknowledge the receipt of a proposition from the New York Yacht Club, to run the Yacht *America* against any number of schooners belonging to any of the Yacht Clubs of the Kingdom upon certain conditions. He will take the earliest opportunity to acquaint the proprietors of schooners throughout the Kingdom of the proposed trial, but as there are a great many Yacht Clubs in Great Britain and Ireland [seventeen in 1851], some little time must necessarily elapse before answers can be received. The members generally of the Royal Yacht Squadron are greatly interested in testing the relative merits of the different models of the old and new world without restriction as to rig or otherwise, and with this view have offered a cup, to be sailed for by vessels of all rigs and nations on the 22nd instant. It would be a subject to them of the highest gratification to hear that the *America* had entered as a competitor on the occasion.

Wilton, Commodore of the R. Y. Squadron

Royal Yacht Squadron House, August 8, 1851.

John Cox Stevens was the sort of man who quickly made up his mind, and it is probable that he had much to do with making up the minds, with equal celerity, of those present with him in the *America* venture, his brother Edwin and Colonel Hamilton. First, he immediately accepted Earl Wilton's suggestion that the *America* be entered in the Royal Yacht Squadron regatta of the 22nd (a race around the Isle of Wight) open to yachts of "all rigs and nations," and then in a note to the Earl dated August 9 he added:

> Yet as the issue of a regatta is not always the test of the merits of the vessels engaged in it, I now propose to run the yacht *America* against any cutter, schooner, or vessel of any other rig of the Royal Yacht Squadron, relinquishing any advantage which your rules admit is due to a schooner from a cutter, but claiming the right to sail the *America* in such manner, by such booming out, as her raking masts require; the course to be in the English Channel with not less than a six-knot breeze; the distance to be not less than twenty nor over seventy miles out and back, and in such a direction as to test the qualities of the vessels before and by the wind. Although it would be most agreeable to me that this race should be for a cup of limited value, yet if it is preferred, I am willing to stake upon the issue any sum not to exceed ten thousand guineas. [roughly $50,000].

Lastly, John Cox Stevens moved a bit afield and approached the Royal Victoria Yacht Club, a rival of the Royal Yacht Squadron. The clubhouse and anchorage of the Royal Victoria was at Ryde, a town on the Isle of Wight coast a few miles to the southeast of Cowes. The annual regatta of the Royal Victoria was to begin on Wednesday, August 13, with a race for yachts of a size comparable with that of the *America.* In response to the overtures of Stevens, the officials of the Royal Victoria quickly agreed to welcome the *America* as a participant.

Thus, for the moment at least, it looked as though the yacht from New York would see some action, although there was no immediate response to the challenge of her owners for a race in the English Channel for a wager approximating two and a half times the vessel's cost. With reference to the $50,000 (or 10,000 guineas) proposed, James Steers noted in his journal, "This was a staggerer for them all." And in so noting, the keeper of the journal—in spite of the biting criticisms of John Cox Stevens he had written and would continue to write—expressed an admiration for the Commodore's daring that he could not conceal.

The Steers brothers made a friend of Robert Underwood, the pilot employed by the *America*'s owners, described by James Steers as "A fine old 'sojer,' by the way, who can take his pint of ale and not wink at it. He's about as broad as he is long." Underwood introduced George and James Steers to his brother-in-law, Michael Ratsey, the great yacht-builder of Cowes, and on August 10 they were invited to the Ratsey home for Sunday dinner. With his usual attention to what he put into his stomach, James Steers wrote, "We visited the shipyard until dinner was ready, which was about 1 o'clock. We had roast veal, mutton and a fine boiled ham with peas, beans, potatoes, etc. After that was cleared off, we had a currant pie with cream, then came the gooseberries, almonds, raisins, etc.; then cheese, wine, ale, etc. After dinner we took a walk."

On Sunday evening the Stevens brothers, influenced by Englishmen of their acquaintance, decided that the *America* needed to carry more canvas for the wind conditions peculiar to Isle of Wight racing grounds. Specifically, she needed a second jib—variously described as a "flying jib" or "topsail jib"—which would be footed on a new boom, and the boom, in turn, would constitute a lengthy extension forward of her bowsprit, which was already quite long. "Old Dick" Brown voiced serious disagreement with the idea, but his objections were overruled.

So early Monday morning, George and James Steers and the latter's two sons went off to procure this new equipment. They combined the main purpose of the expedition with a secondary one, however—a fact not publicly revealed until more than a quarter of a century later. In 1877, in a talk before the Seawanhaka Yacht Club of Long Island, Henry Steers (by then 41 years of age and a successful New York shipbuilder) told of his boyhood experience:

Well, my father and uncle wanted to make part of our expenses after coming so far. We went from one place to another trying to get a little money on the race, but our success was not brilliant. We were rigged pilot-boat fashion, no foretop-mast and no flying jib-boom, and as some thought we could do better with a flying jib, we went to Ratsey to get him to make the spar, and my uncle bet him the price of it that we could beat any boat that he could name, and he named the *Beatrice*. Well, then we went to a sailmaker [George Ratsey, a relative of Michael] to have a flying jib made, and we bet the price of this sail on the race. We heard there was someone else nearby who wanted to bet, but it turned out he wanted to "book it," as they do over there, but we wanted the cash put up, and so this wager fell through. So, after all, all that we got on the race was the price of the flying jib-boom and the sail.

The race cited was that for which the *America* was entered open to yachts of "all rigs and all nations" to be held by the Royal Yacht Squadron on August 22. But, as has been related, the *America* was also scheduled to race in the August 13 regatta of the Royal Victoria Yacht Club of Ryde—or so it was believed by those concerned with the *America* until the day before the Ryde event. On Tuesday, August 12, the disappointment of James Steers was spelled out by this entry in his journal:

A beautiful morning. Was down to the beach about 6 o'clock waiting for the boat to come off for us. Went to the yard, got the boom, towed it aboard, got breakfast, after which got the boom out, stay up, sail fitted, and everything ready. About 2 P.M. a messenger brought off a note to the Commodore containing the decision of the Ryde Yacht Club refusing to allow us to enter tomorrow's race. The objections are these: According to "standing" rules, every yacht has to be the whole property of one individual. There being several owners of our boat, she was rejected. This made us all downhearted. "Old Pig" got mad, went ashore, asked if our challenge of $50,000 was accepted, was answered in the negative.

For whatever actual reason the *America* was denied permission to enter officially the regatta of the Royal Victoria Yacht Club, she could not be stopped from doing so unofficially. Nor was she. For on the day of the race—Wednesday, August 13—James Steers wrote:

> This day begins with no wind at all. We got ready to take a sail with the racers, but they did not start [on time], not having any wind. The vessels entered were the schooners *Brilliant,* 360 tons; *Bacchante,* 160; *Enchantress,* 180; *Capricorn,* 230; cutters *Alarm,* 193; *Arrow,* 150; *Eclipse,* 130; *Liverpool, Cygnet,* etc. About 3 P.M. a breeze sprang up from the southwest and they started. The race was around the Isle. About 4½ P.M. they came abreast of us going down. We got under way with only our jib and foresail, slipped our anchor, put after them, and, as I hope to sleep sound tonight, we kept up with that sail. We left them at the Needles and came back to our anchor.

The *America* again taunted the yachtsmen of the Royal Victoria on Friday, August 15. Members of the Ryde club staged the second race of their regatta on that day, and during its running the *America,* once more assuming her gadfly role, showed the contestants how a really fast yacht could be sailed.

> About 10 o'clock got under way [James Steers wrote]. Wind NW. Light breezes. Beat down to the Needles. Later the breeze sprang up. We turned around and made for the race boats. They were at least three miles ahead. We beat the whole fleet of about thirty sail.

But James Steers was not gratified by all that happened that Friday. He continued irked by the social gulf which placed his brother, his sons, and himself on one shore and the *America*'s owners on another, and his injured feelings are acutely reflected in his final journal entry for the day:

> At 6 P.M. came to anchor at Ryde. Got supper of jerked beef, fried spuds and stinking chicken. The second mate wanted a smoke, went up to Mr. Hamilton and addressed him with "Can

you give me some segars for some poor men?" There were six of them. Captain, second mate, chief mate, carpenter's mate and pilot, six all told. The gentleman gave him *four segars* to divide among the six. Now how were they to divide them? At 10, "Johnny" [John Cox Stevens] and the aristocracy went ashore to the ball at Ryde.

Mid-August was the height of the yachting season throughout the Isle of Wight. Leading British newspapers, including the most influential of them all, *The Times* of London (nicknamed "The Thunderer") had correspondents there. Soon the *Times* man learned of the *America*'s difficulties in entering any but the forthcoming Royal Yacht Squadron's race of August 22, and in prose that was at once incensed and sensitive he let loose a blast at British sportsmanship that only a Briton could write and that only a newspaper as fearless as *The Times* would dare publish in Britain. The dispatch was datelined "Cowes, Saturday, August 16," and is given here in part:

Most of us have seen the agitation which the appearance of a sparrowhawk in the horizon creates among a flock of wood-pigeons or skylarks, when unsuspecting all danger, and engaged in airy flights or playing about over the fallows, they all at once come down to the ground and are rendered almost motionless by fear of the disagreeable visitor. Although the gentlemen whose business is on the waters of the Solent are neither wood-pigeons nor skylarks, and although the *America* is not a sparrow-hawk, the effect produced by her apparition off West Cowes among the yachtsmen seems to have been completely paralyzing.

I use the word "seems," because it cannot be imagined that some of those who took such pride in the position of England as not only being at the head of the whole race of aquatic sportsmen, but as furnishing almost the only men who sought pleasure and health upon the ocean, will allow the illustrious stranger to return with the proud boast to the New World that she had flung down the gauntlet to England, Ireland and Scotland, and that no one had been found to take it up. If she were victorious, all that could be said was that the American builder had put together a lighter, swifter and better made mass of wood and iron than any the English builders had matched against her. No one could affirm there was the least disgrace attached to us from the fact.

But if she be permitted to sail back to New York with her challenge unaccepted, and can nail under it, as it is fastened up on one of her beams, that no one dared touch it, then there will be some question as to the pith and courage of our men, and yachting must sink immeasurably in public estimation, and must also be deprived of the credit which was wont to be attached to it, of being the nursery for bringing up our national naval spirit to a respectable and well-grown maturity. The discomfiture, I repeat, would be as nothing if we were beaten after a well-fought field, compared to the discredit of running away or evading a contest with a vaunting but certainly an honorable enemy.

And what, after all, if we are afraid of a phantom! I do not mean for a moment to assert that the *America* is not the most formidable competitor against which any yacht could be matched; but suppose she has her weak point of sailing, what a chuckle her owners would have over us for not trying to find out! . . . The vessel never yet was built that could sail equally well on all points and in all weathers. I trust that, whether she runs or not in the Cowes regatta, her qualities will be tested to the utmost by some of our first class yachts in a long run. . . .

There is something strange about the sudden start . . . [her] challenge has given the clubs. They have been reading month after month of the giant races, 3,000 miles long, over the Atlantic, between British and American steamers, without the least notion that anything afloat could touch their yachts. They heard it said that the Americans were improving vastly in shipbuilding. . . . They knew that the New York pilot boats were matchless for speed and seagoing properties in their class; but they are as much petrified in beholding an American yacht anchor in Cowes, and at getting a challenge from her, as if she were a Chinese war-junk or a Malay praha.

For some reason or other, though there was a whole armada of yachts at Ryde on Friday, there was great difficulty in getting up a race. . . . At last . . . schooners of the Royal Victoria Yacht

Club entered. . . . The event of the day, however, was the appearance of the Yankee [as an unofficial contestant]. I suppose she was tempted out by the breeze of wind, which was not, however, quite good for six knots, by the sailing of several crack schooners from Cowes, and by the desire to run past Osborne decorated for the *fête,* and with the royal yachts lying dressed in the roads, close under the house, so that the Queen might see what a craft Brother Jonathan could turn out.

Whatever the reason, out she came, with the wind on her quarter (after some three or four schooners had got well ahead of her), under mainsail, foresail, and her new jib. She went along very steadily and well up to Ryde, but did not show any great superiority till she was off the pier . . . when she seemed as if she had put a screw in her stern, and began to "fly" through the water.

She passed schooners and cutters one after the other, just as a Derby winner passes the "ruck," and as the breeze freshened slid with the speed of an arrow out toward the Nab, standing upright as a ramrod under her canvas, while the schooners were staggering under every inch they could set, and the cutters were heeling over under gaff topsails and balloon jibs.

It was remarked by the crowd on the pier-head that there was scarcely any foam at her bows, nor any broken water raised in a mass before them; but that the waves appeared to fall away under her keel and sides, offering the *minimum* of resistance to her course, owing to the peculiar form of her "entry."

Still, the nauticals looked knowing, and said, "Oh, aye, this is all very well for a schooner on this wind—let us see how she'll come back, when the wind will be a point or so worse for her!"

The *America* soon gave them an opportunity of judging on this point too. She went about in splendid style, a little short of the Nab, spinning around like a top, and came bowling away towards Cowes as fast if not faster than ever. As if to let our best craft see she did not care about them, the *America* went up to each in succession, ran to leeward of every one of them as close as she could, and shot before them, coming to anchor off Ryde at least two miles, as it seemed to me, ahead of any of the craft she had been running against.

Having landed the Messrs. Stevens for the ball at the clubhouse, she made sail in the evening for Cowes, and bowled away like a seagull, leaving all the boatmen and yachtmen with a deep sense that she was a "tartar," the former, in particular, being duly offended with the liberal display of stars and stripes on her ensign and burgee on such a crack craft, and irritated with the "gentlemen" for not accepting her challenge.

This blast of criticism from *The Times* shook British yachtsmen. They reddened and fidgeted like a group of delinquent schoolboys chastised by a teacher they respected. If ever the Royal Yacht Squadron had considered rescinding its invitation extended the *America* to sail in the race of Friday, August 22, such a thought suffered immediate banishment from the Squadron's collective mind.

Indeed, the article in *The Times* gained the prospect of a new opponent for the *America.* The proprietor of the challenging yacht turned out to be a man, well known to the Stevens brothers, who bore a name similar in sound to their own. He was 47-year-old Robert Stephenson, a Member of Parliament and a builder of railroads and bridges. In past years, his work had taken him to Canada and the United States, where he had visited the Stevens family at Hoboken. Robert Stephenson owned the 100-ton schooner yacht *Titania,* as much of an innovation in her day as the *America,* for she boasted an iron hull. After friendly dickering, it was agreed that on Thursday, August 28, the *America* and the *Titania* would race in the English Channel for a wager of £100 a side.

Throughout Saturday and Sunday, August 16 and 17, the aristocracy of the Isle of Wight visited the *America* in droves, and the yacht's owners entertained them with rich food and heady drink. The Steers brothers found themselves in the awkward position of being neither hosts nor guests, and apparently Commodore Stevens did nothing to put them at their ease. Consequently, they absented themselves as much as possible from the yacht and while away took steps toward carrying through a resolve they had considered earlier. This was to make arrangements for returning to New York.

Young George wanted to go home with them, but 15-year-old Henry begged to stay. So James Steers allowed him to, placing him in the care of "Old Dick" Brown. The last entry in the journal of James Steers, dated Monday, August 18, reads: "After supper, we left the boat, bound for York. Dick looked as though he had lost all his friends. He said if we would stay until after the race on Friday he would leave and come home with us, but we had engaged our passage on the *Atlantic* which left on the 20th from Liverpool. He came ashore with us and we took a parting drink."

There is nothing to indicate what George Steers said or how he felt. Perhaps on leaving Cowes he turned and regarded with a lingering look of affection the most noble of his many creations, the *America.* It is to be hoped he did, for while during the decades to follow she visited New York on several occasions, he never saw her again.

THREE

"A Crop of Glory . . . A Crop of Wisdom"

An article printed in an 1851 issue of a British newspaper contained this description of the water surrounding the Isle of Wight: "It is notoriously one of the most unfair to strangers that can be selected—and, indeed, does not appear as a good race-ground to anyone, inasmuch as the currents and tides render local knowledge of more value than swift sailing and nautical skill."

The Isle bears the shape of an irregular diamond. From its northern extremity at Cowes to its southern one at St. Catherine's Point, it measures close to 13 miles, while from its western end at the Needles to its eastern limit at Bembridge Point, it falls a bit short of 23 miles. The two southern faces of the Isle lie exposed to the English Channel, and its two northern ones are separated from the mainland by narrow, shoal-infested bodies of water called The Solent and Spithead. A feature of the area fronting on the Channel is the range of chalk cliffs towering to a height of 500 feet, portions of which, throughout the ages, have broken off and tumbled into the sea, leaving behind them deep ravines and creating where they have plunged hazards to navigation now and again made all the more hazardous by lying submerged.

The best known of the hazards are The Needles. Centuries ago it was written that "they protrude from the choppy waters like the gaunt fingers of a sinking giant. They are a terror to sailors on account of the double tide of the sea, which whirls away the ships, dashing them against the rocks on one side, or the neighboring shore on the other." By "double tide" was meant the rushing in and rushing out of the tide through the two apertures on the northern sides of the Isle—The Solent and Spithead. Proof that these dangers still existed and were recognized in 1851 is the fact that the Isle was then encircled by strategically situated lighthouses, lightships, and light buoys to the number of fifteen.

The wonder is that the Isle ever became a yachting center. The explanation rests in a historical aspect of British yachting. The earliest of the vessels were not racers and therefore required no lengthy race course. They were simply pleasure barges of the aristocracy, built for comfort and gaily decked out. In the beginning—and for a long while to follow—the English meaning of the term "regatta" merely signified a procession or parade of private craft, and such functions required only a short stretch of quiet water. For this purpose the few tranquil, protected coves in the vicinity of Cowes and Ryde were entirely adequate, and there was no call for ventures beyond them.

Inland the Isle is the opposite of its rugged coast. The temperate and warm seasons come early in the year, and fruits, flowers, and vegetables grow in abundance. Keats wrote some of his poetry there, as did Tennyson later on. For more than a century prior to 1851 a select group of Britain's wealthier noblemen established summer residences on the Isle, and from their loins sprang a progeny of yachtsmen. When competitive racing rescued the sport from its processional beginnings, these aristocratic sailors kept in stroke with the times, yet continued using waters close at hand, for their yacht basins, yacht-builders, and the edifices of their yacht clubs were already on the Isle. Moreover, races *around* the Isle seemed only reasonable to them, for this course of between 50 and 60 miles offered the advantage of permitting cheering spectators to witness both the starts and finishes of races from a single location. Indeed, not until quite a while after the *America* arrived at the Isle did they realize that the same goal could as well be gained if the yachts raced from Cowes or Ryde out into the English Channel and around a judges' ship posted at a given distance, and then returned to finish at the point from which the start had been made.

By 1851 the Isle had lost much of its earlier exclusiveness. This was because of the advent of steam transportation and the consequent easy accessibility of the Isle both from Southampton, across The Solent, and from Portsmouth, across Spithead, by regular steamer. Excursionists came not alone to watch yacht races, but to catch a glimpse, perhaps, of Queen Victoria or some member of her family. They wanted to know, first of all, if it were true that the Queen breakfasted to bagpipe music, and, secondly, if thirty cooks were employed during her summer stay at Osborne House. Since these crowds required shelter and feeding, hotels and boarding houses sprang up at Cowes, Ryde, and elsewhere, and for the commercial entertainment of the crowds a "pleasure pier" a half-mile in length was built off Ryde. The builders of the pier might better have directed their efforts toward endowing Ryde with a public waterworks and a sewerage system, for it possessed neither until 1855. Possibly because of this lack, the Isle was swept by a cholera epidemic in 1849 and by an outbreak of scarlatina during the yacht races of 1851.

The trophy offered for the race of Friday, August 22, was officially designated "The Royal Yacht Squadron's One Hundred Guinea Cup," presumably because it cost that much. The trophy had been voted at a meeting of Squadron members held in London on May 9, 1851, six days after the launching of the *America* thousands of miles away. While the race was open to yachts of "all rigs and nations," the *America* was the only alien vessel to participate. In stories of the race, the trophy has often been called mistakenly "The Queen's Cup," and even Commodore Stevens, in a speech, was once guilty of this error. The man who did the most to foul up the truth, however, was G. W. Sheldon, the writer who, in the July 1882 issue of *Harper's New Monthly Magazine,* told the far-fetched tale of the English spy who disguised himself as a French pilot in order to learn something of the *America's* sailing qualities. In that same contribution to *Harper's,* Sheldon declared that Queen Victoria, feeling that the *America* had been discriminated against, presented "the Steers brothers" with "a precise duplicate of the Queen's Cup for which they had not been allowed to compete. That is the cup which was brought home by them, and deposited by Mr. John C. Stevens and his friends in the hands of the New York Yacht Club, where it still lies safe, in spite of repeated efforts of foreign yachts to capture it."

A writer of a far different character and caliber was the correspondent of *The Times* of London who followed the great August 22 event—the world's most famous yacht race—from start to finish and reported it as accurately as any one man could, in all of its colorful detail. But this is not to say that the *Times* writer avoided all difficulty. The race finished so late that he could not send to his paper the whole of his story within the limits of its deadline for August 23, and the remainder was of necessity forwarded for appearance in the next issue. The following, then, represents the bulk of both dispatches, with certain duplications and other extraneous matter eliminated:

Cowes, Friday, August 22.

The day that has been looked forward to here with so much anxiety, . . . as pregnant with the most important results to the fame of the Royal Yacht Squadron, has at length arrived, and a few hours will soon set at rest the many thousand conjectures as to whether the Squadron is invincible, or whether that honor is henceforth to rest with our transatlantic brethren.

On no occasion, we understand, since the establishment of the Squadron, has so general an interest been manifested as to any particular vessel as has for some weeks pervaded all classes with respect to the American clipper. Her appearance in the water, as she rides quietly at anchor, has a singularity that cannot fail to be observed. She sits upon it like a duck, and, taken with her clean build and saucy, raking masts, she evidently looks bent on mischief.

Things have come to a pretty pass when a New Yorker challenges all England in Cowes Roads and all England hesitates about accepting the challenge. From the moment of our leaving the Waterloo Road station [in London] on Thursday evening, until our arrival at Cowes, nothing else was talked of by railroad and steamboat passengers. Good-humored surprise was expressed by some, ill-natured annoyance by others. But the most singular unanimity of opinion prevailed through all that "the Yankee" (as she is most improperly styled) was able to outsail creation.

Yet still the lurking hope, which ever filled Mr. Micawber's bosom, that "something might turn up" to save the honor of the Old Land, was lingering around many a heart; and now and then the cheerful assurance would burst forth that, even if the *America* carried off the cup this time, there would be half a score of English schooners this time twelvemonth ready and able to beat her.

Southampton was filled with visitors. Cowes was crammed—scarcely a bed to be found for love or money. Wanderers were moving about the streets long after midnight, knocking at impracticable doors and drawing nightcapped heads from windows, only to receive the unpleasing information that there was no room for them.

Towards morning there was a slight fall of rain, for which the yachtsmen were extremely thankful, as the cloudy atmosphere bore promise of a breeze. Shortly after nine o'clock the yachts were at their stations, off the Club House, the *America* lying considerably astern—a strange looking craft enough, with her long, low black hull, and thick, stiff looking rakish masts, not at all the sort of phantom ship that Fenimore Cooper loves to paint. A big-boned skeleton, she might be called, but no phantom. Hers are not the tall, delicate, graceful spars, with cobweb tracery of cordage, scarcely visible against the gray and threatening sky; but hardy sticks, prepared for work, and up to everything that can be put on them. She carries no foretopmast, being apparently determined to do all her work without one. And how she can do it this day will probably show better than any of the short and accidental courses that she has hitherto run against yachts of the Royal Yacht Squadron and others.

Cowes, Saturday, August 23.

A large portion of the peerage and gentry of the United Kingdom left their residences and forsook the sports of the moors to witness the struggle between the yachtsmen of England, hitherto unmatched and unchallenged, and the Americans who had crossed the Atlantic to meet them. All the feelings of that vast population which swarms in our southern ports and firmly believes in "Rule Britannia" as an article of national faith; all the prejudices of the wealthy aristocracy and gentry, who regarded the beautiful vessels in which they cruised about the Channel and visited the shores of the Mediterranean every summer as the perfection of naval architecture, were roused to the highest degree, and even the Queen of England did not deem the occasion unworthy of her presence.

Until within the last few days no Englishman ever dreamed that any nation could produce a yacht with the least pretensions to match the efforts of White, Camper, Ratsey, and other eminent builders. In the *Yacht List* for this very year there is an assertion which every man within sight of sea water from the Clyde to The Solent would swear to—that "Yacht building was an art in which England was unrivalled, and that she was distinguished preeminently and alone for the perfection of science in handling them."

From the Royal Cork Club, which was founded in 1720, to the Royal London, founded in 1849, there are 17 yacht clubs in various parts of the United Kingdom—ten English, four Irish, two Scotch, and one Welsh, and not one of them had ever seen a foreigner enter the lists in the annual matches. [Until] the *America* came over, the few who were aware that there was a flourishing club at New York did not regard it as of the slightest consequence, or as at all likely to interfere with their monopoly of the glory of the manliest and most useful of all sports.

The few trial runs the *America* made after her arrival proved she was possessed of great speed, and that her owners were not so little justified as at first they had been thought in offering to back an unproven vessel against any yacht in our waters for the large sum of £10,000, or for a cup or a piece of plate. As the day of the Royal Yacht Squadron's grand match drew near the entries became numerous, and 1851 will be celebrated for the largest number of starters for the Derby and for the £100 Cup respectively, that were ever known, so far as I can gather. The conduct of the Americans since their arrival in The Solent has been bold, manly and straightforward—qualities which Englishmen respect wherever they are found, and love to see even in an opponent.

In the memory of man Cowes never presented such an appearance as upon Friday. There must have been upwards of 100 yachts lying at anchor in the roads; the beach was crowded from Egypt [an entertainment area] to the piers—the esplanade in front of the Club thronged with ladies and gentlemen, and with the people inland, who came over in shoals, with wives, sons and daughters for the day. Booths were erected all along the quay, and the roadstead was alive with boats, while from sea and shore arose an incessant buzz of voices mingled with the splashing of oars, the flapping of sails, and the hissing of steam from the excursion vessels preparing to accompany the race.

Among the visitors were many strangers—Frenchmen *en route* for Havre, Germans in quiet wonderment at the excitement around them, and Americans already triumphing in the anticipated success of their countrymen. The cards containing the names and colors of the yachts described the course merely as being "round the Isle of Wight;" the printed program stated that it was to be "round the Isle of Wight, inside Noman's Buoy and Sandhead Buoy, and outside the Nab." The distinction, it will be seen, might have been productive of larger consequences than could be imagined.

The following yachts were entered, listed in the order in which they were placed from Cowes Castle, the first being the nearest. They were moored in a double line. No time allowed for tonnage:—

	Tons	Owners
Beatrice, schooner	101	Sir W. P. Carew
Volante, cutter	48	Mr. J. L. Cragie
Arrow, cutter	84	Mr. T. Chamberlayne
Wyvern, schooner	205	The Duke of Marlborough
Ione, schooner	75	Mr. A. Hill
Constance, schooner	218	The Marquis of Conyngham
Titania, schooner	100	Mr. R. Stephenson
Gipsey Queen, schooner	100	Sir H. B. Hoghton
Alarm, cutter	193	Mr. J. Weld
Mona, cutter	82	Lord A. Paget
America, schooner	170	Mr. J. C. Stevens, et al.
Brilliant, 3-mast. schr.	392	Mr. G. H. Ackers
Bacchante, cutter	80	Mr. B. H. Jones
Freak, cutter	60	Mr. W. Curling
Stella, cutter	65	Mr. R. Frankland
Eclipse, cutter	50	Mr. H. S. Featon
Fernande, schooner	127	Major Martyn
Aurora, cutter	47	Mr. T. Le Merchant

The mist which hung over the fields and woods from sunrise was carried off about 9 o'clock by a very gentle breeze from the westward, which veered round a little to the south soon afterwards, and the morning became intensely warm. At 9.55 the preparatory gun was fired from the clubhouse battery, and the yachts were soon sheeted from deck to topmast with clouds of canvas, huge gaff topsails and balloon jibs being greatly in vogue, and the *America* evincing her disposition to take advantage of her new jib by hoisting it with all alacrity.

The whole flotilla not in the race was already in motion, many of them stretching down towards Osborne and Ryde to get a good start on the clippers. Of the list above given the *Titania* and the *Stella* did not start, and the *Fernande* did not take her station. Thus only 15 started, of which seven were schooners, including the *Brilliant* (three-masted schooner), and eight were cutters. At 10 o'clock the signal gun for sailing was fired, and before the smoke had well cleared the whole of the beautiful fleet was under way, moving steadily to the east, with the tide and a gentle breeze. The start was effected splendidly, the yachts breaking away like a field of racehorses; the only laggard was the *America,* which did not move for a while after the others. [Fifteen-year-old Henry Steers, who was aboard the *America,* in later years explained what had happened. "The yachts were allowed to get up their sails after the first gun," he said. "But we found that we constantly overran our anchor and slewed around, and we had to lower our sails, and so all the yachts got off ahead of us. However, we had a large crew and got our sails up again very quickly. The slight delay made no difference."]

Steamers, shore-boats and yachts of all sizes buzzed along on each side of the course, and spread away for miles over the rippling sea—a sight such as the Adriatic never beheld in all the pride of Venice. Soon after the yachts started a steamer went off from the roads with the Earl of Wilton, Commodore of the Royal Yacht Squadron, and the members of the Squadron's sailing committee. The American Minister, Mr. Abbott Lawrence, and his son, Colonel Lawrence, attaché to the American Legation, arrived too late for the sailing of the *America,* but were accommodated on the committee's steamer, and went around the island in her, and several steamers chartered by private gentlemen or for excursion trips, also accompanied the match.

The *Gipsey Queen,* with all her canvas set and in the strength of the tide, took the lead after starting, with the *Beatrice* next, and then, with little difference in order, the *Volante, Constance, Arrow,* and a flock of others. The *America* went easily for some time under mainsail (with a small gafftopsail of a triangular shape braced up to the truck of the short and slender stick which serves as her maintopmast), foresail, jib and forestaysail [flying jib]; while her opponents had every cloth set that the club regulations allow. She soon began to creep upon them, passing some of the cutters to windward. In a quarter of an hour she had left them all behind, except the *Constance, Beatrice* and *Gipsey Queen,* which were well together, and went along smartly with a light breeze.

Once or twice the wind freshened a little, and at once the *America* gathered way, and passed ahead of the *Constance* and *Beatrice.* Another puff came and she made a dart to pass the *Gipsey Queen,* but the wind left her sails, and the little *Volante* came skimming past her with a stupendous jib, swallowing up all the wind that was blowing.

As the glorious pageant passed under Osborne House the sight was surpassingly fine, the whole expanse of sea from shore to shore being filled as it were with a countless fleet, . . . the green hills of Hampshire, the white batteries of Portsmouth, and the picturesque coast of Wight, forming a fine frame-work for the picture.

As the *Volante* passed the *America* great was the delight of the patriotic, but the nautical *cognoscenti* shook their heads, and said the triumph would be short-lived; the breeze was freshening, and then the sprightly cutter must give way, though she was leading the whole squadron at the time. At 10.30 the *Gipsey Queen* caught a draught of wind and ran past the *Volante,* the *Constance, America, Arrow* and *Alarm* being nearly in a line. At 10.45 the breeze freshened again for a short time, and the *America* passed the *Arrow, Constance* and *Alarm,* but could not shake off the *Volante* or come up with the *Gipsey Queen,* and exclamations were heard of "Well, Brother Jonathan is not going to have it all his own way," etc.

Passing Ryde the excitement on the shore was very great, and the great ichthosaurus-like pier was much crowded; but the *America* was forging ahead, and lessening the number of her rivals every moment. . . . The yachts were timed off Noman's Land buoy, and the character of the race at this moment may be guessed from the result:—

	H.	M.	S.
Volante	11	7	0
Freak	11	8	20
Aurora	11	8	30
Gipsey Queen	11	8	45
America	11	9	0
Beatrice	11	9	15
Alarm	11	9	20
Arrow	11	10	0
Bacchante	11	10	15

The other six were staggering about in the rear, and the *Wyvern* soon afterwards hauled her wind and went back towards Cowes. At this point the wind blew somewhat more steadily, and the *America* began to show a touch of her quality. Whenever the breeze took the line of her hull, all the sails set as flat as a drumhead, and, without any careening or staggering, she "walked along" past cutter and schooner, and, when off Brading, had left every vessel in the squadron behind her . . . with the exception of the *Volante,* which she overtook at 11.30, when she very quietly hauled down her jib, as much as to say she would give her rival every odds, and laid herself out for the race around the back of the island.

The weather showed symptoms of improvement, so far as yachting was concerned; a few seahorses waved their crests over the water, the highlands on shore put on their fleecy "nightcaps" of clouds, and the horizon looked delightfully threatening; and now the "Yankee" flew like the wind, leaping over, not against, the water, and increasing her distance from the *Gipsey Queen, Volante* and *Alarm* every instant.

The way her sails were set evinced superiority in the cutting which our makers would barely allow; but, certain it is, that while the jibs and mainsails of her antagonists were "bellied out," her canvas was as flat as a sheet of paper. No foam, but rather a water-jet, rose from her bows; and the greatest point of resistance—for resistance there must be somewhere—seemed about the beam, or just forward of her mainmast, for the seas flashed off her from her sides at that point every time she met them. While the cutters were threshing through the water, sending the spray over their bows, and the schooners were wet up to the foot of the foremast, the *America* was as dry as a bone. She had 21 persons on her deck, consisting of the owners, the crew, cook and steward, a pilot named Underwood, and some seamen who had been lent her. They nearly all sat aft, and when the vessel did not require any handling crouched down on the deck by the weather bulwarks.

At 11.37 the *Arrow, Bacchante, Constance* and *Gipsey Queen* stood away to the north, to round the Nab, imagining, most probably, that it was requisite to do so, as the usual course certainly is to go outside the lightship, though the cards did not specify it on this occasion. The *America* and most of the other yachts kept their course round the Foreland and by Bembridge. She ran past the white and black buoys at a tremendous rate, and at 11.47 tacked to the west, and stood in toward the Culver Cliffs, the nearest yacht being at least two miles to leeward astern of her.

At 11.58 she stood out again to the southeast, and, having taken a stretch of a mile or so, went about and ran in towards Sandown. The breeze died off at this point, and to keep the cutters and light craft off, the *America* hoisted her gafftopsail. . . . Under Shanklin Chine the set of the tide ran heavily against her, but still there was nothing to fear, for her rivals were miles away, some almost hull down!

While running under Dunnose at 12.58 her jib-boom broke off short. It may be remembered she procured this spar from Ratsey, of Cowes, but no blame attaches to him. The boom was broken by mismanagement on the part of the men when straining on it with the windlass, and did not snap from action of the sail. [Young Henry Steers, in telling of this incident long after the race, declared, "I remember that Dick Brown said he was damned glad it was gone, as he didn't believe in carrying a flying-jib to windward."]

This accident threw her up in the wind, and gave an advantage of about a quarter of an hour to her opponents, while she was gathering in the wreck. But it was of little use to them. Looking away to the east, they were visible at great distances, standing in shore or running in and out most helplessly astern. . . .

The wind fell off very much for more than an hour, and it was but weary work stretching along the coast against a baffling tide. . . . Soon after 3 o'clock the *Arrow* managed to run on the rocks to the east of Mill Bay; and the sailing committee's steamer the *Queen*, an excursion boat *Her Majesty*, and the yacht *Alarm*, at once made in to her assistance. . . .

Meanwhile minute after minute the "Yankee" was gaining ground, and at 3.30 was flying past St. Lawrence towards Old Castle, while the *Bacchante* and *Eclipse*, which had been working along honestly and steadily, were about 2½ miles to leeward behind her. Further away still were visible five or six yachts, some hull down. . . . The *America* had by this time got the wind on her quarter, having gone around Rocken-end, and thus having a tolerably fair course from the South to NW up to the Needles, the wind being light and the water somewhat broken.

The persons on board the steamers were greatly astonished at seeing ahead of the *America*, after she had rounded Rocken-end, a fine cutter with a jib and foresail together—"two single gentlemen rolled into one"—bowling away with all speed, as if racing for her life, and it was some time before they could be persuaded she was not the *Aurora;* but she was in reality the *Wildfire*, 42 tons, Mr. F. Thynne, of the Royal Cork Club, which was taking a little share in the match to herself [without being entered, and starting far ahead of the others], and had passed the End at 3.40. The *America*, however, bore straight down for the cutter, which was thoroughly well sailed, and passed her after a stern chase of more than an hour....

At 5.40 the *Aurora*, the nearest yacht actually in the race, was fully 7½ miles astern, the *Freak* being about a mile more distant, and the rest being "nowhere." The *America* at this time was close to the Needles, upon which she was running with a light breeze all in her favor. Two of the excursion steamers ran into Alum Bay and anchored there to see the race around the Needles. While waiting there in intense anxiety for the first vessel that should shoot around the immense pillars of chalk and limestone which bear the name, the passengers were delighted to behold the *Victoria and Albert*, with the Royal standard at the main, and the Lord Admiral's flag at the fore, steaming around from NW, followed by the *Fairy*....

Her Majesty, the Prince, and the Royal family, were visible by the aid of a glass from the deck of the steamers. The royal yacht went past the Needles, accompanied by the *Fairy*, at 5.35, but quickly returned and at 5.45 lay to off Alum Bay. The *Fairy* was signalled to proceed round the Needles, to bring tidings of the race, and at once started, Ariel-like, on her errand. Soon after the royal yacht anchored a boat put off from her, in the stern sheets of which were Prince Albert and the Prince of Wales [Albert Edward, then ten years old, crowned King of England on the death of his mother, Queen Victoria, a half-century later], who wore his white sailor's suit and tarpaulin hat. They landed, attended by two gentlemen, on the beach under the cliff at Alum Bay, with the aid of the boatmen, and it was some time before the saunterers from the steamboats, who were climbing up toward the heights, were aware of the presence of such distinguished visitors. They proceeded a short way up the narrow winding path which leads to the heights, but a wet drizzle drifted before the wind, and rendered the walk unpromising, and the royal party soon returned to the beach, the young prince dancing down the shelving with boyish vivacity.

After a stay of eight or ten minutes, the royal party returned to the yacht. The *Fairy*, which had returned to signal, again stood out past the Needles, but all doubt and speculation, if any there could have been, was soon removed by the appearance of the *America* hauling her wind round the cliff at 5.50. The breeze fell dead under the shore, and the *America* lowered out her fore sail and forestaysail so as to run before it. All the steamers weighed to accompany her, giving three cheers as she passed, a compliment which owners and crew acknowledged with waving hats.

At 6h. 4m.... the schooner... had got almost in line with the *Victoria and Albert*. Though it is not usual to recognize the presence of Her Majesty on such occasions as a racing match, no more, indeed, than a jockey would pull up his horse to salute the Queen when in the middle of his stride, the *America* instantly lowered her ensign—blue with white stars—the Commodore took off his hat, and all his crew, following his order and example, remained with uncovered heads for some minutes—a mark of respect to the Queen not the less becoming because it was bestowed by republicans....

[It was now] evident that the *America* had won the cup, unless some light cutter ran up with a breeze in the dusk and slipped past her. The steamers... returned towards Cowes, and the royal yacht, having run by the *America* under half-steam for a short distance, went on towards Osborne.

Off Cowes were innumerable yachts, and on every side was heard the hail, "Is the *America* first?"—The answer, "Yes." "What's second?"—The reply, "Nothing." As there was no wind, the time consumed in getting up from Hurst Castle to the winning flag was very considerable, the *America*'s arrival first not having been announced by gunfire till 8.37. The *Aurora*, which slipped up very rapidly after rounding the Needles, in consequence of her light tonnage and a breath of wind, was signalled at 8.45; the *Bacchante* at 9.30; the *Eclipse* at 9.45; the *Brilliant* at 1.20 A.M. August 23d. The rest were not timed.

Thus the *America* made good all her professions. It is with great pleasure I have to state that a protest which had been entered against her receiving the cup, on the ground that she had not followed the course marked out, was withdrawn, and that the Messrs. Stevens were presented by the Royal Yacht Squadron with the well-won cup.

After the race there was a very brilliant and effective display of fireworks by land and water along the clubhouse esplanade, at which 6,000 or 7,000 persons were present. A reunion took place at the clubhouse, and the occasion was taken of Ambassador Abbott Lawrence's presence to compliment him on the success of his countrymen. His Excellency acknowledged the kindness in suitable terms, and said that, though he could not but be proud of the triumph of his fellow citizens, he still felt it was but the children giving a lesson to the father.

A portion of this patently factual account in *The Times* was grist for the mills of the makers and purveyors of myths. They found it necessary to alter the part which read: "Off Cowes were innumerable yachts, and on every side was heard the hail, 'Is the *America* first?'—The answer, 'Yes.' 'What's second?'—The reply, 'Nothing.'" Barely had news of the *America*'s victory had time to reach the United States before the story was so radically changed that it invoked the name of Daniel Webster, the New England orator. Webster, while delivering an address at the State House in Boston, was alleged to have glanced at a message handed him by a page, and then to have digressed long enough to announce triumphantly to his audience, "Like Jupiter among the gods, the *America* is first and there is no second!"

John Cox Stevens bears a modicum of guilt in spreading and giving distorted color to the myth. On October 2, following his return to New York from England, he made a speech and during the course of it attributed the questions

"Who is first?" and "Who is second?" not to the throngs at Cowes, but to a "high personage." Quite naturally, this was taken to mean Queen Victoria, and inasmuch as the speech was reported in the *Spirit of the Times,* it received widespread circulation and was assumed to be gospel.

Consequently, almost all of the stories about the famous August 22 regatta appearing since then—written by reputable writers for equally reputable publications—have contained some such anecdote as this:

> The *America* ran ahead so fast that when she returned to the starting point, Cowes, the following memorable colloquy took place between the Queen and one of her officers:
> Her Majesty—"Signal Master, are the yachts in sight?"
> "Yes, may it please your Majesty."
> "Which is first?"
> "The *America.*"
> "Which is second?"
> "Ah, your Majesty, there is no second."

While actually there is no basis in fact for the story at all, the pity is that there is not. For had Victoria really participated in the dialogue imputed to her, so dedicated a yachting enthusiast was she that she would doubtlessly have approved the questions asked by her fictional self.

The day after the great race, on Saturday, August 23, the Queen demonstrated her great interest in yachting and in yachts by coming aboard the *America.* Colonel Hamilton, in his *Reminiscences,* gave this picture of what occurred:

> Colonel Phipps [an equerry to the Queen] informed Commodore Stevens by a note that if the *America* would fall down to opposite Osborne House her Majesty would visit the *America,* to which, in the absence of the Commodore, I replied that the yacht would be at anchor opposite Osborne House at four o'clock P.M. After getting all things in order this was done. Lord Alfred Paget, who was one of the Queen's attendants, then off duty, went down with us. Her Majesty and the Prince Consort, with four gentlemen and two ladies (Lady Desart and Miss Bing)

came off with her barge, sailed around the vessel, and came to at the port gangway; where she and her husband were received by the Commodore and conducted to the quarter-deck—the attendants, ladies and gentlemen, remaining forward of the main rigging, the two ladies on one side, and the gentlemen on the other. Lord Alfred presented us by name, and we had an agreeable chat, her Majesty congratulating us on our success at the regatta. To our surprise, and that of all present, the reserve and those forms generally observed in the presence of majesty were entirely done away. When I remarked upon this at the Club, the explanation given was that as we were her hosts, of course, we were put upon an equality with her Majesty. After awhile, she expressed a wish to go below. The Commodore took her Majesty's hand to help her to the cockpit, and then took her through the vessel, as I did the Prince. Her Majesty was particularly struck with the arrangement of the ballast, which was peculiar, and asked to see the accommodations for the crew. The whole thing went off well. . . .

In spite of what Colonel Hamilton wrote, legend has it that "Old Dick" Brown showed the Prince Consort through the *America*'s cabins, staterooms, and forecastle. No respecter of royalty, Captain Brown insisted that the Prince wipe the mud from his shoes before proceeding below. And legend also has it that the Queen was so impressed with the cleanliness of the *America* that she afterwards sent Captain Brown a gold-encased pocket compass with a note expressing the hope that he would keep it as bright and shining as he did the yacht. According to *Bell's Life,* the Queen, before leaving the *America,* gave to each member of the yacht's crew a gold sovereign.

But members of the royal household were by no means the only Britishers interested in the *America.* The curious hundreds who swarmed around her in small boats prior to the August 22 regatta afterward increased several-fold as she lay at anchor off Cowes or took brief runs along The Solent. For the word had been spread that for motive power she was not dependent on the winds and her sails alone. Concerning this, Colonel Hamilton wrote:

> There was at one time a very general impression among the lower orders of the people about the docks at Cowes that the *America* had a propeller which was artfully concealed; and our crew amused themselves by saying to the boatmen who came alongside with visitors: . . . "In the stern-sheets, under the gangway, there is a grating which the Commodore does not allow any person to open." And indeed this opinion was entertained by persons not of the lower classes alone. A sporting clergyman said to a gentleman, who repeated it to me: "I would not wager a guinea against the Yankee craft, but I will give a hundred to see her bottom."
>
> The old Marquis of Anglesey went out with his yacht, the *Pearl* (one of the best sailers of the squadron), taking with him one of our seamen, to sail about the harbor. The *America* went after her under a mainsail and jib only, and passed her without difficulty. The master of the *Pearl* said, "Your lordship knows that no vessel with sails alone could do that." When the *America* went slowly, he said, "Now it is stopped;" and when she went on, "Now it is going." These remarks of the master were not unheeded by the Marquis, and our seaman said nothing to contradict them—he enjoying the joke. When the vessels came to anchor, the Marquis' boat was manned; he came aboard the *America;* and after a salutation he went to the stern, leaned over so far that the Commodore grabbed him by his peg leg to prevent him from falling in. He was looking for the propeller.

The throngs interested in examining the *America*'s bottom had an unexpected opportunity to do so on Wednesday, August 27, the day before she was scheduled to race the *Titania.* Early that morning, as she was limbering up off her anchorage at Cowes, the tides of The Solent played her dirty and she struck bottom, thereby knocking off a part of her outer shoe.

> This rendered it necessary that we should haul her out [John Cox Stevens later explained], and we repaired to the govern-

ment dock at Portsmouth [about 10 miles across Spithead from Cowes] for this purpose. On the instant the application was made an order was issued by the admiral to repair her in the shortest time possible. . . . She was docked at twelve and finished at eight o'clock that evening. For this important service no remuneration, in any shape or way, would be listened to. The admiral, in expressing the pleasure it gave him to do us a service, endeavored to prevail upon us to believe the obligation to be altogether on his side.

With reference to the crowds led to think that the *America* possessed some form of mechanical propulsion, Colonel Hamilton wrote, "The day was wet, but notwithstanding hundreds went to Portsmouth to see her on the ways. Thus alone was that illusion destroyed."

But not all who hurried to the dry dock for a look at the *America*'s bottom were motivated by gullibility or mere curiosity. Some, according to *Bell's Life,* could be ranked among Britain's "most talented and scientific naval constructors," eager to study those portions of her anatomy hitherto concealed by water. Indeed, one member of this group made an on-the-spot scale drawing of the unique lines of the yacht while her hull was thus exposed.

After undergoing repair, the *America* took leave of the Portsmouth dry dock and sailed back to Cowes. While she had experienced a wearying day and night, the next morning found her possessed of her usual energy. Or so she seemed to the correspondent of *Bell's Life* who that day covered her race with the *Titania.*

This schooner-rigged yacht was as new as the *America,* but not quite as large. While in length over all she missed by 4 feet, and in breadth another 4 feet, matching her rival's dimensions, in draft they were virtually on a par. The *Titania*'s iron hull, however, followed in contour the "wave line" theories of John Scott Russell, Britain's leading nautical designer. Russell was, in fact, a founder of the Royal Institution of Naval Architects, and served at that very time as Secretary of the Great International Exhibition in Hyde Park, London, so dear to Queen Victoria's heart.

The story of the race between the *America* and the *Titania* appeared in the August 31 issue of *Bell's Life.* But in a previous number the editors of this sporting journal had explained to their readers that the contest would take place in the English Channel and had defined the course. The yachts would start abreast of the Nab Light, to the east of the eastern extremity of the Isle of Wight, and after running out and back—guided by a judges' steamer—an aggregate distance of 40 miles, would finish where they had begun. Following are the highlights of the *Bell's Life* report:

> The long-talked-of challenge given by the American Commodore Stevens to sail against any British yacht for any amount, having been accepted in the most friendly manner by Robert Stephenson, M.P., the terms and conditions being left by both parties with the noble Commodore of the Royal Yacht Squadron, the match was appointed to come off on Thursday last, provided there was the necessary "six-knot breeze" for the purpose. . . .
>
> The day opened with every appearance of a strong wind for the contest, and in the morning the yachts left Cowes for the rendezvous off the Nab, the *Queen* steamer, Captain Corke, having been expressly engaged to proceed out as the station vessel. At 9 o'clock the steamer left Cowes, having John Bates, Esq., the Squadron's secretary, on board, and our reporter, and proceeded to the appointed place. The wind was strong from N.N.W. throughout the forenoon, and in the afternoon a fresh gale prevailed. A more fitting opportunity or better day could not have happened for so interesting a trial. . . .
>
> At 9:7, with a strong wind, the *Titania* weighed from Cowes Roads and proceeded out to the east end. At 9:35 the *Titania* hove to off the quarantine station, apparently waiting for her adversary, which, up to this period, was observed at anchor in Cowes Roads. Some little anxiety was manifested about her, as there was no doubt that, owing to her having been undocked only the night before, some little preparation ere she could get

ready to sail was necessary. At length she got ready and proceeded to her station.

At 10:14 the *Queen* steamer took her departure from the Nab and steered S.E. by S., and having got about an hour's start in advance of the yachts, took a bearing at 11:15 which gave a distance of 10½ miles. At this time we observed the two schooners under weigh steering in the direction of the steamer, and accompanied by the *Xarifa* [Commodore Wilton's flagship] and four other yachts. At noon Culver Cliff bore N.W. and Dunnose about W.N.W.; an increasing breeze from N. by W. with strong ebb tide, and the distance from Nab 14 miles.

In running towards us the yachts were frequently observed to alter their positions. From hence the steamer veered S.E. by S. until 12:46, when the only bearing was Dunnose, which bore from her N.W. The Culver Cliffs being out of sight, the steamer was judged to have reached the required distance, and she hove to, and hoisted a blue ensign as a signal to round. *America* now bore from the steamer N.N.W. ten miles, the *Titania* in company. To all appearances they were following close upon each other, the *America* being the leading vessel.

At 1:30 the hull of the *America* was fast rising, but the *Titania*'s hull was invisible. Five minutes afterward she was seen to jibe, but seemed to be steering wild, the *America* being well handled, both being under a cloud of canvas. At 1:46 the *America* prepared to round the steamer. The manner in which she came on, "as easy as a Limerick glove," was admired by all on board. The following is the order and time of rounding the steamer:

America	2 hrs., 3 min., 50 sec.
Titania	2 hrs., 8 min., 2 sec.

Thus there was a difference of 4 min. 12 sec. in favor of the "Yankee." As the *America* rounded, they informed us that they had carried away the jaws of their main gaff, but had secured it.

There was now a fresh gale from the northward, and the steamer's head was turned inshore; the wind "dead on end" and plenty of it to test the relative merits of these vessels, the *America* being perfectly upright and "slipping gracefully through it." On the contrary, the *Titania* "bowed" or rather "dipped her nose into it." We watched their progress minutely. The *Titania* wetted her sails, but all efforts to even recover her former position appeared useless.

The difference between the two yachts increased, and became visibly "more and more" as they progressed inshore. At 3:20 they tacked to the westward. The Culver Cliff bore N.W.½N. from the steamer; the *America* from the latter E.N.E., and the *Titania* S.E. by E. At 3:30 the yachts had a strong wind to contend with, and both worked toward the Nab with the ebb in their favor.... The *Titania* was then observed with her topmasts struck and under her three jibs, foresail and mainsail, the *America* with mainsail, foresail and jib, all without a reef in, and as "upright as a top."

At 4:08 the *America* lay four miles dead to leeward of her antagonist. The *America* tacked to the northward, the *Titania* keeping her reach to the southward. At 4:30 the *America* again tacked to the westward, and laid "well up" for the island.

At 4:50 the steamer returned to the Nab light vessel, and made fast to her, and remained to watch the motions of the yachts and note their return. The *America* reached in towards the island, distant from the Nab 2½ miles, the *Titania* keeping her reach to the southward and westward, and was now "half mainsail down." At 5:30:15, the *America* having passed us, and brought the Nab to bear from her S.W., was timed as the winner.

Unfortunately there was no gun aboard to give either of the vessels a welcome, and a little smoke and steam from "the big tube" of the steamer was all that could be resorted to. The match was at an end, and the *America* stood on for Cowes and went to her moorings in Cowes Roads. At 5:57 the *Titania* was seen making toward us, she having been nearly out of sight. At 6:22:15, having reached the proper bearing, she was thus timed as arriving at the goal, being exactly 52 minutes behind the *America* out and home....

Thus has terminated the match in favor of the *America,* which, had such an idea been only imagined a few weeks ago, the poor mortal guilty of the heresy would have been doomed to some asylum. But the really skeptic now freely admit the *America's* superiority over anything in these waters. Our shipbuilders have looked forward to the breeze, to learn how she answered, and have nobly and generously conceded her to be without a rival in this country. Whatever may be the rule adopted for yacht architecture, there is this much to be said and learnt—that unless our sailmakers will also take a notion by what they have witnessed, and abolish old ideas, the alterations of the builders will be futile.

The day following the *America*'s victory over his brainchild, John Scott Russell took a moment off from his duties as Secretary of the Great International Exhibition to express his beliefs in a few amiable and logical words. "This challenge of America to England was of incalculable benefit to England," he confessed. "America reaped a crop of glory; England reaped a crop of wisdom. It was worth the loss of a race to gain so much."

And on the same day that the yacht designer made this frank admission to the British press, Colonel Hamilton received the following from the Earl of Wilton, Commodore of the Royal Yacht Squadron:

Dear Mr. Hamilton:

I must congratulate you upon the success of the *America* yesterday, which was complete. I enclose the stakes that were deposited with me before the race.

My address in London is 7 Grosvenor Square. I must now bid you farewell, as I leave this station for London today; but I hope the period will not be far distant when I shall have the pleasure of seeing you again.

I beg that you will kindly convey my adieus to the Commodore and his brother.

And I am always,

Yours very truly,
Wilton

Also on that day, Friday, August 29, Edwin A. Stevens found time to write his motherless daughter Mary. Only 10 years old, the little girl, in her father's absence, had relatives staying with her at the family mansion in Hoboken. While this letter contributes little to the story of the *America*, as a racing yacht, it does show the very human—and even tender—side of one of her owners, who in public appearances usually stood in the shadow of his older and more flamboyant brother. Lastly, the letter of Edwin A. Stevens serves to focus still another camera of history on Queen Victoria's visit to the *America*. Dated at Cowes, the letter said:

My Dear Mary,

I was very glad to receive yours of the 29th of July and to hear you were all well. I received it last night on my return from the race with the *Titania* and answered it this morning, but had to cut it off short to get it in time for the mail.

I am much pleased to hear that you have learned to swim and am happy to hear that you are all enjoying yourselves at Hoboken. You should be very much obliged to your Uncle Robert for his kindness to you. Tell Aunt Mary I have received hers and hope soon to get time to answer them all and say how much obliged I am to them for their kindness in writing to me.

I feel assured, my dear child, that you have done everything in your power to make your Aunt very comfortable and happy at Hoboken. Tell her how much pleasure it would give me if she and her family would stay with you until my return home, which I hope and expect will be during the month of October.

We propose going to London in the *America*. It will take us some time to see the sights. After a short visit to Scotland we expect to return to Liverpool on our way home by steamer.

I do not know whether I told you of the Queen's visit, with Prince Albert & suite, to the *America*. We took the yacht to opposite her residence at Osborne. She came on board with her Lady in waiting & maid of honor and Lords in attendance on a large and splendid barge rowed by 12 or 16 men with another barge following for fear I presume of accident—it is the usual etiquette on such occasions.

The *America* was as clean as a new pin and looked very well. Her Majesty and the Prince expressed their gratification. They examined every part of the vessel. The Queen is better looking than I had supposed—looks 25 to 30 years old, about as tall as Aunt Libby, with a good complection and moderately good person. She has a pleasing cast of countenance and is courteous and very ladylike in her manners.

As you may suppose, the visit made a great deal of talk and stir here. You cannot conceive how much importance is given to the most trivial action of the Queen's. That her gracious Majesty would condescend to visit the yacht of a private individual appears here very extraordinary and is considered an honor that cannot be too highly prized.

Give my love to all the family and to Aunt Maria and her family.

Your affectionate,
Father

As matters turned out, the Stevens brothers and Colonel Hamilton and his wife did not go to Scotland, nor did they sail the *America* to London. The deterring factor was in all probability a story published in *Bell's Life* that Queen Victoria wished to buy the *America* for the use of her son, the Prince of Wales, when he became somewhat older. Nothing, however, materialized on this score, although while the yacht's owners tarried at Cowes a vastly different proposition was put to them.

This came from local builders of yachts who boasted that, given an opportunity, they could construct a vessel capable of beating the *America*. Young Henry Steers, telling the story many years later, put it in these words: "The people who ran the Cowes shipyards were much chagrined over the *America*'s success. They all said the *America* was a 'mere shell, a Yankee trick,' that we had exhausted ourselves and could never do it again. 'Well,' John C. Stevens said, 'what *will* you do?' They said, 'We will build a boat in ninety days that will beat the *America* for £500.' Commodore Stevens said, 'We'd like to accommodate you, but $2,500 won't pay us for waiting ninety days—not by any means. Make it £25,000 and we'll stay and sail the race.' They wouldn't do this, of course, and so it all came to naught."

Surely there were no sailmakers among the *America*'s critics in this gathering at Cowes. Had there been, and had they dared open their mouths, they would have found themselves instantly silenced. For virtually all British yachtsmen and yacht-builders stood in open admiration of the canvas the *America* carried, made of machine-spun cotton, as opposed to the hemp used in England, and of the way she carried her canvas, laced to the booms. "Put your hand to the lee side of a hemp sail," a Ryde yachtsman suggested, "and you feel a strong breeze blowing through. Do the same with one of cotton, and you are in a complete calm, for the force of the wind is being put to use. Secured as they are, the *America*'s sails stand like boards, a particular advantage in heading to windward. Proceeding in the same direction, our sails belly so that large portions of them are thus thrust about and converted to back sails, doing more harm than good."

While still at Cowes in early September, the Stevens brothers and Colonel Hamilton received a number of offers for the *America* which they rejected as too low. Why they wished to sell the yacht was never publicly explained, although a good guess might be that if they took her back to New York her maintenance and possession would doubtless prove awkward, since six men owned her and they could not divide her up. Happily, a bidder of means soon came along, and rather than tarry in England for an indefinite period, they let the *America* go for £5,000. But this, plus the £100 won on the race with the *Titania,* represented a profit. For the two sums, translated into American money, came to $25,500, while the initial $20,000 cost of the yacht, plus $3,750 in expenses incurred on the junket, left a tidy $1,750 on the credit side of the ledger.

In addition, there was the cup—the 100-guinea cup of silver. When the three triumphant American gentlemen, accompanied by Mrs. Hamilton, boarded a steamer at Liverpool to return home, Commodore Stevens carried the huge cup under his arm. It was not then known as "The America's Cup," but one day it would be, and the British, in their efforts to win it back, would spend, over the decades to come, many, many multiples of the total of all the sums itemized above.

Portraits from *The Lawson History of the America's Cup*, privately published, Boston, 1902.
John Cox Stevens, first Commodore of the New York Yacht Club, headed a syndicate of members who ordered the *America* built.

George Steers designed the *America* and supervised her construction.

The first picture of the *America* published anywhere appeared on the front page of *The Illustrated London News.*

THE ILLUSTRATED LONDON NEWS

o. 474.—Vol. xviii.] FOR THE WEEK ENDING SATURDAY, MARCH 15, 1851. [Sixpence.

New York Nov.r 15. 1850

George L Schuyler Esq

Dr Sir. I propose to build for you a yacht of not less than 140 tons custom house measurement on the following terms –

The yacht to be built in the best manner, coppered, rigged, with joiner's work, cabin & kitchen furniture, table furniture, water closets &c & ready for sea. You are to designate the plan of the interior of the vessel & select the furniture –

The model, plan & rig of the vessel to be entirely at my discretion, it being understood however that she is to be a strong seagoing vessel, and rigged for ocean sailing –

For this vessel complete & ready for sea you are to pay me $30,000 – upon the following conditions –

When the vessel is ready, she is to be placed at the disposal of Hamilton Wilkes Esq as umpire who after making such trials as are satisfactory to him for the space of twenty days, shall decide whether or not she is faster than any vessel in the United States brought to compete with her –

The expense of these trials to be borne by you –

If it is decided by the umpire that she is not faster than every vessel brought against her, it shall not be binding upon you to accept and pay for her at all.

In addition to this, if the umpire decides that she is faster than any vessel in the United States, you are to have the right, instead of accepting her at that time, to send her to England, match her against anything of her size built there, & if beaten still to reject her altogether –

The expense of the voyage out and home to be borne by you –

The test of speed in England to be decided by any mode acceptable to you & consented to by you in writing –

Respectfully Yours &c

W. H. Brown

George L. Schuyler, representing the *America* syndicate, drove a hard bargain with George Steers, the designer and builder of the yacht, and with William H. Brown, owner of the New York shipyard in which the vessel took shape. The letter of contract for the *America* (opposite page) although addressed to George L. Schuyler and signed by William H. Brown (owner of the shipyard that produced the yacht), was probably written or dictated by Schuyler. A shrewd businessman, he insisted on strictures that caused George Steers the loss of $10,000. But in the end Steers got back the money—and more—as a result of the amazing behavior of the *America* and the publicity he consequently received.

Letter and portrait from *The Lawson History of the America's Cup.*

James R. Steers, older brother of the designer of the *America,* crossed to England aboard the yacht and kept an amusing log. From *Harper's New Monthly Magazine.*

Edwin Augustus Stevens, less flamboyant than his brother the Commodore, was present when the yacht won the Isle of Wight race and when Queen Victoria came aboard afterward. Courtesy of Stevens Institute, Hoboken, N.J.

ROYAL YACHT SQUADRON REGATTA, 1851, will take place on Monday, Tuesday, Wednesday, Thursday, and Friday, August 18th, 19th, 20th, 21st, and 22d.
FIRST DAY.—HER MAJESTY'S CUP, open to R.Y.S. cutters from 50 and under 100 tons; closed.
SECOND DAY.—The R.Y.S. annual dinner.
THIRD DAY.—HIS ROYAL HIGHNESS PRINCE ALBERT'S CUP, by large-class R.Y.S. schooners (140 tons and above).
FOURTH DAY.—The R.Y.S. ANNUAL BALL; tickets, 10s each, can be obtained of the secretary, through the introduction of a member.
A SUBSCRIPTION CUP, to be sailed for by any royal yacht club yachts, not exceeding 30 tons o.m.; thrice round the west buoy of the Middle and buoys of the Brambles; entrance 5s each; to close Wednesday noon.
FIFTH DAY.—The R.Y.S. £100 CUP, open to yachts belonging to the clubs of all nations; to close at midnight, Aug 16; no time allowed for tonnage; three vessels must enter and start for each prize, or no race.
Fireworks at 9 p.m., Aug 22d. JOHN BATES, Secretary.

From *Bell's Life,* August 5, 1851.

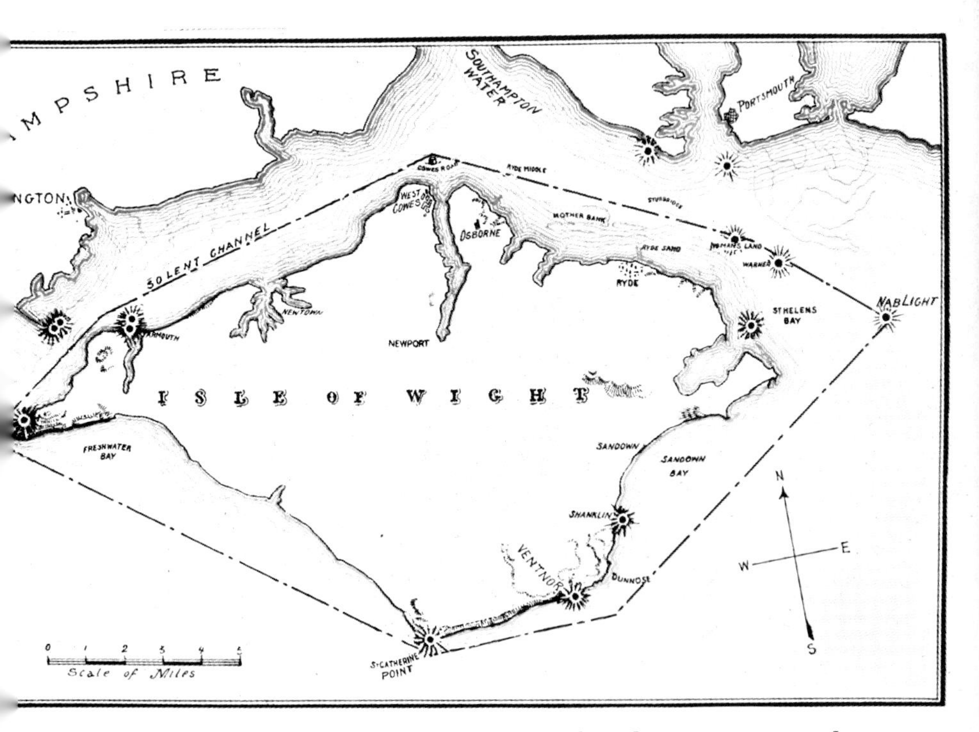

A chart of the Royal Yacht Squadron's diamond-shaped race course around the Isle of Wight, where the *America* competed on August 22, 1851, against a large fleet of the best of British yachts. The race started at Cowes Roads, the northernmost point of the diamond, and encircled the Isle counterclockwise. From *The Lawson History of the America's Cup.*

The most renowned of all yachting prizes, the America's Cup, was called originally the 100-Guinea Cup, for it cost the Royal Yacht Squadron about $500 to have it made. From *The Lawson History of the America's Cup.*

At the start of her famous race around the Isle of Wight on August 22, 1851 (opposite page), the *America* carried more than her accustomed spread of canvas. The extra sail, a flying jib, necessitated the rigging of a spar forward of her bowsprit. "Old Dick" Brown, the *America's* skipper, objected, only to be overruled by her owners, and consequently the yacht answered her helm with less than her usual alacrity. From *The Illustrated London News,* August 30, 1851.

Steamers followed the *America* and the numerous other yachts racing around the Isle of Wight. From aboard one steamer, Abbott Lawrence, the American Minister to Great Britain, saw the *America*'s flying jib carried away by a fierce gust of wind and feared she would lose as a result of the accident. Instead, she handled better and picked up speed. From

At times, the *America* raced with her sails "wing and wing"—that is, with her foresail swung to starboard and her mainsail to port. While in many yacht races of the time this tactic was not permitted, the judges at the Isle of Wight contest allowed it. The original of this painting by Oswald W. Brierly hangs in the McPherson Collection, National Maritime Museum, Greenwich, England. Courtesy of The Mariners Museum, Newport News, Virginia.

LOOK OUT FOR SQUALLS!

American Youth "I GUESS, MASTER JOHNNY, IF YOU DON'T LOOK SHARP, I'LL SHOW YOU HOW TO MAKE A SEVENTY-FOUR NEXT!!"

This cartoon appeared in a September 1851 issue of *Punch*, the British humor magazine, soon after the *America*'s victory at the Isle of Wight. The reference in the caption is to a 74-gun frigate.

During the winter of 1851–2, the new owner of the *America*, Lord de Blaquiere, cruised aboard the yacht in the Mediterranean. This contemporary lithograph from *Hunt's Yachting Magazine* of September 1852 shows the *America* battling a gale off Valetta, Malta, on February 2, 1852.

The January 1853 issue of *Hunt's* included this lithograph (below) of the *Sverige*, a schooner-rigged yacht owned by Nicholas Beckman of the Royal Swedish Yacht Club. Lord de Blaquiere pitted the *America* against her successfully, but it proved to be a most controversial race.

Visible in this picture of George Steers's workroom are models of 27 of the vessels he designed and built alone or as a member of the firm he formed, in late 1851, with his brother James R. and the latter's son Henry. From *Frank Leslie's Illustrated Newspaper,* December 13, 1856.

Shortly before his death in a tragic road accident, September 25, 1856, George Steers carved this half-model of the *America*. He had planned to send it to Queen Victoria, in appreciation of Her Majesty's visit aboard the yacht nearly five years before. Courtesy of The Mariners Museum, Newport News, Virginia.

Stephen R. Mallory, Secretary of the Confederate Navy, bought the *America* at the outbreak of the Civil War from a mysterious Britisher, Henry Edward Decie, who had sailed her to Savannah, Georgia, in 1861. From Series II, Vol. 2, *Official Records of the Union and Confederate Navies in the War of the Rebellion.*

James D. Bulloch, of Georgia, as the chief Confederate agent in England during the Civil War, built and/or equipped such raiders as the *Alabama* and *Shenandoah*. When Edward Anderson and James North reached Britain aboard the *Camilla* (formerly *America*) they reported to Bulloch. From *The Confederate Veteran,* March 1901.

Edward Clifford Anderson—formerly an officer in the U.S. Navy and later Mayor of Savannah, Georgia—kept a diary detailing the events of his perilous voyage to England on the *Camilla* and his work for the Confederacy abroad. Courtesy of Mrs. J. Fred Schwalb, of Savannah, the great-granddaughter of Edward Clifford Anderson.

said, "You are perhaps not aware Captain that I have
order to take passage in the Camilla to England - North of
Navy and myself are to go over with you. I have been
re acquainted with all matters connected with your vessel, an
must understand each other without further mystery - for I
w that the authorities at Montgomery have purchased your vessel

Lines from the Anderson Diary in which he records what he said to Decie about the *America*. From Edward Clifford Anderson Diary, 1861–1862 (Volume 5 of Edward Clifford Anderson Papers), in the Southern Historical Collection, University of North Carolina Library, Chapel Hill, N.C.

HUNT'S

YACHTING MAGAZINE.

SEPTEMBER, 1861.

ALARM AND AMERICA.

A MATCH between these celebrated yachts has for a long time been looked forward to with considerable interest. The event of Monday August 5th. created almost as much excitement as was manifested in 1851 on the first appearance of the America in our waters.

From that period a thorough remodelling of the old school has taken place. Up to that year the Alarm built upon the lines of her owner (Joseph Weld Esq.,) was the fastest cutter yacht afloat, and, owing to the success of the America, Mr. Weld was induced to lengthen his cutter and convert her into a schooner. Ever since her alteration in 1852 she has maintained her reputation against almost everything she has contended with.

This match was originally fixed to take place on the 30th of July, but owing to the Goodwood races occurring that week it was postponed to the 5th of August, the day previous to the Squadron's Regatta. The day at length arrived, and the number of spectators who flocked to witness the start, as well as the 84 vessels of every description—from the Royal Yacht with her illustrious freight down to the humble pilot boat which accompanied the match, was sufficient testimony of the interest and excitement which prevailed.

A decade after her famous victory in the Royal Yacht Squadron regatta at the Isle of Wight in 1851, the *America* participated in a match race with the *Alarm* over a portion of this same course. Curiously, in reporting the event, *Hunt's Yachting Magazine* made no mention of the fact that the name of the *America* had since been changed to *Camilla*, that enormous wagers had been placed on the outcome of the race, and that while Henry Edward Decie sailed the schooner with all the pride of ownership, she was no longer his. Perhaps *Hunt's* did not wish to admit that Britain knowingly permitted a Confederate vessel to frequent her shores.

Charles C. Hemming, 40 years after he scuttled the *America* to save her from Union seizure. At the time of this photograph he was a wealthy banker in Colorado Springs. From John W. Headley, *Confederate Operations in Canada and New York*, Washington, D.C., 1906.

Thomas Holdup Stevens, who found the yacht *America* and caused her to be refitted at a Union base. *Official U.S. Navy Photo*, taken in 1869 after Stevens had made Captain.

The *America*, based at Newport, Rhode Island, from the early summer of 1863 until the end of the Civil War, doubled as a U.S. Naval Academy schoolship and in cruises off the New England coast as a pursuit vessel in chases after Confederate raiders. During this period, the yacht regularly mounted two swivel guns amidships and occasionally heavier cannon at her bow or stern. Aboard her, many "future admirals" got their first taste of war.

In 1870, while she was still owned by the Naval Academy, she made an excellent showing in the first challenge race for the America's Cup. Seventeen yachts participated, and critics claimed the *America* was hampered by her "Navy rig." The man at her helm was Charlie Brown, the son of "Old Dick" Brown, the skipper who had sailed her to victory at the Isle of Wight 19 years before. From Series I, Vol. 2, *Official Records of the Union and Confederate Navies in the War of the Rebellion*.

Shortly before the departure of the steamer from Liverpool, a September issue of *Punch,* the British humor magazine, appeared, and it contained a parody called "The Last Appendix to 'Yankee Doodle,'" which served to further gladden the hearts of the travelers. The first two verses of this epic are here set down:

Yankee Doodle sent to Town
  His goods for exhibition;
Everybody ran him down,
  And laughed at his position;
They thought him all the world behind,
  A goney, muff or noodle;
Laugh on, good people–never mind
  Says quiet Yankee Doodle.

Yankee Doodle had a craft,
  A rather tidy clipper,
And he challenged, while they laughed,
  The Britishers to whip her.
Their whole yacht squadron she outsped,
  And that on their own water;
Of all the lot she went ahead
  And they came nowhere arter.

FOUR

"*What Is a 7-Knot Breeze?*"

SOON after their return to New York, the Stevens brothers and Colonel Hamilton were given a "Welcome Home Dinner" by the New York Yacht Club. It was held on the evening of Wednesday, October 1, 1851, at the Astor House, then on Broadway at Barclay Street, across from City Hall Park. Indeed, it *had* to be held at the Astor House, for no other hotel of the time could have put on such a spread. All told, there were ten courses, consisting of fifty-six dishes, not counting relishes, preserves, fruits, and nuts.

The company of several dozen of New York's most prominent citizens assembled at the Astor bar during the afternoon and were called in to dine promptly at six. The banquet started off reasonably enough with Green Turtle Soup, but then began showing its lavish character. There was "Boiled Salmon Trout, Lobster Sauce" followed by "Young Capons, Garnished, Monmarenci Style," "Roast Saddle of Mutton," "Fillet of Roast Beef, with Truffles," "Boned Partridges," "Fillet of Eels," "Oysters Fried in Butter," "Cutlets of Pigeon, Mushroom Sauce," "Sweet Breads à la St. Cloud," "Salmi of Woodcock," "Reed Birds, Perigreux Sauce," "Roast Grey Duck," "Broiled Rice Birds," "Broiled Yellow-leg Snipe," and seemingly no end of vegetables, breads, and pastries.

Suitable wines accompanied each course, and a rare brandy was served with coffee. Then came the gustatory hit of the evening—"Ornamental Confections." There was one shaped like the New York Yacht Club's clubhouse, another like the Crystal Palace at London's Great International Exhibition, and a final creation of spun sugar depicting the *America* racing, and, of course, beating *Titania.*

The candied replica of the victorious yacht brought forth resounding applause, which concluded only after Commodore Stevens agreed to the shouted demands that he make a speech. He told of the many courtesies he and his associates had received in England and dwelt particularly on the fact that the *America* had been admitted to the ports there with a status normally reserved for British vessels, without customs interference. "From the Queen herself," the Commodore said, "we received a mark of attention rarely accorded even the highest among her own subjects, and I was given to understand that it was not only a courtesy extended to myself and friends, but also a proof of the estimation in which she held our country, thereby giving a significance to the compliment infinitely more acceptable and valuable. Long may the bonds of kindred affection and interest that bind us together at present remain unbroken!"

At this point the toastmaster of the evening demanded that the diners drink to Queen Victoria and her visit aboard the *America.* Other toasts followed—to the President of the United States, to Earl Wilton, to the Royal Yacht Squadron, to Captain Brown and the officers and crew of the *America,* and to the mechanics and artisans employed in constructing and outfitting the *America.*

Sated with both food and drink, the guests at the banquet then lolled back in their chairs, each to pursue his individual inclination—either to catnap or to listen to the principal address of the occasion. This was delivered by Charles King, president of Columbia College. That institution, then located on Park

Place—a block from the Astor House—was many years short of becoming Columbia University and many more years short of moving far uptown to its present location on Morningside Heights.

King talked for the length of time that most college presidents talk, and consequently there is room here for only a fragment of his speech:

> Our honorable guests are our own boys. They are sons of Columbia, and there one, the Commodore, learned—for we teach such things—the science of navigation and shipbuilding. Your Commodore was graduated A.B. from our college, and those magic letters may now typify alike Bachelor of Arts or Accomplished Boatman. . . . As an American, I am proud to pay homage to the Commodore and his associates. With all the courtesy and high bearing of the knights of old, they have struck a blow of which the consequences—and the benefits—and the renown—are national. For this victory of the American yacht in the narrow sea—*Mare Nostrum*—the peculiar domain of England, is a national event.

Considerably after midnight, the banquet concluded with the unveiling and showing of the silver trophy the Stevens brothers and Colonel Hamilton had brought home from England —the Royal Yacht Squadron's 100-Guinea Cup, known henceforth as the America's Cup. While certain of the gentlemen who looked at it with admiration may have been inebriated, none attempted to drink from it, for the cup stood 27 inches high, had a maximum circumference of 36 inches, weighed 8 pounds 6 ounces, and being bottomless would not hold liquid. Actually it was not a cup at all, but took the form of a ewer, boasting as it did an ornate spout opposite to an even more ornate handle. Indeed, its chief feature was the extravagance of its ornamentation, from base to lip, with curlicues entwining its numerous scrolls and the six large shields forming its bulbous middle. The cup bore the hallmark and name of its maker, the

Messrs. R. & S. Gerard, Panton Street, London, and in addition the following engraving:

100 Guinea Cup
won
August 22nd, 1851, at Cowes, England
By Yacht *America,*
At the
Royal Yacht Squadron Regatta
Open to all Nations
Beating

Cutters	Tons
Volante	48
Arrow	84
Alarm	193
Mona	82
Bacchante	80
Freak	60
Eclipse	50

Schooners	
Beatrice	161
Wyvern	205
Ione	75
Constance	218
Gipsey Queen	160
Brilliant	392

Schooner *America,* 170 Tons
Commodore John C. Stevens
Built by George Steers of New York
1851

It should be noted that while fourteen vessels started in the Royal Yacht Squadron regatta with the *America,* the names of but thirteen appear preserved for posterity on the cup. By some error, intentional or otherwise, the cutter *Aurora,* of 47 tons, got left out. And yet the little *Aurora* had come in next best in the race, gliding across the finish line only 8 minutes after the *America.* This omission has served further to perpetuate the myth of the Signal Master's famed reply to his Queen: "Your Majesty, there is no second!"

George Steers attended the Astor House banquet in name only, not in the flesh. It is doubtful that even if invited he would have appeared, for he was far too busy. As soon as the news of the *America*'s victory at Cowes reached New York, both George and his brother James found themselves famous, at least in shipbuilding circles, and their services much in demand. They negotiated with Hathorne, took over the old yard of Hathorne & Steers in Brooklyn, and in addition opened a second yard, under the partnership style of James R. & George Steers, at 11th Street and the East River in Manhattan.

During the next five years the brothers built several yachts, notably the *Silvie*, the first sloop to cross the Atlantic. Her owner, Louis A. Depau, a charter member of the New York Yacht Club, sailed her to England for an Isle of Wight race in 1853, in an attempt to duplicate the *America*'s accomplishments. The *Silvie* lost, but only narrowly.

Also in 1853, the newspapers announced that George Steers planned to build a clipper ship of 2,500 tons along the lines of the yacht *America.* He would own her himself; he calculated she would do 22 knots; and he stood ready to bet $10,000 that she would outsail any vessel in the world. But the newspapers were as wrong as they often are, for when the clipper was launched and christened *Sunny South,* she measured a mere 700 tons. Moreover, she resembled the *America* not at all, and she was bought immediately for $70,000 by Napier, Johnson & Company, who placed her first in the China trade and later on a South American run.

For Edward Knight Collins, proprietor of the United States Mail Steamship Company, the Steers brothers built the *Arctic* and the *Adriatic,* transatlantic liners and sister vessels of other large steamers already owned by Collins, the *Atlantic,* the *Baltic,* and the *Pacific.* On September 27, 1854, while picking her way through a fog off Cape Race, Newfoundland, the *Arctic* collided with a small French steamer, the *Vesta,* and went down, drowning nearly 400 passengers and crewmen. Among those who lost their lives were the wife, son, and daughter of Collins.

Like the black gull of seamen's dreams, tragedy followed in the wake of Collins. In January 1856, the *Pacific* cleared Liverpool for a voyage to New York and was never heard from again. Collins operated under a U.S. Government subsidy of more than $800,000 a year, which was withdrawn by Congressional action soon after the loss of the *Pacific;* and the *Adriatic,* the *Atlantic,* and the *Baltic* were seized by his creditors, whereupon Collins forsook the sea and went into the coal and iron mining business in Ohio. He made no second fortune, but years later a friend described him as "rosy, hearty and not careworn as when he had those mighty American steamships resting on his shoulders."

William Ross Wallace had friends in all walks of life, as befitted a man who was both a lawyer and a poet. While his friendship with Edgar Allan Poe and George Steers has been noted already, it is yet to be said that he was also a friend of Mike Walsh. Born in Ireland and brought to this country as a child by his impoverished father, Walsh grew up in the hurly-burly streets of New York. He became a printer, a journalist, a social reformer, a labor organizer, an eloquent speaker, and a heavy drinker, which provided him with all the requisites for the role he finally assumed—that of a professional politician.

Walsh sat for three terms in the New York State Assembly and in 1852 was elected to Congress. While serving in the latter chamber, he was introduced to George Steers by William Ross Wallace, and the two became immediate friends. Also while Walsh served, the Federal Government appropriated nearly a million dollars for the building, at the Brooklyn Navy Yard, of a screw-driven steam frigate of more than 4,500 tons, capable of carrying twelve heavy guns. By astute lobbying, Walsh won for George Steers the lucrative job of designing the vessel and supervising her construction.

In the course of this work, which took up the bulk of his time for nearly two years, George Steers made another fast friend of Daniel B. Martin, Engineer-in-Chief of the U.S. Navy. The frigate, launched on February 23, 1856, was christened *Niagara.* Her initial duty, far from warlike, consisted of participating, along with the British man-of-war *Agamemnon,* in the abortive early attempts of Cyrus Field to lay an Atlantic cable.

The new prosperity that came to George Steers permitted him to buy a summer house at Great Neck, Long Island, to keep a horse and carriage, and to allow himself more leisure. During certain of his free hours, he prepared a gift for Queen Victoria he had long wanted to send her, for he felt she had done him great honor by visiting aboard his brainchild and the product of his craftsmanship, the yacht *America.* The gift was a mahogany half-model of the hull of the *America,* which he carved to the scale of a half-inch to the foot and mounted on a bird's-eye maple plaque 12 inches by 54 inches. He affixed to the plaque, beneath the stern of the model, an oval silver plate engraved with the yacht's dimensions, and beneath the prow a second plate inscribed with these lines:

To Her Most Gracious Majesty
Queen Victoria
this model of the Yacht
America
is most respectfully presented by
the Designer & Builder
George Steers Esq.
of New York

George Steers's intended gift to the Queen was never sent. He died before he could ship it. Even so, he was not the first of the men prominently concerned with the *America* to be taken by death. As related earlier, Hamilton Wilkes, one of the six original proprietors of the yacht, died at the winter "health" resort of Pau, France, in 1852, of a pulmonary malady. Seemingly he knew he was going to die, for he had set his affairs in order shortly before. These included his interest in the America's Cup. Wilkes signed a legal document giving a friend the authority to concur with whatever disposition the other owners decided to make of the trophy.

Edwin Augustus Stevens married a second time on August 22, 1854, thus providing his daughter Mary, now 13, with a stepmother. The new Mrs. Stevens was the former Martha Bayard Dod, daughter of the late Professor Albert Dod, who had taught mathematics and architecture at Princeton. By his second wife, Edwin Stevens had five sons, three of whom became members of the New York Yacht Club.

Maria Livingston Stevens, the wife of John Cox Stevens, died in February 1855. Her loss so saddened her husband that he closed their mansion on Washington Square, as well as their country place in Dutchess County, and went to live on a 500-acre farm he purchased near South Amboy, New Jersey. He was now 70—too old for much more strenuous yachting, he felt. So he resigned as Commodore of the New York Yacht Club and was succeeded in office by another of the Club's charter members, William Edgar, who was in turn succeeded in 1859 by Edwin Augustus Stevens.

Robert Livingston Stevens, who had designed the yacht *Maria*, the *America*'s trial horse, died on April 20, 1856. Unmarried, he left the bulk of his fortune to his brother Edwin. While famous the world over as a talented engineer, only his friends knew that he was equally talented as a musician.

George Steers died a few minutes after 9 o'clock on the night of Thursday, September 25, 1856, as the result of an accident. That afternoon he had quit work early and hitched up his horse and carriage for a drive to Great Neck. It was his intention to close his summer home there for the season and bring his wife back to their city residence at 91 Cannon Street. But on his way to Great Neck, when he had proceeded only three or four miles from his Brooklyn shipyard and was in the vicinity of Calvary Cemetery, his horse took fright and bolted. The carriage overturned, and he was thrown out. Friends found him lying in the road and yet only barely recognized him, for his head was so bloody. They took him home to Cannon Street and called a doctor, but nothing could be done to save him.

The next day *The New York Times* said, "It is with a feeling of profound sorrow that we announce the death of George Steers, the celebrated naval architect, the builder of the yacht *America,* of the steam frigate *Niagara* and of the Collins steamer *Adriatic.* He was a man of rare genius, of the noblest instincts and of incorruptible integrity of character. His knowledge of shipbuilding seemed to be an inspiration. Probably no man who ever achieved so great a reputation by his works owed so little to book learning. His untimely death is a national loss."

For a long while, Mrs. Steers kept the model of the yacht *America* her husband had carved and mounted for Queen Victoria. It was her original intention to follow through with his plan and pack it up and ship it off to England. But each time she began the chore, she found herself so overcome with emotion that she could not complete it. Meanwhile she had numerous offers for the model, for ever-increasing amounts of money, all of which she turned down. Finally she gave it to Daniel B. Martin, the U.S. Navy's engineering chief, for she considered him George Steers's best friend.

Martin came from South River, New Jersey, and has descendants still living there. From generation to generation the model was handed down in the family until 1949. Then the Martins, feeling that the keeping of the model should be a public and not a private trust, decided to present it to some nonprofit institution. The one they chose was the Maritime Museum, at Newport News, Virginia, and the model has been on display there ever since.

In 1854 Mike Walsh ran for a second term in Congress. John Kelly, his opponent, contended that Mike, born in Ireland, was the son of an unnaturalized alien, and having never himself taken out naturalization papers, was constitutionally disqualified. The truth or falsity of the charge never became a court issue, for Mike lost the election in the usual way, by failing to receive a majority vote. Also, in his usual way, Mike took the edge off the pain of defeat by dulling it with drink. Not long after his friend George Steers died, the ex-Congressman followed suit. After a wild night, he was found dead the next morning in an areaway near his home, and the police reported that he had probably been the victim of foul play.

During the last year of his life, John Cox Stevens suffered from "kidney disease" compounded by "enlargement of the heart." He moved from his 500-acre farm at South Amboy back to the family's "Castle" at Hoboken, where he had been reared. Like many an aging and ailing rich man before him, aware that the grave was not far ahead, he made offerings to his God. He built an Episcopal church at South Amboy and endowed a home there for indigent widows and orphans.

The ex-Commodore died at Hoboken on the afternoon of Wednesday, June 10, 1857, and was buried the following Saturday. During the period of mourning intervening, flags on Hoboken–New York ferries flew at half-mast.

The dead man's memory was also honored by an obituary of a column and a half in the *New York Tribune,* a paper owned and edited by his friend Horace Greeley. "Statesmen and soldiers often *save* a country," the obituary pontificated, "while such men as John Cox Stevens *make* a country." But in a sense the *Tribune* contradicted itself by complaining that although the subject of its eulogy quite properly had been, in politics, a staunch Whig "in principle," lamentably he had not voted in ten years.

Finally, the *Tribune* estimated the worth of the estate of the late John Cox Stevens at $1,500,000, and gave a run-down of his family history. For three generations, the paper declared, members of the clan had been prominent in various forms of steam and other types of transportation, in sport, and in society. But nothing was said of the social status of John Stevens, the great-grandfather of John Cox Stevens and the progenitor of the tribe in America. This original John Stevens had come to these shores in 1699 as an indentured law clerk.

The terminal illness of John Cox Stevens once more raised the question first posed when Hamilton Wilkes neared his end at Pau, France, five years earlier. The question was: What would be the eventual disposition of the America's Cup, now that all members of the owning syndicate had not proven themselves immortal?

John Cox Stevens, prior to the death of his wife, had been the chief custodian of the America's Cup and usually kept it displayed at his New York City mansion on Washington Square. But for balls and dinner parties given by other members of the syndicate, the trophy was now and again "loaned out" temporarily. Then when Mrs. Stevens lay stricken and bedridden a long while, somehow the Cup got banished to a closet.

Following the death of his wife, John Cox Stevens employed extra help to assist in closing his city residence. A maid unfamiliar with the house encountered the Cup, and so tarnished was it that she thought it worthless. But for the quick and knowledgeable eye of the Stevens butler, the trophy so highly prized would have been hauled off to a junk heap embedded in a wagonload of rubbish.

With John Cox Stevens relocated in South Amboy, he and the other syndicate survivors discussed the Cup's future. A proposal that it be melted down and the silver from it cast into medallions suitably engraved, one for each of its owners, was for a time considered. Happily for the future of American yacht racing, this plan was not adopted.

Later, after John Cox Stevens, fatally ill, had made his final move home to Hoboken, the others in the syndicate agreed to present the America's Cup to the New York Yacht Club as a perpetual challenge trophy. They drew up a paper to this effect which they sent their ex-Commodore. He signed it, but through some oversight those attending him failed to return it immediately. Thus the paper, which was not signed by his fellow syndicate members until July 8, 1857—and is so dated—presents a seeming chronological puzzler. It appears to have been signed by John Cox Stevens nearly a month after his death on June 10.

The paper is known as the America's Cup "Deed of Gift," or with greater exactitude as the "First Deed of Gift," for it has since been twice revised. It is addressed to the Secretary of the New York Yacht Club and reads in part as follows:

> The undersigned, members of the New York Yacht Club and late owners of the schooner yacht *America*, beg leave... to present to the Club the Cup won by the *America* at the Regatta of the Royal Yacht Squadron at Cowes, England, August 22, 1851.
>
> This Cup was offered as a prize to be sailed for by yachts of all nations, without regard to differences of tonnage, going round the Isle of Wight, the usual course for the Annual Regatta of the Royal Yacht Squadron, and was won by the *America*....
>
> The Cup is offered to the New York Yacht Club, subject to the following conditions:
>
> Any organized Yacht Club of any foreign country shall always be entitled, through any one or more of its members, to claim the right of sailing a match for this Cup with any yacht or other vessel of not less than 30 or more than 300 tons, measured by the Custom House rule of the country to which the vessel belongs.
>
> The parties desiring to sail for the Cup may make any match with the Yacht Club in possession of the same that may be determined upon by mutual consent; but in case of disagreement as to terms, the match shall be sailed over the usual course for the Annual Regatta of the Yacht Club in possession of the Cup, and subject to its Rules and Sailing Regulations—the challenging party being bound to give six months' notice in writing, fixing the day they wish to start. This notice to embrace the length, Custom House measurement, rig, and name of the vessel.
>
> It is to be distinctly understood that the Cup is to be the property of the Club, and not of the members thereof, or owners of the vessels winning it in a match; and that the condition of keeping it open to be sailed for by Yacht Clubs of all foreign countries, upon the terms above laid down, shall forever attach to it, thus making it perpetually a Challenge Cup for friendly competition between foreign countries....

During the very month that John Cox Stevens died, a handsome yacht was launched from a shipyard at Port Jefferson, Long Island, and christened *Wanderer.* Although like the *America* she was schooner-rigged, she measured larger than her predecessor by roughly 80 tons, and soon phrases of infamy rather than glory would attach to her name. Her original owner, a member of the New York Club, sold her in less than a year to William C. Corrie, about whom nothing was known in yachting circles. Regardless, on May 29, 1858, Corrie was elected to membership in the Club, without careful screening, and the *Wanderer* continued to fly the Club's burgee.

Corrie sailed her to Charleston, South Carolina, where he turned her over to his employer, Charles A. L. Lamar, for whom he had been fronting. Had Lamar attempted to buy her himself, it is certain he would not have succeeded, and even had he done so the New York Yacht Club would have rejected him. For Lamar was a blustering, fire-eating Southerner from Savannah, Georgia, of whom most of Savannah disapproved. His business was slave-running, pursued long after the United States had joined with Britain in outlawing the traffic. During the late 1850s Lamar had suffered the seizure of two of his slave-ships, and he needed such a vessel as the *Wanderer,* to all appearances a pleasure craft, to continue his illegal activity.

During late 1858 and early 1859, the *Wanderer* made two voyages to the African coast and brought back to Georgia captive Negroes. Following the first, the yacht was impounded by Federal authorities and put up for auction. But Lamar got her back for $4,000 by threatening potential rival bidders with physical violence should they bid against the dummy he had employed to act for him. No longer, however, could he hoodwink the New York Yacht Club. At a meeting on February 3, 1859, the Club struck the *Wanderer's* name from its squadron list and expelled William C. Corrie from membership.

After the *Wanderer's* second round trip to Africa, Lamar outfitted her for a third. But one night in the absence of her captain, her mate had a change of heart about continuing such a loathsome venture. Aided by similarly inclined crewmen, he ran off with the yacht and delivered her up to a U.S. Marshal north of the Mason-Dixon line. Lamar contended she had been stolen from him and once more got her back, but only after posting a high cash bond guaranteeing the validity of his claim.

Charles A. L. Lamar was the 35-year-old son of a crafty and wealthy father who labored under the name of Gazaway Bugg Lamar. The father possessed vast business interests in Georgia —in cotton, banking, railroads, and shipping—and in addition he was president of the Bank of the Republic in New York City, where he lived most of the time. Gazaway Lamar deplored his son's "blackbirding" activities, first on economic and next on humanitarian grounds. He felt that Charlie, with little hope of profit, was making a fool of himself. Charlie, in fact, had gone so far as to challenge, by letter, the editor of the influential *New York Times* to a duel as a consequence of that paper's biting criticism of him, and such behavior reflected on the integrity, stability, and financial wisdom of his parent.

A heated exchange of letters between Gazaway in New York and Charlie in Savannah ensued. The father ordered his son to dispose of the yacht so tarnished in reputation, and for a long while Charlie refused to obey. But eventually he did, sending the *Wanderer* to Cuba to be sold. Soon after, the Civil War broke out.

Early in that war—in April 1861—another yacht dropped anchor off Savannah. She was the *America,* now sailing under a different name. Charlie Lamar undoubtedly saw her, and it is probable he met her British owner. A dozen years later, in 1873, Gazaway Bugg Lamar claimed—and it was claimed for him by the trickiest of tricky lawyers—that he had bought the *America* during her visit to Savannah, that she was still his, and that he would go to court if necessary to regain possession of her.

But the Briton with whom Lamar contended he had dealt was not the purchaser of the *America* back in September 1851. During the decade following, she had changed hands several times. When the Stevens brothers and Colonel Hamilton sold the yacht at Cowes for £5,000, the man who paid over the money was John de Blaquiere, a captain in the British Army.

Captain de Blaquiere came from an old and prominent Huguenot family. His forebears, to escape persecution for their religious beliefs, fled France in the late 1600s and found sanctuary in England. A century later, with the shoe on the other foot, Captain de Blaquiere's grandfather did his bit toward helping the English hush dissonant Irish voices. For his efforts he was created Baron de Blaquiere of Ardkill, County Londonderry, Ireland, and he received in addition a grant of office of Great Alnager of Ireland. The one award gave him social status and 3,000 acres of land, the other money. For being Great Alnager meant that he collected for the Crown a tax on every pound of wool produced in Ireland, a sizable part of which he retained as his tax collector's fee.

Captain de Blaquiere's uncle became the second Baron de Blaquiere and died unmarried in 1844. Then the Captain's father succeeded to the title and the property that went with it, yet paid little attention to either, so interested and proficient was he in military matters. At the age of 35 he wore the insignia of a major general in the British Army, and eventually he became a lieutenant general and finally a full general.

But his military success and dedication ruined his marriage. His wife, Harriet, daughter of the Marquess of Townshend, left him when their first son, John, was not quite 2 years old, and at a time when she was three months pregnant with their second son, William. On reaching manhood, this second son became an officer in the Royal Navy, where he served with distinction for thirty-five years.

John de Blaquiere, on the other hand, followed his father in the army, yet proved himself nowhere near so successful nor so swift in gaining promotion. While he saw active service in the Afghan campaign in 1842 and in consequence rose from lieutenant to captain, he was still a captain nine years later when he bought the *America* in 1851.

That year was an eventful one for Captain de Blaquiere. In July 1849, a few weeks after his 37th birthday, he married for the first time. His bride, Anna, was the daughter of John Christie, a gentleman of means, and the combined incomes of the newlyweds permitted them to live well and to travel extensively when the Captain took leaves. While on one such junket, after less than two years of a childless marriage, Anna de Blaquiere died in February 1851, on the island of Madeira.

Another tragedy soon followed. In the fall of 1851, only a few weeks after Captain de Blaquiere bought the *America,* his father, the General, contracted smallpox, at that time a disease always disfiguring and often fatal. But in this case its victim preferred to meet death like a soldier on a battlefield, by a bullet. On November 12, 1851, General William de Blaquiere, the third Baron de Blaquiere of Ardkill, shot himself in his quarters in the Norwood section of London, and his son, Captain John de Blaquiere, became the 4th Baron.

As such, the Captain was henceforth addressed as Lord de Blaquiere. He joined the Royal Western Yacht Club, at Plymouth, and the Royal Victoria, at Ryde, for among the members of both he had numerous friends. He seems not to have gone into deep mourning for his father. On the contrary, while many of his fellow yachtsmen were hauling out and shrouding their craft for the approach of winter, Lord de Blaquiere hired a sailing master and twelve seamen and readied the *America* for a Mediterranean cruise.

While doing so, he received a letter from Commodore Stevens in New York which must have cheered him considerably, for the intelligence it contained relieved him of the necessity of spending as much as he had planned on supplies for the *America* in the way of liquid refreshment. The substance of the letter was later made public in the columns of the *Spirit of the Times* by Commodore Stevens's friend, W. T. Porter, who edited and published that sporting journal. As Porter told the story, this is what happened:

> Before the *America* sailed [in June 1851, from New York] Mr. Stevens placed on board two dozen bottles of the celebrated Bingham wine, derived from the cellars of the late Mr. Bingham of Philadelphia, father of the wife of the late English minister to the United States, Lord Ashburton. It was more than a half-century old, and the Commodore designed to drink it to the health of Her Majesty. It would appear that the Commodore's excellent wife, in setting to rights various little matters in relation to the outfit of the *America*, concealed these two dozen bottles in a secret cranny in the vessel, so that when he sold her, without his knowledge the wine went with her. He presumed that through some oversight it must have been taken ashore, and never discovered the mistake until his return home, when he immediately wrote Lord de Blaquiere that if he would look in a certain hidden locker in the *America* he would find some wine "worth double the price of her," of course making him a present of it.

Lord de Blaquiere's cruise with the *America* to the Mediterranean lasted for seven and a half months. How he managed to obtain a leave of this length from his duties as an infantry officer in the British Army has never been publicly explained. While conceivably it was granted him out of respect for his late father, there may be another answer: Perhaps he was not on leave at all.

Many of the score or more ports the *America* visited during her cruise were of strategic military importance. Had a British warship called at them, local authorities might have restricted the movements of her officers. But the *America* by now had an international reputation as a yacht dedicated solely to racing, and Lord de Blaquiere, divested of his uniform, looked the part of a happy-go-lucky sportsman. In such a guise, if guise it was, His Lordship had an immediate entree anywhere, and there was nothing to prevent him from collecting information for subsequent inclusion in intelligence reports.

The *America* cleared Plymouth on November 27, 1851, and reached Lisbon a week later. On New Year's Eve she dropped anchor at Cadiz, Spain, where she remained for nearly three weeks before passing through the Strait of Gibraltar. The long run of more than a thousand miles from Gibraltar to the Mediterranean island of Malta was accomplished, at its end, in less time than those aboard wished. For as the yacht neared the rock-bound entrance to the harbor of Valetta, the chief port of Malta, she encountered winds and seas eager to carry her hurtling along, perhaps to her doom.

These extracts from the *America*'s log for the afternoon and evening of Sunday, February 1, and for the morning of Monday, February 2, 1852, will provide some idea of the severity of the storm:

> At 1 hr. P.M.—Barometer 29.60. Strong winds and tremendous easterly sea. Kept her south while setting up bowsprit shroud.
>
> At 3 hr. P.M.—Glass falling and sea rising from the southeast, and every appearance of an approaching gale. Reefed jib. Secured and lashed everything about the deck and sailed her under the storm main-try-sail, and reduced jib.
>
> At 4 hr. P.M.—Barometer 29.57.
>
> At 8 hr. P.M.—Strong gale from N.b.E. with frightful sea.
>
> At 1 hr. A.M.—Barometer 29.59. Strong gale and frightful sea, all of a boil. Yacht behaving well, but pitching and tossing heavily.
>
> At 2 hr. A.M.—Valetta light, Malta, bearing SSW. Hove the *America* to, head to the NE.
>
> At 4 hr. A.M.—Strong gale and clear.
>
> At 8 hr. A.M.—Same weather. Bore away for the harbor. Set fore-sail and shook out reefs in jib.
>
> At 8 hr. 30 m.—Entered harbor of Valetta. Heavy sea on, almost to breaking at the entrance. Moored with both anchors. Dried sails.

From Malta the *America* sailed to Albania and touched at Zante and other islands off the coast of Greece. In March she was at Ithaca and Corfu, and in April she passed from the Ionian Sea through the Strait of Messina into the Tyrrhenian

Sea. During May and early June, along the west coast of Italy, she visited Naples, Civita Vecchia, and finally Leghorn.

While his yacht rode at anchor off Leghorn, Lord de Blaquiere took a train for a look at Florence, inland from the sea some 50 to 60 miles. There he met an American tourist—member of a breed not so ubiquitous then as now—in the person of Colonel John Winthrop, of New Orleans, and the two took a liking to one another. This resulted in an experience about which Colonel Winthrop wrote at some length, and his narrative found its way, during September 1852, into the columns of at least two New York newspapers and perhaps others across the country. The following is a part of what Colonel Winthrop said:

> It is now some eight or ten weeks ago that I was invited by Lord John de Blaquiere to join a small party in running down from Florence to pass a day on board of the yacht *America*, then lying in the port of Leghorn, two hours and a half distant. On the way down I had a great deal of conversation with Lord de Blaquiere in reference to the vessel, her rig and performance. Her greatest run, he said, had been from Malta to Albania, when during the entire distance she had averaged more than ten knots, making in some thirty-odd hours what was ordinarily accomplished by other yachts in five days. She was dry and easy in the heaviest weather, and had never carried away a spar or a rope of the slightest importance.
>
> She was off Malta, in February last, in the heaviest gale that had been known there in fifteen or twenty years, during which an Austrian ship with all hands on board was lost in sight of Valetta, the British fleet sustaining damage to the extent of £40,000 and the neighboring shores of the Mediterranean were strewed with wrecks. She rode through the whole of the brunt of the hurricane, and came into Valetta harbor towards the conclusion of it with flying colors and perfectly uninjured.
>
> I then approached another subject upon which I was extremely anxious to have his opinion. I had seen it remarked, I said, in English papers that the *America* was a mere racing craft; that comfort had been sacrificed to speed; that no gentle-

man would think of making an extended cruise in her, there being not sufficient room either for stowage, crew or passengers.

At this he expressed his extreme surprise. So far from this being the case, he said that she was as comfortable, capacious and roomy as any yacht of her size he had ever seen—indeed, she was more so—and he told me he would satisfy me of the fact when we reached Leghorn.

On boarding the *America,* Colonel Winthrop was delighted with what he found. In terms of rig, sails, hull, and interior fittings, the yacht remained exactly as she had been described following her victory at Cowes in August 1851. "Even her paint is the same color," Colonel Winthrop wrote, "and I am happy to add that the beautifully carved eagle still remains to adorn her stern, attracting the attention of all by its graceful proportions and spirited action."

Indeed, Lord de Blaquiere had made but one addition to the yacht, and that an improvement. Her bulwarks being low, he had surmounted them at appropriate intervals with waist-high iron stanchions and between the stanchions had strung taut lengths of heavy rope (except at the gangways), thereby creating a protective rail. "It is used simply for safety in heavy weather," Colonel Winthrop concluded his communiqué, "and when in port to prevent any of the crowds who visit her from tumbling overboard."

After clearing Leghorn, the *America* called at the French ports of Toulon and Marseilles, and she was back at Gibraltar for a mere overnight stop on June 28. Then she began the long Atlantic run north—900 air miles, but 1,500 zigzag sailing miles—home to England. She made this voyage in thirteen days, reaching the anchorage of the Royal Western Yacht Club at Plymouth on July 12.

Two days later, Lord de Blaquiere had her at Portsmouth, where she was hauled out for a scraping of her bottom and where her paint was touched up. But the work had to be done hurriedly, for her owner planned to enter her in a Royal Victoria Yacht Club race scheduled for July 22 at Ryde.

This race was truly a Queen's Cup event, for the trophy at stake had been donated by the Crown. A newspaper's description of the cup said:

> It is very richly decorated in the *cinco-cento* style and is valued at 100 guineas. It stands upon an ebony base, and upon two of the panels project the royal arms. Upon one panel is an allegorical representation from the Odyssey, Book X, "The seamen of Ulysses thinking to discover riches within the bag (given to the master by Aeolus), unfasten the mouth. The winds contained therein burst out, and the result is a terrific storm." The other panel contains the following inscription:—"The gift of Her Most Gracious Majesty Queen Victoria to the R.V.Y.C., July 22 1852." Upon the shoulder of the cup are figures representing the winds.

The work on the *America* at Portsmouth was not finished until the morning of July 21, the day before the Queen's Cup event. As soon as his yacht was released, Lord de Blaquiere sailed her across Spithead to Ryde. He struck luck in being able to obtain for the race the services of the pilot Underwood, who had guided the *America* to victory in the Royal Yacht Squadron regatta eleven months before. Moreover, the course to be covered was virtually the same as formerly: eastward to Nab Light, then around the Isle of Wight for a distance of some 50 to 60 miles, with the starting line doubling as the finish line. The only seeming difference was that in this Royal Victoria event the contenders would start and finish off Ryde Pier instead of off the Royal Yacht Squadron clubhouse standing atop the neighboring promontory at Cowes.

And yet there was a subtle difference not taken into account by Lord de Blaquiere on the eve of the race. The day of its running was Election Day—the day the voters of Britain would choose their Parliamentary representatives. Consequently the crowds normally attracted to the scene of an important sporting event remained in their home bailiwicks in order to participate actively in the regatta of politics.

Considered practically, the absence of a cheering multitude should have no effect on the speed of a yacht. And yet an actor performs with difficulty if he receives no applause, and a horse runs only sluggishly unless urged on by roars from the grandstand.

On the morning of the contest, the *America*'s competitors at the starting line were four cutters and a schooner. But at 10:30, when the gun was fired, two of the cutters remained at anchor, for seemingly the wind was not to their liking. This left in the race with the *America* her fellow schooner *Zephyretta,* of exactly her tonnage, *Mosquito,* and *Arrow. Hunt's Yachting Magazine* described the race at length, and this is part of what was said:

> There was a good stiff breeze blowing from the southwest. The *Mosquito* was the first to get under weigh and soon showed her bowsprit ahead of the *Arrow,* who followed closely in her wake. The *America* was somewhat tardy in getting her gaff topsail set, which gave the others a decided advantage in the start; but that was of trivial account when the extent of the course is considered. The *Zephyretta* was the last to get away. . . . In this order they passed the No-man Buoy, beating up against the tide.
>
> On rounding the No-man the *Zephyretta,* which was lying close astern, passed the *America* a little to windward on the starboard tack, and got round the Nab Light one minute before her. From this point the *Mosquito* kept heading the *Arrow* a very little towards the White Cliff at the back of the island, which was now against flood tide. . . . One great thing in the *Mosquito*'s favor was the power of being able to make short tacks quicker than the longer and larger vessels, and the *Mosquito* held a much better wind than the *Arrow.*
>
> The *America* held a good wind, but, being a larger vessel and schooner-rigged, she was unable to get up to the *Mosquito,* who met with the light breeze that just suited her. . . . But after rounding St. Catherine's, the *America* began to overhaul the *Arrow* very fast and finally passed her off Freshwater Bay. . . .

The *Mosquito* was only four minutes and a half ahead of the *America*, and the latter about eight minutes in advance of the *Arrow*. After these yachts got inside the Needles the wind shifted to WNW, and the *America* overhauled and passed the *Mosquito*, thereby becoming the leading vessel.

By the time the *Mosquito* reached Lepe the *Arrow* passed her. From thence the yachts stretched across the Solent towards Old Castle Point, where the three met together, and the *Arrow* and *Mosquito* shortly afterwards closed the *America* and passed her.

The whole now ran up and passed Osborne with the wind dead aft. The *America* "goose-winged," the same advantage being taken by the cutters, they also booming out their foresails. It was here evident that as long as the cutters could run under their two sails they had the advantage. Eventually they arrived at the goal, it being almost a neck and neck race between the *Arrow* and *Mosquito*, the former being about the length of her bowsprit in advance.

They were timed as follows:—

	h.	m.	s.
Arrow	6	59	30
Mosquito	6	59	31
America	7	1	20
Zephyretta	7	39	0

Thus it will be seen it was a most exciting match. . . . But it was generally remarked that however well the *America* may have been sailed and attended during the match, and with the same canvas as when sailed by her former American crew, her sails did not present that "cardboard" appearance we have been accustomed to witness; nor did she present that smooth appearance in displacing or going through the water as formerly, when her motion was almost imperceptible.

The *Arrow* and *Mosquito* fouled when abreast of Peel Bank, mid-way between Old Castle Point and Ryde, by the *Mosquito's* boom dragging the larboard side of the *Arrow*. The eighteenth regulation of the Royal Victoria Yacht Club states, "That two yachts touching will both be disqualified unless it can be proved to the satisfaction of the committee which is the aggressor."

Immediately following the race, no one made a move toward invoking the regulation. Mr. Chamberlayne, owner of the *Arrow*, could not have been more satisfied, for his yacht had been the first to cross the finish line. Nor did Lord Londesborough, owner of the *Mosquito*, speak up, since it was apparent to all that his yacht had been at fault; she had drawn too close to her competitor, and her skipper had inaccurately estimated the amount of clearance available for the swing of her boom.

It was apparent to all, that is, excepting Lord de Blaquiere. He seemed to consider it a blight upon his name that his cherished *America*, in an all-day race, should have lost by less than 2 minutes. And so in an absurd attempt to eradicate the fancied stain—and grab the Queen's Cup—he proved himself other than reasonable.

He insisted that the Royal Victoria's racing committee conduct an investigation. Appalled, the committeemen did so, and in a matter of seconds announced their verdict: The *Mosquito* had been clearly the aggressor, and the victor's trophy therefore rightfully belonged to Mr. Chamberlayne and his *Arrow*.

Lord de Blaquiere's truculence did nothing to increase his popularity in British yachting circles. Although by now the height of the regatta season had arrived at the Isle of Wight, His Lordship found the lists already filled whenever he proposed entering a race, and his collection of friends in the yacht clubs rapidly waned. Owning the *America* had apparently gone to his head, displacing his awareness that he should have remained genial and fair-minded.

But on September 11 a yacht from a foreign land sailed up and dropped anchor in Cowes Roads, and she would soon prove a worthy foe for the *America*. She was the new schooner *Sverige*, owned by Nicholas Beckman of the Royal Swedish Yacht Club, and this was her maiden voyage. According to contemporary press accounts, she had sailed from Gothenburg in four days, but the report must have been in error unless she was towed by a herd of speedy dolphins.

> The illustrious stranger [said *Bell's Life*] flies a blue swallow-tailed flag with a yellow cross, in the middle of which is a royal initial. The general appearance of the yacht resembles in the hull that of the *America,* but we think she is handsomer about the stern and in size she exceeds the *America* by possibly 70 tons. She has considerable spring forward, more so than the *America,* and is higher out of the water. The spring referred to is not unsightly, the eye being relieved from the monotonous black by all above the planksheer forward being painted white. The *Sverige* has no cutwater, but has a raking stern and flaring bows; her bowsprit, which is only 8 feet outboard, makes an agreeable finish. The royal Swedish arms, in a shield, is on the stem, and branching therefrom on both sides are gilded scrolls instead of trailboards, which give her a sightly appearance. On her stern are also the Swedish royal arms exquisitely carved. She is a fore-and-aft schooner, her masts very taunt and close together. The spars are of extraordinary dimensions—mainmast 92½ feet, with 18-ft. topmast; foremast 87½ feet, with 18-ft. topmast; main boom 58½ feet; gaffs 30 feet each. Her deck is flush, length overall 111 feet, extreme breadth 25 feet, depth of hold 11 feet. She carries a crew of 17, and is altogether a splendid craft.

Lord John de Blaquiere lost no time in making the acquaintance of Nicholas Beckman and challenging him to a race. The Swedish gentleman, while agreeable, declined to sail for the wager of £400 a side Lord de Blaquiere named and instead suggested £25—enough, he said, to cover expenses. Eventually there was a compromise of £100 a side; the date set for the race was Saturday, October 9, "should that day provide a 7-knot breeze, and if not, on the first week-day thereafter that such a breeze shall blow;" and the course of the race was agreed upon and marked on a chart. It would start off Ryde Pier, near the clubhouse of the Royal Victoria Yacht Club, go southeast to the easternmost end of the Isle of Wight, then circle a mark-vessel moored 20 miles out in the English Channel, and return to the place of starting.

When Saturday arrived, Lord de Blaquiere, on learning that

Underwood, who had piloted the *America* in 1851 and again in the recent Queen's Cup race, was now aboard the *Sverige* to act as her pilot, loudly objected. It would not be fair, he claimed, for Underwood knew all the *America*'s faults. A pilot named Caws went aboard the *Sverige* as a replacement, and Underwood left dismayed. Later a newspaper commented that if Lord de Blaquiere's complaint were valid, and if validity of that sort were extended throughout the small world of British yacht racing, then all pilots were reduced to the role of serfs, each bound for a lifetime to serve but a single master.

In the midst of the hassle the wind blew strong. While Mr. Beckman contended that the breeze had reached 7 knots, Lord de Blaquiere thought otherwise, and the Royal Victoria's judges, with some reluctance, sided with His Lordship. Whereupon Mr. Beckman invited several officers of the Royal Navy to go with him for a sail and on their return the officers attested that the *Sverige* had averaged 9.2 knots and at one point had zipped along for several miles at 11 knots.

> So much [said *Bell's Life*] for the opinion that there was not a 7-knot breeze. But when the "faculty" disagrees, what are the "students" to do? The breeze continued throughout the afternoon, and the public and those more immediately interested in the result were greatly disappointed. A better day could not have been selected for the race. [And *Hunt's Yachting Magazine* added:] The question is, what *is* a 7-knot breeze? This puzzles many heads—and whether it means the wind to *travel* at the rate of seven nautical miles, or whether it means the wind to propel a vessel seven nautical miles, has not been defined. If the latter, what description of vessel is to be propelled seven knots? A man-of-war, a horse boat, a collier, or a racing yacht?

On Monday, October 11, no one could argue about wind conditions, for there was a definite, depressing calm. It persisted, in fact, throughout Monday night and breakfast-time Tuesday. Consequently, no crowd gathered at Ryde to watch the *America* and the *Sverige* lie lazily at anchor; the waters were free of excursion steamers accustomed to follow yacht races;

and the only journalist up and about was a *Hunt's Yachting Magazine* correspondent, who felt fairly certain he would have the day to himself.

But as matters turned out, this reporter soon got busy. Almost on the dot of 11 o'clock starting time, a strong breeze rushed up from the ENE, and the Royal Victoria's referee announced that the race was on by firing two guns. Aboard the judges' steamer, the man from *Hunt's* followed the race, and later he turned in this story:

> *The Start*—The *Sverige* was under weigh first and took the lead on the lee bow, but the *America* prevented her passing. After reaching about a quarter of a mile, the *Sverige* tacked, but could not weather the *America*. They each set main-sail, fore-sail, stay-sail and top-sails. There was afterwards but little variation in them till they rounded Bembridge Ledge, when they both set a square-sail. Here the *Sverige* tried to pass the *America* on her weather side, which the latter prevented by taking a more easterly course; upon which they put up the *Sverige*'s helm, and passed under the *America*'s stern; the *Sverige* accordingly got the lead, and improved it, rounding the mark vessel, thus—
>
> *Sverige* .... 3 hrs. 37 min. 4 sec.
> *America* .... 3 hrs. 45 min. 30 sec.
>
> *The Beat Back*—Now came the struggle. Unfortunately in rounding the steamer, the *Sverige* carried away the jaws of her main-gaff, which was temporarily lashed up; but for the last twelve miles she could not set her top-sail at all; and the superiority of the sails of the *America*, in a dead beat, became again manifest. The flood tide having set in, the vessels made Freshwater Cliff on the first reach; they then tacked toward St. Catherine's, and for one hour and twenty minutes, both close hauled, they kept neck and neck, till off St. Catherine's Light House, when the *America* passed on the Swede's weather bow; and shortly the *America* tacked, and stood towards Dunnose; and the *Sverige* stood to the eastward, and through fear of the main-gaff being carried away if she frequently tacked, night coming on with hazy weather, and the Nab not visible, the

> *Sverige* overreached herself twenty minutes. After passing the Nab, the *Sverige* gradually improved her position, but all chance of winning, after injuring her main-gaff, was hopeless. They arrived at the goal, as follows:—
>
> | | |
> |---|---|
> | *America* .... | 8 hrs. 5 min. |
> | *Sverige* .... | 8 hrs. 31 min. |
>
> There seems to be a general opinion that the *Sverige* was very badly sailed. As an instance we cite the great mistake in overreaching so much at the Nab Light, but there were many others. . . .

The correspondent concluded his story by giving what he considered the cause of the mishandling of the *Sverige*. First, the abrupt withdrawal of Pilot Underwood brought about the employment of Pilot Caws. Mr. Beckman, owner of the *Sverige*, so resented the substitution that he insisted on steering the yacht himself, and not knowing local waters, did a bad job of it. Next, the *Sverige*, shortly before the race, added to her regular crew of Swedish sailors a number of Britishers. Neither group understood the language of the other, with a result not unlike that at the building of the Tower of Babel.

Mr. Beckman took the criticism with good grace and sailed his *Sverige* back to Sweden. Not so Lord de Blaquiere. The *America* won, he insisted, only because she was the faster yacht. "I do not see how this question can be better or more satisfactorily settled," he wrote *The Times*, of London, "than by some crack vessel racing against the *America*. I, therefore, now challenge the yachts of all countries—America excepted—not exceeding the *America* in tonnage, to sail with my yacht, for a sum not less than £500, and not more than £1,000, on any day and in any place—in short, over any course—that would give scope for testing the sailing qualities of the *America* and her opponents, under all points, in a nine-knot breeze. I beg, in conclusion, to state that this challenge will be open until the 15th of November, and cannot be extended beyond that day, as the *America* . . . must go into harbour to refit for another trip to the Mediterranean."

His Lordship's published challenge received three acceptances, all from yachtsmen of stature. Two agreed to race for £1,000—or for more, if desired—and the third for £500. But none of the three could do so immediately, as the season had grown late. Their yachts, laid up for the winter, would have to be specially refitted, and this would take time.

The threat of delay gave Lord de Blaquiere an out, if such he was seeking, and subsequent events certainly suggest he had written *The Times* with a pen dipped only in the ink of bravado. Instead of outfitting the *America* for another cruise to the Mediterranean, the eccentric nobleman put her up for sale—in January 1853—and meanwhile his own activities were of a romantic rather than an aquatic character.

On November 25, 1852, at St. James's, Westminster, Lord de Blaquiere married for the second time. His bride, only four years more than half his age, was Eleanor Amelia, daughter of William George Hylton-Jolliffe, the first Baron Hylton. The couple went off—not aboard the *America*—on a lengthy honeymoon.

On their return they found the War Office busy recruiting troops. Trouble brewed between Russia and Turkey, and France and Great Britain possessed interests along the shores of the Bosporus they had no inclination to forsake. Among the numerous British officers recalled from extensive periods of leave was that zealous yachtsman and not-so-zealous Captain of Infantry, Lord John de Blaquiere.

Britain and France declared war on Russia in January 1854, and soon thereafter the bloody Crimean War began in earnest. Lord de Blaquiere, placed in command of a unit in the 41st Foot on July 7, resigned his commission—or "sold out," as the British call it—exactly seven weeks later. Perhaps His Lordship's estates in Ireland needed his attention, or it may have been that his young wife objected to being left at home alone.

The Crimean War—in which 45,000 Britons died—ended with

the signing of the Treaty of Paris in March 1856. While hostilities lasted, British yachting suffered severe curtailment, and the *America,* up for sale throughout the war, found no purchaser. But as soon as peace was declared, the yacht was acquired by the most unlikely of buyers—Henry Montagu Upton, the second Viscount and third Baron Templetown.

The Honorable Henry's grandfather on one side had been Clerk Comptroller to the Princess Dowager of Wales and his grandfather on the other the 5th Earl of Sandwich. His father, a member of the House of Commons before elevation to the peerage, for years had as a mistress a Miss Rietz, a natural daughter of the King of Prussia. His father's mother, a woman of great liberality and learning, kept up a lively and friendly correspondence with Miss Rietz as long as the affair lasted. On occasions they wrote in French, on others in German. Lady Templetown did this, she explained, to improve her language proficiencies.

As a young aristocrat should, the Honorable Henry received his education at Eton and then at Christ Church, Oxford, and emerged fully equipped to lead a life of leisure, which is precisely what he did.

On the death of his father in 1846, the newly created Lord Templetown inherited Castle Upton, in County Antrim, Ireland, and more than 24,000 acres of land. In rents, the land brought in £19,000 a year, give or take a thousand or so. But with a castle and all this property, His Lordship—who never married—preferred to live at a London hotel, the Albany, in Piccadilly.

He lived there, that is, except during yachting seasons. Then he shifted about from one yacht club to another, and at times was a member of the Royal Thames, the Royal Western, the Royal Victoria, or the Royal Yacht Squadron, and often he maintained his membership in two, three, or all four at once.

In a like manner, he owned more than one yacht. In 1853, he bought the *Smokie Piga,* a cutter of but 12 tons; later the *Gurida,* a somewhat larger cutter; still later the *Magic,* a schooner of 83 tons; and finally the *America,* whose tonnage was considerably greater than that of all the other three put together.

Almost as soon as Lord Templetown added the *America* to his fleet, he realized he should not have done so. Essentially she was a racing yacht, and he was not a racing yachtsman, nor did he aspire to become one. He liked to drift or sail about in a mild breeze, preferably in shallow water, in the company of a few like-minded friends.

Had some aggressive, yet personable, chap thought of asking His Lordship for the *America,* he might have given her away. But no one did, and so, after using her but a single season, he laid her up in a mud berth at East Cowes, and there she remained until 1858.

Indeed, she might have stayed even longer had not gossip gone the rounds that Lord Templetown was guilty of permitting the world's most famous and perhaps most beautiful yacht to end her days the victim of rot. When the shameful whisperings reached His Lordship's ears, he rose from his lethargy sufficiently to advertise the *America* for sale. In May 1858, Henry Sotheby Pitcher, a shipbuilder, bought the yacht—reputedly for a sum so small that ordinarily it would not have purchased the enormous amount of extra tackle and gear that went with her—and caused her to be towed to his yard at Northfleet on the Thames, a few miles below London.

It is good, however, that Pitcher got the yacht cheap. For he rebuilt her with a view toward reselling her—at a profit, of course—and the low price permitted him to take his time and do the topnotch job of which he was supremely capable.

For the frames of the yacht in need of replacement, Pitcher used stout English oak, for the bottom planking elm, and for topside planking teak. But he changed her lines barely an iota, for he was too great an admirer of the artistry of the late George Steers to commit such sacrilege.

Pitcher found the *America*'s mainmast and foremast sound except for a few feet at the butt of each. So he cut away these deteriorating lower extremities and restepped the masts at their original angles of rake. To compensate the spars for the loss of their accustomed feet, he gave the mainmast a taller topmast, and for the foremast he provided a fore-topmast—a stick the yacht had rarely sported previously.

When it came to replacing the *America's* suit of ragged sails, Pitcher could not find in all of England the same sort of machine-spun cotton canvas. That material, while thick and so tightly woven that it would hold every whisper of a roaring wind, nevertheless remained pliable and easy to handle. The trouble was that such fine sailcloth could be obtained only in the land the *America* came from—America. So Pitcher did the best he could with top-quality hemp from the English market.

Finally, as the Northfleet shipbuilder neared the end of his work, the *America* looked—and seemed to feel—very much like her old self. She was lacking, however, the gilded spread eagle that had graced her transom on leaving New York. At some point during the yacht's lengthy sojourn in Britain, the eagle had disappeared, and no one seemed to know its whereabouts.

But this was a minor mystery, as compared with another, for after a few years the eagle turned up, hanging as a sign above the portal of a pub called "The Eagle," on the Isle of Wight. The second mystery proved deep—even dark in certain of its aspects—and infinitely more complex. This second mystery involved the man who bought the *America* from Pitcher, changed her name to *Camilla,* and eventually changed her character from that of a racing yacht to a vessel in need of a racer's speed to avoid destruction by gunfire.

FIVE

"The Brief History of My Captain"

THE PURCHASER of the *Camilla,* formerly the *America,* obtained from Henry Sotheby Pitcher the usual bill of sale. This he presented to the Registrar of British Ships, at Portsmouth, where he filled out a Declaration of Ownership. In the Declaration he gave the yacht's rig, measurements, and tonnage, and she was awarded Official Number 15984. He correctly dated the document July 30, 1860, put down his address as Clipstone House, Northhamptonshire, and signed what purported to be his name—Henry Edward Decie.

There is not now and was not then any community in Northhamptonshire—or anywhere in Britain—called Clipstone House. There is, however, on the northern edge of Northhamptonshire, about 90 miles north of London, the very old inland village of Clipston (spelled without an "e"), boasting only a thousand or so residents. In 1860 an edifice called Clipston House stood in the village, and it was then the home of a family named Harrison. But today these Harrisons are no more, and if a Henry Edward Decie ever lived there, he left no lasting imprint.

Also, prior to 1860, Decie's name had never appeared in the yachting press. Reputedly he was a member of the Royal Western Yacht Club of Plymouth, but even this lacks confirmation. During World War II, German planes bombed Plymouth, and the Royal Western's clubhouse and records suffered total destruction.

Reputedly, too, the man who was actually named or who used the name Henry Edward Decie made a cruise aboard the *Camilla* to the Mediterranean immediately after buying her. Such seems hardly possible, however, for eighteen days following the purchase—on August 17, 1860—the yacht's new owner raced her in a regatta at Plymouth open to entrants not necessarily members of the Royal Western.

In this match, the *Camilla's* only competitors were two other schooners, the *Galatea* and the *Wildfire,* owned respectively by T. Broadwood, Esq., and J. Turner-Turner, Esq. Sports writers of the time gave the event scant coverage, probably because they felt the outcome a foregone conclusion—that the *Camilla* would win. And so she did, although she spotted the *Wildfire* 15 and the *Galatea* 9 minutes. The course was off the Plymouth Breakwater to a mark-boat out at sea, twice around. In a race lasting roughly five hours, the *Camilla* beat *Wildfire* 20 and the *Galatea* 30 minutes, and won a prize of £80, according to *The Illustrated London News,* but only £60, if the report in *Hunt's Yachting Magazine* is preferred. The two periodicals also differed in a second particular. While the former spelled the name of the victorious yachtsman "Decie," the latter printed it "Ducie."

During the next few years, Henry Edward Decie—or whoever he was—must have become inured to such variations, for on one side of the Atlantic or the other, in print or in longhand, his name was spelled nine additional different ways: Dacie, Dacier, Dacy, Dasy, Deacie, Deacy, Deasy, Decey, and Decri. Also, while usually addressed as "Mister," he was often called "Captain," and on at least one occasion, in a letter penned by a Lieutenant Commanding in the U.S. Navy, he was referred to as "Lord Dacy," for the author of the letter, from the rumors prevailing, apparently believed the title justified.

Further, there were differences of opinion concerning Decie's nautical abilities. Some who knew him contended that, given a seasoned crew, he knew how to keep the *Camilla* in trim and get the best out of her while sailing. Others thought him slipshod and neglectful. Soon after winning the regatta at Plymouth, Decie outfitted the yacht for what he announced would be a long cruise to the West Indies, and disappeared from Britain, not to return for more than ten months.

Information concerning where Decie spent the first eight of the ten has proven elusive. Decie's own later account, revised from the version in which the West Indies was to have been his destination, has defied verification. Success, however, has rewarded efforts to trace many of the movements of Decie from April 1861, until early February 1862, with the latter date marking the end of the period during which the *Camilla* remained under his control.

In large measure, this success is due to the diaries kept by two men, Edward Clifford Anderson, of Savannah, Georgia, and James Heyward North, of Charleston, South Carolina. The two sailed together in the *Camilla* with Decie. Anderson was then a major of artillery in the Army of the Confederate States of America, and North a lieutenant in the Confederate Navy. The yacht took them from the Confederacy to Britain—and thus chalked up for herself a third Atlantic crossing.

During the century following, the diaries, as cherished heirlooms, were handed down in the Anderson and North families. Only recently did both diaries find their way into the Southern Historical Collection of the University of North Carolina Library, at Chapel Hill. Here in this book, for the first time—with the permission of James W. Patton, Director of the Collection—has use been made of the diaries to provide material for important portions of the biography of the yacht.

James Heyward North, aged 50 when his native South Carolina seceded from the Union in December 1860, entered the U.S. Navy as a midshipman in 1829. After a decade of sea duty, he was promoted to a full lieutenancy and, except for about a year (late 1857 and much of 1858), he was permanently stationed at the Norfolk Navy Yard, charged with building, repairing, and arming warships. During the excepted 1857–8 period, he had his first encounter with a vessel designed and constructed by the late George Steers. This was the frigate *Niagara,* temporarily assigned by the Navy to Cyrus Field to assist in his early efforts to lay an Atlantic cable. As part of the deal, North and other naval officers went along and actively participated.

Seemingly North possessed only modest private means. Even so, he married early—in 1835, before he was drawing a lieutenant's pay—and he and his wife Emily, also a South Carolinian, enjoyed a close and loving relationship that was productive of several children. So close were they, in fact, that when North went to Britain aboard the *Camilla,* he took with him his wife and their adolescent daughter Annie.

North resigned his commission in the U.S. Navy three weeks after South Carolina's secession. He did so with frankly admitted reluctance, for at the Norfolk Navy Yard he had found for his family and himself a secure and comfortable berth. But other South Carolinians, in the U.S. Army as well as in the Navy, were resigning, and North was not a man to buck the tide.

North's diary notations, obviously never revised, were mainly brief jottings. They show him to have been beset by envy, various real or fancied bodily complaints, mental and physical lassitude, a morbid dislike for bad weather, and a lack of both ingenuity and daring. On the other hand, he was fond of music, he read his Bible often, he attended religious services at every opportunity, and he appears to have made numerous fast friends among the naval officers at Norfolk.

The Provisional Confederate Government, formed at Montgomery, Alabama, in February 1861, commissioned North a lieutenant in its then nonexistent Confederate Navy and sent him off scouting for ships around which to build a Navy. While the South possessed a fair quantity of sailing vessels, she was in dire need of steamers. North visited Baltimore, Philadelphia, and New York, but in all three cities found that agents of the

U.S. Navy had gone ahead of him and scooped up the cream of available ships. The steamers left were either too old and broken down or too high-priced. Whereupon, North returned to Montgomery to report his findings to Confederate Secretary of the Navy Stephen R. Mallory, whose name he erroneously entered in his diary "F. R. Mallory." On April 12, while North was at Montgomery, Confederate General Beauregard began the bombardment that two days later forced the surrender of Fort Sumter—the opening curtain on the great four-year drama of the Civil War. Although the name "Sumter" was on every tongue and emblazoned in newspaper headlines, North misspelled it "Sumpter"—this in spite of the fact that the fort stood in the harbor of his native Charleston.

Mallory refused to accept his agent's lament that suitable steamers were not to be had and ordered him north again. On this second trip the Lieutenant got no farther than Baltimore, where, according to his diary, a friend informed him that in Washington a warrant had been issued for his arrest. So warned, North retreated back home to Charleston and from there reported his lack of success by letter to Mallory at Montgomery, 400 miles distant.

At this early stage of the war, seasoned officers, never plentiful in the Confederate Navy, were in terribly short supply. Also, facilities for building warships in the South were virtually nonexistent, except for those few shipyards already seized by the Union. Eventually the Confederate Congress recognized some of the realities of the situation and passed a bill appropriating $2,000,000 for the purchase in England, or elsewhere in Europe, of "six steam propellers of moderate size, fully armed, and two steam ironclad warships fully armed." But implementing the bill by placing abroad loyal and competent agents and supplying them with the actual cash or negotiable letters of credit needed were duties the Congress blithely delegated to Secretary of the Navy Mallory. At the outset Mallory was able to obtain from the Confederate Treasury only half of the amount appropriated, and that by dribs and drabs.

For his initial overseas agent Mallory made a happy choice. He picked James Dunwody Bulloch, scion of an old and distinguished Georgia family, whose half-sister Martha, not long before, had given birth to a future President of the United States, Theodore Roosevelt. Bulloch, at the start of the Civil War, was 38. Three years after the death of his first wife, he had married the daughter of a prominent Marylander. Like North, he had once been an officer in the U.S. Navy, but there the resemblance stopped. Bulloch was a man of great physical and mental vigor, boldness, and resourcefulness. Throughout his career in the U.S. Navy he had sought sea duty and had been rapidly promoted. But the Navy's idea of rapidity was not fast enough to suit him, and some years before the Civil War he resigned to launch a successful shipping business in New York.

As soon as his native Georgia seceded from the Union, Bulloch wound up his New York affairs and headed for Montgomery. He entered the service of the Confederate Navy as a civilian, but was in time commissioned commander. A practical man, he questioned in advance the ability of the Confederacy to obtain credit abroad until after she had received formal political recognition from foreign powers, and insisted that funds be made available to him through the Liverpool branch of the Southern banking house of Fraser, Trenholm & Co. After leaving Montgomery, Bulloch followed a simple route to England—via Canada and a steamer across the North Atlantic—previously taken by Captain Caleb Huse, a purchasing agent of the Confederate Army.

Huse, aged 30, was the first and the youngest Confederate agent to be sent abroad. Moreover, he was the only such agent not a native Southerner. Born in Massachusetts, he received an appointment to West Point from that commonwealth and was graduated in 1851. Stationed in Florida during the year following, he met and married a Southern girl and then began a teaching career at West Point while Robert E. Lee was Superintendent. Huse became a great admirer of Lee, and even earlier he had developed a fondness for the South. Following a leave from the faculty at West Point, which lasted until February 1861, Huse resigned his commission as a first lieutenant in the U.S. Army and accepted the post of Commandant of Cadets at the University of Alabama.

The Army of the Confederacy was as nearly destitute of the matériel of war as its Navy. Needed particularly were pistols, rifles, rifled cannon, cartridges and shells, surgical instruments, quinine, and opiates. Charged with the duty of meeting the demand, Leroy P. Walker, the Southern Government's first Secretary of War, found the few manufactories within his bailiwick incapable of quantity production. He therefore looked to England and for an officer to send there, and since the University of Alabama and its Commandant of Cadets were handy to Montgomery, he chose Caleb Huse. Commissioned a captain in the Confederate Army, the man who had only recently resigned as a lieutenant in the U.S. Army took off, and not until some while after his departure did the thought occur to anyone that he might prove disloyal.

This shocking possibility had the whole Southern hierarchy agog, when Edward Clifford Anderson, at a most appropriate time, wrote to Montgomery offering the Confederacy his services. In his diary, Anderson revealed what followed, and the details will be best told in his words later. It is enough to say for the moment that the Confederate War Department invited Anderson to Montgomery, with a view toward dispatching him to England. Since this meant that the Army would then have two representatives overseas to the Navy's one, Secretary Mallory hurriedly decided to send another. He telegraphed Lieutenant James H. North, at Charleston, to proceed immediately to Montgomery.

Anderson, 45 in the spring of 1861, came from an honored and socially prominent Savannah family. Appointed a midshipman in the U.S. Navy as a youth, he saw most of his service aboard the 20-gun warship *Falmouth* and thus learned a lot about the sea and even more about ordnance. He rose rapidly and was commissioned a lieutenant, but resigned in 1849. He had married early, and he and his wife Sarah had several children. Moreover, the Anderson clan owned three large plantations near Savannah, and there was no other male member of comparable competence to supervise their operation.

Prior to the Civil War, Anderson served a two-year term as Mayor of Savannah, and after the War two four-year terms. Had he wished, he might have gone far in public office, for he was ruggedly handsome, personable, and blessed with the sort of boundless energy born of good health. If he had a fault, it was the size of his ego, which seems to have been somewhat swollen. On subjects other than his own abilities, however, he thought straight and to the point, and if the hundreds of thousands of words he left written on paper are indicative of how he talked, he must have been a colorful, amusing, and effective speaker.

Anderson's Civil War diary is more than a diary; it is a running narrative of much that he thought, heard, saw, and did during those anguished and yet exciting four years. Unlike James H. North's jottings, often cryptic and only barely legible, Anderson wrote complete, well-constructed sentences and paragraphs, with due regard for clarity in both penmanship and meaning. Internal evidence suggests he had posterity in mind, and that portions of his narrative were first roughed out, corrected, and polished before being entered in final form.

While eventually Anderson had a great deal to say about the activities of the yacht *Camilla* and her owner, he did not tell much concerning the initial phase of their Savannah sojourn, for during it he was absent from Georgia. Others, however, had such contact soon after the yacht put in at Savannah—on or about April 25, 1861—and subsequently reported what they heard and observed.

William Howard Russell, the correspondent for *The* (London) *Times* who would one day be knighted for the excellence of his newspaper work, sensed the coming of civil war in America well in advance, and to cover its inevitable opening left England in February 1861. He tarried in New York first, then in Baltimore and Washington, before taking the plunge below the Mason-Dixon line. While the stories he sent his paper were in the main concerned with major political and military events, he picked up fascinating scraps here and there which he entered in his notebook and later published in a series of magazine articles and in two books, one for British and the other for American consumption.

From Washington south, Russell was accompanied by two men in disguise. Theodore R. Davis, a young artist-correspondent for *Harper's Weekly,* a Northern periodical with strong Union sympathies, traveled, according to Russell, as "Deodore F. Moses" and pretended to represent *The Illustrated London News.* And Sam Ward, brother of Julia Ward Howe, the famed Abolitionist editor and writer, went along on the junket posing as Russell's secretary. Actually Ward, for years a Congressional lobbyist, was a spy for William Henry Seward, Lincoln's Secretary of State, and the intelligence reports he compiled were forwarded to Seward under the cover of Russell's newspaper dispatches. Today these reports, signed "Carlos Lopez," are among Seward's papers in the Rush Rhees Library at the University of Rochester in Rochester, N.Y.

This conglomerate trio left the North soon after the fall of Fort Sumter, spent a few days in North Carolina, a few more in South Carolina, and arrived by train at Savannah on April 20. Charles Green, an Englishman, met them with his horse and carriage and took them to stay at his home, the finest mansion in the city. Green was related by marriage to the Low family, and he and certain of the Lows, with great success, operated the Savannah branch of Isaac Low & Co., an important Liverpool mercantile house. Also, Green had close business and financial ties with Gazaway Bugg Lamar, the Savannahian who ran the Bank of the Republic in New York City and was, too, the disapproving father of Charles A. L. Lamar, once owner of the slave yacht *Wanderer.*

In 1861 Savannah had a population of 14,000 whites and 8,500 Negroes. Three railroads converged and maintained their shops there, and in addition the city boasted iron foundries, numerous cotton presses, rice mills, and sawmills. Although a seaport, Savannah actually lay 18 miles from the sea. The Savannah River provided excellent deep-water communication with the Atlantic, and at the mouth of the river stood Fort Pulaski, recently taken over by Confederates.

Russell and his companions must have enjoyed themselves in Savannah, for they remained about two weeks. They visited Fort Pulaski, and Theodore Davis made a sketch there of Russell, with Sam Ward standing by, pretending to sight a cannon—a drawing which subsequently appeared in *Harper's Weekly.* On the evening of April 30, Charles Green gave a dinner party for his house guests, and Russell, in his notebook, listed, along with numerous prominent Georgians who attended, "a Britisher, owner of the once renowned *America* which, under the name of *Camilla,* was now lying in the river (not perhaps without reference to a little speculation in running the blockade, hourly expected). . . ."

On May 1, when a junket out of Savannah was about to begin, Russell went hunting Theodore Davis and discovered that ". . . the young artist, for some reason known to himself, had gone on board the *Camilla.*" The yacht lay in the middle of the river "moored to a floating dock, with her club ensign flying. These are the times for bold ventures, and if Uncle Sam is not very quick with his blockades, there will be plenty of privateers and the like under C.S.A. colours looking out for his fat merchantmen all over the world."

So far in his notes, Russell did not name the yacht's owner. And yet, in a dispatch sent *The Times* on that very day and printed by the paper on May 28, Russell said of Savannah, "There were very few ships in the river; the yacht *Camilla,* better known as the *America,* the property of Captain Deasy, and several of those few sailing under British colours. . . ."

It developed that the business of Theodore Davis aboard the *Camilla* was to interview Decie. *Harper's Weekly,* in its issue for June 1, published the result. Davis wrote that "Captain

Decri" was now the "fortunate possessor of the *Camilla,* formerly the *America,"* and then declared:

> The Captain is a gentleman of independent fortune, with a most charming wife and family, who with him sail from country to country in the yacht in as comfortable and homelike a manner as one can well conceive of. During a recent run from the Cape de Verdes the little vessel made the distance of seven hundred miles in two days, thus more than retrieving the laurels she lost while in the hands of Commodore Stevens' successor. She won a race at the Plymouth last fall, which emboldened her present proprietor to challenge all England for a sail, without finding a competitor. The pride of our yacht marine had lain neglected for years, and been suffered to go to decay. But ships, unlike mortals, can have their skeletons clothed in the new beauty of line and strength of skin; and the *Camilla,* having undergone this "Frankenstein" process, "now walks the water like a thing of life" again.

While there are at least two errors in this story, it is impossible to say whether Theodore Davis committed them on his own or whether Henry Decie—or Deasy, or Decri—misinformed his interviewer. Decie had raced his yacht at Plymouth not in the "fall" of 1860, but on August 17, and following the race there was no report that he had unsuccessfully challenged "all England" for another.

The *Harper's Weekly* representative sent off his Savannah dispatch not immediately, but further along in his travels after he had reached the Confederate capital, over which held sway a Chief Executive bearing a surname identical with his own. Then he datelined the story "Montgomery, Alabama, May 8, 1861," and made some additions to it, including this bit of intelligence: "The lady of the President, Mrs. Davis, held a morning *levée* yesterday, which was largely attended. . . . Mr. Russell, Mr. Samuel Ward, of New York and Captain Decri were received with marked attention. . . ."

Concerning the same matinal reception, Mary Boykin Chesnut, the wife of an aide to President Jefferson Davis, wrote in her famous, later-published diary, "Mrs. Davis was in fine spirits. Captain Dacier was here. Came over in his own yacht. Russell, of the London *Times,* wondered how we had the heart to enjoy life so thoroughly when all the Northern papers said we were to be exterminated in such a short time."

Apparently Henry Decie, Theodore Davis, Sam Ward, and William Howard Russell had all journeyed from Savannah to Montgomery together, or hard on one another's heels. In his notes, Russell described Montgomery as a city "too hot, dirty and ugly to call itself a capital." Jefferson Davis, however, impressed the *Times* correspondent as "certainly a man of far more polish than Abraham Lincoln, the chief executive of the Union in Washington." And yet Russell deplored the caliber of various of the hangers-on who surrounded President Davis, for he found them "uncouth, unmannerly and patently self-seeking."

Russell included in this category George Nicholas Sanders, a lumbering bear of a man he had previously encountered abroad. Sanders, once a Kentucky horse trader, had gone on to embarrass the United States while tentatively serving as consul at Liverpool. He had joined a nefarious group of exiled French and Italian "liberals" who advocated the assassination of Napoleon III, and had employed the immunity of U.S. diplomatic pouches to transmit their inflammatory literature. "But here he is a slavery man," Russell commented, "and a friend of an oligarchy. Your 'Rights of Man' man is often most inconsistent with himself, and is generally found associated with the men of force and violence."

Russell might have been even more critical of Sanders had he followed his history since his recall from Liverpool. Within days of taking office as President of the United States, James Buchanan awarded Sanders the juicy appointment of navy agent at New York. And as soon as Charles A. L. Lamar, a Sanders crony, heard of his pal's landing the job, he put slave-running out of his mind temporarily in favor of another way of turning a fat and fast dollar. On April 1, 1857, Charlie Lamar wrote Sanders:

> Let me congratulate you upon your appointment. I'm glad to see it, independent of any selfish motive—and I'm glad on that account too. I want none of the offices of "Honor and Trust," but want a contract for making money. You have the power of disposing of the contract for the supplying of timber and lumber at the Navy Yard, and I have the means and ability of supplying. Will you give me the point to enable me to get it? I have 11,500 acres of pine land which is just the ticket. . . .

On the morning of May 8, 1861, Russell booked passage for himself and his companions aboard a steamer leaving Montgomery on the afternoon of the day following for Mobile, some 400 miles down the long and winding Alabama River. Also on May 8 he confided to his notebook the belief that "the owner of the *Camilla* might be tempted to part with his yacht by the offers made to him." Later in the day he recorded further: "I resisted a vigorous attempt of Mr. G. N. Sanders to take me to visit a planter some miles outside Montgomery. He succeeded in capturing Mr. Deasy."

Decie was absent all night from the Montgomery hotel at which he, Russell, Sam Ward, and Theodore Davis stopped. "Much dilapidated," wrote Russell on May 9, "Mr. Deasy returned about noon. The planter was drunk when he went over and kept him up until all hours. When he fell asleep, the planter awakened him and refreshed his glass. This planter owned a large tract of land and a good stock of slaves, but he must have been a 'mean white.' "

Russell, Sam Ward, Theodore Davis, and Henry Decie boarded, at four that afternoon, what Russell described as the "castle-like hulk of the *Southern Republic.* It was nothing more than a vast wooden house, of three separate storeys, floating on a pontoon which upheld the engine, with a dining-hall or saloon on the second storey and a nest of smaller rooms with sleeping berths above that. On the metal roof was a 'musical instrument' called a 'calliope.' As landings were approached the calliope played the wild strains of 'Dixie' and when landings were made at night the gangway of the vessel was brilliantly lit by torches of pine oozing resin."

The *Southern Republic* reached Selma, Alabama—about a quarter of the way to Mobile—around midnight. Russell bade farewell to one of his companions, and noted the parting thus: "Here Mr. Deasy, being attacked by illness, became alarmed at the idea of continuing his journey without any opportunity of medical assistance, and went on shore."

So far as is known today, neither Russell, nor Sam Ward, nor Theodore Davis ever saw Decie again. It is probable that on the night of May 8, while in the company of Sanders—ever the political opportunist—Decie, instead of drinking at some plantation, was closeted with officials of the Southern Government dickering concerning his yacht. Perhaps Sanders warned Decie against making any frank disclosure of his dealings to his traveling companions, for Sanders, Washington wise, knew of Sam Ward's intimacy with Seward. If so much is true, it follows that Decie may have feigned suffering from a shattering hangover, since such a debility would have given him a plausible excuse for debarking from the *Southern Republic* at Selma. And if Decie's act was in fact an act, he proved himself a competent actor. While the Seward papers at the University of Rochester contain military and political intelligence gleaned by Sam Ward in both Savannah and Montgomery, there is no mention whatsoever of Decie or his yacht.

From Selma, Decie returned to the *Camilla* at Savannah, either by way of Montgomery or by some alternate route. On May 12, Lieutenant North, in response to Secretary Mallory's bidding, once more appeared in Montgomery, and for the next few days he remained there studying the plans and models of ironclad warships. On May 17, Mallory handed North his orders, which read in part: "Sir: You will proceed to Savannah and join the ——— and proceed thence to London. You will land at some convenient point in Ireland and reach London by the ordinary steam and rail route. At London you will call upon the commissioners of the Confederate States." North was told that while abroad he was to concentrate on buying or building, in France or England, two ironclad vessels of war each to be armed with six 80-pound Armstrong breech-loaders. He was to associate himself with James D. Bulloch, who had preceded him to Europe. "Instruct Mr. Bulloch," the orders continued, "to place on board the ——— such Armstrong guns with their equipment and shells as Mr. ——— shall be willing to receive, with percussion caps and any other ordnance stores which he may be disposed to bring us. Secrecy and dispatch are equally essential throughout your labors. . . ." North was informed orally that the blanks in his orders referred to the yacht *Camilla* and her British captain.

On May 20, while at home in Charleston, North had his "likeness" taken by a photographer, as did his wife, and they exchanged pictures. That evening, North called on his clergyman, the Reverend Dr. Backman, and the next morning left for Savannah. There he found Edward Clifford Anderson "at the Lows"—the British establishment of Isaac Low & Co.

Earlier in the war, Anderson had spent much time in Richmond, Virginia, at the Tredegar Iron Works, expediting the casting of cannon ordered by Joseph E. Brown, the Governor of Georgia, for Georgia regiments. It was following the completion of this assignment that he wrote offering his services to the Confederacy—an offer quickly snapped up.

> Soon after my arrival in Savannah [Anderson noted in his diary], I received a dispatch requesting my presence in Montgomery. My heart was very heavy within me. I disapproved entirely of the rash course of the politicians of the country North and South. I had been reared under the U.S. flag in the Navy and was to the innermost recesses of my nature attached to its folds. Yet the die was cast and my lot as a Southern man with it.

At Montgomery, Anderson sought out Robert Toombs, a former U.S. Senator from Georgia then serving as Confederate Secretary of State. Together they called on President Jefferson Davis, who told Anderson of the confidential mission of Captain Caleb Huse to England to buy arms and other supplies for the Army, and that the Government had reason to "mistrust his fidelity."

[It was therefore desired, Anderson wrote,] that I should proceed to England at once and examine into his conduct, with full powers in the event of my finding Huse treacherous or not trustworthy, to supersede him immediately and send him back to this country. To this end I was to sail in the yacht *America* (*Camilla* then called) from Savannah and lose no time in getting across. This yacht had been recently purchased by the Confederate authorities from Captain Deacy for twenty-six thousand dollars, with an additional sum of six thousand dollars as a fund to equip and provision the vessel to England and back. Lieut. James North of the Confederate Navy was to accompany me across as an agent of Mr. Mallory's.

I received the appointment from the President as Major of Artillery. My instructions were drawn up and I do not think any copy was taken. Verbally I had *carte blanche* given me and in fact was to be the Secretary of War in England. I was entirely independent of the Commissioners then in that country, was not instructed or required to confer with them, and in fact was clothed with unlimited powers in all matters appertaining to the purchase of war materiel and the control of the special fund connected with this purpose.

Anderson's meeting with Jefferson Davis took place on May 18. The next morning he caught a train for home.

Soon after my arrival in Savannah [he wrote], I called at the Pulaski House to see Captain Deacy of the yacht *Camilla.* I found him lounging in the hall in front of the office and was struck with his dapper, sailor-like appearance. He was dressed in a suit of white duck, and seemed to me about as well satisfied with himself as anybody I had seen. On my enquiring of

> him when he proposed to sail, he affected the most profound ignorance of his movements & of the Confederate interests. I took him into the south east parlor of the Hotel and looking steadily in his eye said, "You are perhaps not aware Captain that I have an order to take passage in the *Camilla* to England. North of the Navy and myself are to go over with you. I have been made acquainted with all matters connected with your vessel, and we must understand each other without further mystery, for I know that the authorities at Montgomery have purchased your vessel and that you are now waiting for final instructions from them." We then conversed freely together. North was absent at the time in Charleston and it was arranged that as soon as he arrived, and the despatches from Montgomery came along, we would take our departure for England.

To be in readiness for this departure, Decie, on May 21, dropped the yacht down the Savannah River off Fort Pulaski and anchored in Tybee Roads. By that evening North was on hand, as were the dispatches. The next morning, Charles Green, of Isaac Low & Co., ran North and Anderson down the river to the yacht aboard a steamer, only to find that such a gale was blowing inland from the Atlantic that no sailing vessel could get out, and weather predictions warned that the storm would persist. Consequently, North and Anderson returned to Savannah.

On the following morning, Thursday, May 23, North telegraphed his wife inviting her to go to England with him, and she replied she could not be ready until Saturday. Apparently the Norths had previously discussed this possibility, and it is also probable that North had obtained the assent of Anderson and Decie. While so far in their diaries, Anderson had spelled the yachtsman's name "Deacy" and North had written it "Dasy," both would eventually come around to calling him "Decie."

Throughout Friday the unfavorable wind persisted, and Savannah suffered record high tides. But on Saturday the wind changed its direction and blew happily from the west. When the afternoon train from Charleston got in, not only did North's wife Emily alight, but so did his daughter Annie. The steamer *Everglade* ran Anderson and the North family down to the *Camilla,* and once they were aboard, towed the yacht over the bar and then cast off.

On this same Saturday, May 25, Gazaway Bugg Lamar, on his first trip south for many months, arrived at Savannah by train from Virginia. He may have been aboard the same train that, on passing through Charleston, picked up Mrs. North and her daughter. Lamar's second wife, the former Harriet Casenove, had died at their home, 42 University Place, New York City, earlier in May, and Lamar accompanied her body to her family's burying ground at Alexandria, Virginia.

Shortly before leaving New York, Lamar wound up his business affairs there, which included resigning as president of the Bank of the Republic. But this did not mean that he was done with banking. On May 27, two days after reaching Savannah, he was elected president of the Savannah Bank of Commerce.

In spite of Lamar's later claim, it is doubtful that he had any contact with Henry Decie, for there is nothing in the Anderson and North diaries to indicate it. Indeed, Decie had been aboard the *Camilla* in Tybee Roads for some days prior to May 25, and throughout that day he was still aboard, readying the yacht for her Atlantic crossing.

Under date of May 25, Anderson noted in his diary:

> At half past six P.M. we were fairly launched on the broad bosom of the Atlantic. With a light breeze we made all sail, waved our adieus to our friends aboard the *Everglade* and gently sped along. The yacht *Camilla* on which my destinies were now embarked was a small schooner. Originally the famous yacht *America,* she had been sold in England after beating the whole English yacht squadron, and after various changes had come into the possession of my friend Deacy. She was a little gem of a thing with a splendid cabin and her bulwarks so low in the water that you could step from a boat alongside on to her deck without any trouble.

The *Camilla,* Anderson reported, flew not only the English flag, but the pennant of the Royal Victoria Yacht Club. This pleased him, for he felt that should the yacht run afoul of some Union vessel, her Confederate mission would be doubly masked. But darkness fell with no other craft of any sort in sight. While at this stage of the war the Southern coast was nominally blockaded, it was far from being actually so. In a matter of months, however, the U.S. Navy, with a constantly lengthening arc of armed and vigilant ships, would establish a cordon difficult and dangerous to pierce.

By Monday, May 27, the yacht was off Hatteras, and by Tuesday noon off the Capes of Virginia.

> The *Camilla* moves so quietly through the water [Anderson wrote] that it is difficult to realize her speed. I asked Deacy how fast she was going. He replied by asking me my opinion. I said about eight knots. He said ten at least. The log and second glass were measured and we found she was bowling along at the rate of *thirteen* knots. I have never seen anything like the speed of this vessel in all my naval experience, and yet we have only a moderate breeze which ordinarily would drive the common run of fast sailing ships about seven knots.

On Wednesday, May 29, Anderson's remarks concerning the *Camilla* were not so complimentary. In the absence of steadying winds and yet with turbulent swells transforming the sea into a roller coaster, the

> schooner groaned and creaked in her timbers as if her little heart were breaking. She is so very sharp in her build and has such heavy spars, that her bearings are not sufficient to give her buoyancy in her struggles. Although reefed down, she pitched all night long. Dear me, how she did exercise herself. At one moment my heels were at an elevation of forty-five degrees in my berth and my head would bring up with a thump against the panel work. The next, I would find myself standing almost upright on my feet, and so we seesawed the blessed night through.

While on this occasion North failed to complain to his diary how he felt, he did write concerning his wife and daughter: "Poor Emmie has been sick. Annie gets sick, but is always ready for her meals." Perhaps Anderson and Decie breakfasted, lunched, and dined separately from the Norths, for Anderson frequently observed that he and Decie alone were ready to partake of food when summoned to the table by the yacht's cook. As described by Anderson, the table was sensibly constructed. It had no legs, but hung suspended from the ceiling of the dining saloon by rods working in hinges, and thus its surface remained more nearly horizontal when the yacht pitched and yawed. Even so, the table had to be watched. Swinging wildly as it sometimes did, it could deliver to the unwary a nasty blow.

The *Camilla*'s course was at first northeast and then when off the Newfoundland banks almost due east. In the northern latitudes, where icebergs were occasionally sighted, the thermometer dropped to a point where Anderson and Decie, to warm themselves and lift their spirits, occasionally converted the swinging dining table into a bar and sat drinking hot toddies made of rum, sugar, and water heated in a tin can over a whale-oil lamp. While the sessions were productive of but little intoxication, they did encourage considerable narration of an autobiographical sort, especially on the part of Decie. According to Anderson's diary, this is what he learned about his companion:

> The Captain was a rattle-brained fellow, an Irishman by birth, who had been for a time an officer in the British Navy. He left the service under these circumstances. He was sent out in charge of a boat expedition on the coast of South America in search of a piratical craft which had been annoying the merchantmen, and one night seeing a rakish looking vessel in the offing, he had without assuring himself of her character, dashed alongside of her, carried her by boarding, and after killing and wounding several of her crew, discovered that he had raided upon a Brazilian man of war brig. Deacy paid the penalty of

> this rashness by retiring from Her Majesty's service and returning to England. His brother, a Bishop, helped him to purchase the yacht *America,* and sent him off to sea on his own account. Meantime Deacy had connected himself with a buxom English girl, and with six rosy children as the result of his love scrape, he embarked with his family and sailed over to the Cape de Verd Islands where he amused himself until he heard of the Civil War in America, when he sailed into the Savannah river with his family on board, anchored off the Exchange, and before long found himself in Montgomery, where he sold his vessel to the Confederate Govt. His "wife" and children were sent to Virginia, where four out of the six children died of typhoid fever. Such was the brief history of my Captain. He was the quintescence of carelessness, and yet he had influential connexions.

While Anderson's thumbnail biography of Henry Decie contains certain of the elements to be found in the *Harper's Weekly* account written by Theodore Davis, the similarity does not ensure that either was entirely true. Just as Anderson did not himself see Decie's alleged mistress and their alleged brood of children, it may be that Davis, in preparing his magazine story, simply took Decie's word for all he wrote. Recently, for the purpose of this book, an expert in British maritime history searched the personnel listings of the British Navy for several decades prior to 1860 without finding any record of service under the name Henry Decie, nor under any of its nine spelling variants. There was once in Ireland, however, a William Beresford, created Baron Decies, who by the Church of England was successively named Bishop of Dromore, Bishop of Ossory, and Archbishop of Tuam. But the Baron could not have been the Bishop brother who allegedly assisted Henry Decie in buying the yacht *America* on July 30, 1860, for His Grace had died more than forty years before, on September 6, 1819.

In his diary, Anderson had more to say about Decie:

> He is without exception one of the most courteous men I have ever met with, always good natured and pleasant. But as a sailor

man, he is deficient in attainment, with a carelessness in the watchfulness of his vessel that is alarming. The navigation is done by an English youth, and we have no lookouts at night, hence I have quietly taken the observations each day and have insisted upon lights in the rigging after dark, and a watch stationed forward to keep an eye against being run over by passing vessels. Our crew consists of two mates, twelve able seamen, two cooks and two cabin boys from the Cape de Verd Islands who speak only Portuguese—in all eighteen hands. Deacy, North, his wife, child and myself make up the complement of 23 souls on board. The chief mate's name is Sweetman, whilst the second officer is called Light, both excellent and trusty men. As a whole they are the quietest set of fellows I have ever seen on board ship, and at the same time the slowest. The orders are given in an undertone and are obeyed as leisurely as though there was a question of their necessity. This I suppose is the custom of the English yacht service and is in vivid contrast to the brisk, bear-a-hand order of things in our Yankee men of war and merchantmen.

On Sunday, June 9, when the yacht was something more than two weeks out of Savannah, North noted in his diary, "The day was rather a gloomy one," and on Monday, June 10, he wrote, "Squally appearances, wind baffling with rain." During the ensuing week, one day proved "very disagreeable," another was marked by an uncomfortable "gale," and on still another "the schooner shipped more seas today than any day yet."

On Monday, June 17, the *Camilla* spoke a British ship, the A. & A. She had cleared Charleston, S.C., on the morning of the day the *Camilla* cleared Savannah in the early evening, which meant the yacht had outsailed her by more than 150 miles. On Wednesday, the 19th, Anderson wrote, "The Captain makes us only 378 miles from Cork, Ireland, but he is wrong in his reckoning. We are more than that by some sixty miles."

As Ireland neared, Anderson, who had demonstrated no liking for North, described with a trace of sympathy the difficulties he felt his fellow officer faced:

> Mr. Mallory, the Secretary of the Navy, has sent him across to England to buy imaginary iron clads, ready built to his hands. He has neither Sterling Bills or letters of credit on our Financial Agents abroad, but is to wait like Micawber for funds to turn up. I reminded him that Iron Clads were too costly an article to be found lying loose for a market, and that he would have to build such ships if he expected to send any over to the Confederacy. He seemed however to think that he and Mallory knew more about the matter than I did, so I left him in his opinion. His wife is a very charming lady who bears with great patience the oddities of her husband.

The *Camilla* sighted Cape Clear, on the southern coast of Ireland, at nine on the morning of Saturday, June 22. She spent the day sailing eastward for Cork Harbor and at midnight dropped anchor at the mouth of the harbor, some 60 miles from Cork itself.

> The next morning, Sunday [Anderson wrote], we commenced working into the Harbor and about One P.M., at Queenstown, came to anchor close to the Custom House Dock. An officer hailed to enquire where we were from and was answered by Deacy that we came from Ryde in the Isle of Wight. Nobody boarded us. Got up our luggage and landed at the dock nearby. We went up to the Queen's Hotel close at hand and ordered dinner prior to taking passage in one of the small steamers for Cork.

Decie and the *Camilla* remained for the time being at Queenstown, while Anderson and the Norths, after reaching Cork, took a train for Dublin, then a steamer across St. George's Channel to Holyhead and another train from Holyhead to Liverpool, where they found James Dunwody Bulloch and Caleb Huse and the officers of Fraser, Trenholm & Co. and Isaac Low & Co. But Anderson and North, before parting with Decie, had made arrangements for a future meeting. Indeed, Decie, on an unfilled page in North's diary, had written his name and two addresses at which he might be reached, thus:

Henry Decie Esq
Fenton's Hotel
St. James St
London
or
Royal Victoria
Yacht Club
Ryde
Isle of Wight

Whether Anderson and North knew it or not, Decie had cause for remaining at Queenstown. The year before, the British Admiralty had approved the founding of a yacht club there, to be called reasonably enough the Queenstown Yacht Club, and member vessels were authorized to fly the Red Ensign, with a lion rampant on a green shield clutching a sprig of shamrock. Moreover, the Queenstown Yacht Club had a regatta scheduled for the very near future, with a race for cutters to be run on June 27 and another for schooners on the day following. The prize for the schooner race, in which Decie entered the *Camilla,* was a chronometer valued at 40 guineas, plus a purse of 30 sovereigns.

The *Camilla*'s competitors were *La Traviata, Echo,* and *Urania.* The only contemporary account of the race to survive is so short that its brevity interferes with its clarity. It fails to state exactly where off Queenstown the race started and ended and to give the length of the race course. But it does say:

> The day was squally and showery, but still a grand sailing day—wind at WNW to NW, veering and hauling. Much interest was evinced from the fact that the American was entered to contend.
>
> The starting gun was fired at 1hr 30m. *La Traviata* took the lead in gallant style, closely followed by the American. The *Urania* and *Echo* got, unfortunely, foul; but with admirable smartness they were speedily got clear, and hard upon the tracks of their flying antagonists. Shortly after rounding the Spit

Lighthouse the American rapidly overhauled and passed *La Traviata*, and the *Urania* passed the *Echo*.

In very much the same order the remainder of the course was performed, the American endeavoring in vain to shake off her determined little foe, *La Traviata;* the latter was uncommonly well handled, and beating up to the flag she astonished some who had pinned their faith on the windward qualities of the famous Yankee crack. One thing, however, must be said in her behalf. She had only just arrived from Savannah, and a long cruise to the West Indies, and consequently was not in the same order as *La Traviata.* The American was very sluggish in stays in the narrows, and here *La Traviata* made the most play with her. Their times at the flagship were:—

	h.	m.	s.
Camilla	4	13	0
La Traviata	4	14	3
Urania	4	28	40
Echo	4	31	5

By the terms of the handicap, the *Camilla* had to allow *La Traviata* 10 minutes, the latter vessel thus winning by 8M. 57S.

Even as the *Camilla* ran this race in Ireland, there was talk of her on the other side of the Atlantic. The talk buzzed around Washington, where Gideon Welles served as Secretary of the Navy in Lincoln's Cabinet. Like Seward, Welles employed spies in the Confederacy, and one of them, on June 22, had sent in a report containing intelligence about the yacht accurate in some respects, but erroneous in others. When Secretary Welles received the report, he forwarded a copy to Flag Officer Silas H. Stringham, who temporarily commanded the Union's Atlantic Blockading Squadron, and endorsed the copy: "It is very desirable that the vessel referred to should be captured." As for the text of the report, this was what the spy had written:

From a source entitled to credit I learn that the commander, Decey, of the yacht *Camilla* (formerly *America*), went to Montgomery, and afterwards, about June 1, sailed from Savannah

> with two ordnance officers (Lieutenant North and Colonel E. C. Anderson) to Europe, to, it is supposed, procure rifled cannon and bring back the commissioners of the Confederate States. It is probable the yacht has gone to Liverpool, as the agent in Savannah is Andrew Low, a branch of the house of Isaac Low & Co., of Liverpool. The yacht is very fast, and will probably attempt to run the blockade, passing into some shallow inlet on the Southern coast with the British flag flying.

The commissioners referred to were William L. Yancey, Pierre A. Rost, and A. Dudley Mann. None of the three planned returning to the Confederacy in the near future, nor did they ever consider doing so aboard the yacht. Their primary job was to seek among European powers recognition of the Confederacy as an independent nation, and while the trio—as well as other Confederate diplomats who followed—failed in this task, they were of eventual assistance in raising money for the Southern cause by floating loans in Europe backed by "cotton collateral."

By the early summer of 1861, however, none of these loans had come through. The problems of operating without either sufficient amounts of cash or established lines of credit faced Anderson and North as soon as they reached Liverpool and were particularly acute with North. James Dunwody Bulloch, courteous though he was in social matters, plainly resented the fact that the Confederate Navy had sent abroad an officer to assist him on his mission and bluntly refused either to delegate to North any duties connected with furthering the building and buying projects he had initiated or to share with him the slender naval funds available through Fraser, Trenholm & Co. and Isaac Low & Co. so that North might function on his own.

Coupled with Bulloch's resentment of North was his low estimate of the man's energy, judgment, and ability to operate so secretly that Union agents in Britain and on the Continent would not know what he was about. Bulloch felt that North was too trusting, too indiscreet, and not enough of a sophisticate to engage in activities of a conspiratorial sort. Events in

1864 proved Bulloch right. By then, at a cost to the Confederacy of nearly a million dollars, North had occupied himself for more than two years supervising the building in Scotland of a huge ironclad frigate destined never to serve the South. For shortly before the frigate was to be launched, word of her true nationality leaked out, and to prevent her seizure by Britain as a violation of Queen Victoria's proclamation of neutrality in the American Civil War, North was forced to sell the vessel to Denmark at a distressing loss.

Major Anderson, on the other hand, found the climate of cloak-and-dagger operations in Britain precisely to his liking. First off, he put Captain Caleb Huse through a quiz session and determined that the officer was a loyal, dedicated, and competent Confederate. Moreover, Anderson conducted his interrogation of Huse with such finesse that the Captain never realized suspicion had existed concerning his integrity. Thereafter, for the few months that Anderson felt it necessary for him to remain abroad, he and Huse—now and again in cooperation with Bulloch—worked together in perfect harmony.

Anderson particularly enjoyed frustrating and confusing detectives employed by the U.S. consuls at Liverpool and London to follow him as he went the rounds bargaining with arms dealers. Just as the detectives adopted disguises, so did he. On learning of the interception of telegrams he sent and received, Anderson made no complaint. Instead, he sent to himself and to nonexistent persons messages calculated utterly to confound the detectives by hurrying them off to cities all over England on wild-goose chases.

As that first summer of the Civil War progressed, the Confederate War Department proved itself more efficient than the Navy in transmitting funds to its agents abroad. Rarely now were Anderson and Huse out of pocket. But once when Anderson found himself broke, he appealed to Edmund Molyneaux, the British consul at Savannah who happened to be home on leave in Liverpool, and Molyneaux immediately took him to his own banker and in a matter of minutes obtained for him a loan of £10,000.

Perhaps this encounter with Molyneaux caused Anderson to dwell on the esteem with which consular offices were generally regarded. For not long afterward, when Anderson noticed in the warehouse of a London arms dealer a choice lot of Enfield rifles already sold to a Union buyer, he managed to wangle them away, and the only bribe he employed was a promise. As soon as the South won the war, Anderson assured him, the dealer would receive from Jefferson Davis the appointment of Confederate States consul at London.

The Civil War in America proved a bonanza for dealers in military equipment not alone in Britain, but all over Europe. Arms hitherto discarded as defective reappeared on the market. Lest he buy guns more likely to kill friend than enemy, Anderson insisted on a rigid inspection of all his purchases, but to obtain a competent inspector required ingenuity. Anderson hired one right out of a British War Office arsenal by first wangling for his recruit an extensive "sick leave."

During a quick trip to Paris in late July, Anderson found guns aplenty, but no one trustworthy to test them, and he consequently bought nothing. The visit, however, added to his store of knowledge as a man of the world. While in Paris he wrote in his diary, "The French are an odd people. Walking along one of the most fashionable boulevards I saw a Frenchman deliberately leave a lady, and going to one side of the walk do something that nobody else could do for him, whilst the lady waited with the most matter of fact demeanor until her companion rejoined her."

At about this same time, Lieutenant North and his wife and daughter left Liverpool and took lodgings at 108 Jermyn Street in London. For his personal expenses North had less than £800, money he must have spent sparingly, since it lasted him nearly two years. In London, he and his family visited the Crystal Palace one day, saw the changing of the guard the next, and during the day following strolled through the Botanical Gardens.

Henry Decie called on the Norths in London, and he and the Lieutenant inspected the *Warrior,* a new British warship. While on this junket, Decie informed North that the yacht *Camilla* was at the Isle of Wight and apparently invited all the Norths down. On July 29, North lamented in his diary, "I have been so worried at the news from America, especially when I think how little I am doing for my poor country. The only consolation I have is that the fault is not mine & I am ready and willing to do anything in the world for her."

Hard on this patriotic announcement, North betook himself and his wife and daughter to the Isle of Wight, and by Saturday, August 3, they were installed, bag and baggage, in the main cabin of the *Camilla.* "Mr. Decie," North wrote, "insisted upon our coming on board to live." And in a diary entry for the next day, Sunday, he added: "I was so very sick this morning that Mr. Decie went on shore and brought the Doctor off. He remained with me for hours & then called again in the evening."

But by Monday, August 5, North had experienced a remarkably quick recovery. "Very pleasant day with a light breeze," he noted. "Find that this Yacht (*America*) and the Yacht *Alarm* are to run a match race for £100 a side. At 11 A.M. the gun fired, made a beautiful start. . . ."

It appears that this race had been pending since soon after Decie's return to Britain. Indeed, the rich, 84-year-old Joseph Weld, owner of the *Alarm* (and the owner, too, of ancient Lullworth Castle at Wareham, Dorsetshire), had been for years awaiting an opportunity to match his yacht once more against the American vessel. For in the Royal Yacht Squadron regatta of 1851, the *Alarm* had been one of the contenders for the 100-Guinea Cup won by the *America,* and Weld, who prided himself on his ability as a racing yachtsman, still smarted from that defeat.

As a copyist, however, Weld felt no shame. While a decade

ago his *Alarm* had been a cutter, he had since had her redesigned and rebuilt in close imitation of the *America.* With her bow lengthened 20 feet and the whole of her sharpened and hollowed away, she was now, with a second mast stepped and with that mast and her original mast set at smartly raking angles, a swift and handsome schooner of 248 tons.

To captain the expert crew of the *Alarm,* Weld regularly employed John Nicholls, the most seasoned and knowledgeable man of his profession in all England. Decie was lucky to get Underwood, who had guided the *America* to success ten years before. But there Decie's Irish luck—if, in fact, he *was* Irish—ceased. With the race originally scheduled for July 30, the *Camilla*'s "regular" crew struck work two days before for a reason or reasons not clearly defined. Presumably this crew was the one headed by Sailing Master Sweetman and Mate Light, who had so successfully taken the *Camilla* across the Atlantic to Savannah and back. The race was then postponed until August 5, although not solely because of Decie's crewless condition; the first date was found to conflict with another important British sporting event. Thus Decie received a grace period of six days to hire and break in a pickup crew, and meanwhile the North family paid him a visit. However, in its extensive reports of the race, the British press not once attributed its outcome to the *Camilla*'s having a Jonah aboard. Rather, fault was laid to the former *America*'s having a new suit of unsuitable "bellying" sails and to Decie's own actions. Throughout the race he insisted on giving orders, often contradicting those already issued by Underwood, with the result that the crew handled the yacht in a fashion calculated to ensure her defeat.

The race was run over the "inside" course off the Isle of Wight, in the channels known as Spithead and The Solent, which separate the Isle from the shores of Sussex and Hampshire. The race started in Cowes Roads, opposite the Royal Yacht Squadron clubhouse; then proceeded southeastward past Ryde, Ryde Pier, and the clubhouse of the Royal Victoria Yacht Club; then around the Warner Light Vessel; then to the northward around the Calshot Light Vessel; then westward back to the point of starting, twice around. The course once around measured about 25 miles, and thus the whole of the race covered some 50 miles.

A correspondent for *Hunt's Yachting Magazine* counted 84 spectator vessels, which meant that the race, with but two yachts competing, had drawn a surprisingly large crowd. Among the spectator vessels was the royal yacht *Fairy,* gaily bedecked, with the Prince Consort aboard. Another, the steamer *Medina,* had been chartered for the day by G. R. Stephenson, who invited his family and friends to follow the race with him and witness how well or how poorly the *Camilla,* formerly the *America,* had matured since beating his *Titania* a decade ago.

The *Camilla* behaved brilliantly at the start, but soon got in trouble. Her crew, in attempting to haul down her topsail, allowed it to get adrift. The sail then became fouled up in the yacht's rigging. For a quarter-hour it acted as a back sail, and thus a deterrent to progress, before it was cut loose and let go. This bit of mismanagement seemed to so demoralize those aboard the *Camilla* that other errors both of judgment and of action followed. At the end of the first round, the *Camilla* trailed the *Alarm* by 18 minutes and 20 seconds, and in the late afternoon the *Alarm* won the race by 37 minutes and 5 seconds.

The Times of London reported the match with nearly a full column, and in the doing took a crack at Decie. Had it been known that he was to command the *Camilla,* the paper said, "odds to any amount could have been obtained that he would lose the race." As matters stood, the betting seems to have been heavy—indeed, extremely heavy. *The Illustrated London News* claimed that on the outcome of the match "upwards of £80,000 were pending in wagers between the members of the Royal Victoria Yacht Club and the Royal Yacht Squadron"—and in those days such a sum was the equivalent of nearly 400,000 U.S. dollars. While *The Illustrated London News* did not say which club backed the *Camilla,* the assumption is that the Royal Victoria cast itself in that unhappy role. Decie's yacht had flown the Royal Victoria's pennant. Moreover, on the Friday night following the Monday race the Royal Yacht Squadron, possibly to celebrate the *Alarm*'s victory, gave a "magnificent ball . . . at which upwards of 200 ladies and gentlemen . . . were present." Whether on account of this race or because of some other matter, the Royal Victoria has remained remarkably uncommunicative concerning whatever it may have in its files about the man either actually named or who used the name Henry Edward Decie. During a recent search for biographical data on the *Camilla*'s owner of more than a century ago, inquiry made of the Secretary of the Royal Victoria failed to elicit a reply.

The day of the race, on Monday, August 5, *The Times* carried an account of a more important contest. This story concerned the overwhelming victory of the Confederates in their first large-scale encounter with Union troops, at Manassas, Virginia, on July 21—the Battle of Bull Run. North did not see the *Times* account until Tuesday, August 6, and on that day wrote in his diary that he was "thankful to Almighty God." Anderson, however, had got the news much earlier—on the morning of Sunday, August 4. The fast packet bringing the word from America had touched first at Queenstown, and from there it was telegraphed to major British cities. When apprised of the victory, Anderson was in the company of Huse at Liverpool, and according to Anderson's diary this was what they did:

> We jumped into a cab and drove out rapidly to Prioleau's country seat to give him the intelligence and to run up the Confederate flag on his housetop. He was absent at church in attendance on a christening, but we found his sister at home & soon mounted to the roof & threw out our banner. Meantime the churches had finished their services & the congregations were pouring out into the street. I had given our cab driver a half crown to cheer lustily as soon as our flag was run up, and as it floated out to the breeze, he mounted on the roof of his vehicle and made the welkin ring with his cheers. People for a moment thought him mad or drunk, but were soon undeceived & enter-

> ing heartily into the enthusiasm gave us lusty cheers. When Mr. Prioleau returned he opened some old wine and we drank success to our cause.

The hospitable dispenser of the wine was Charles K. Prioleau, a man as wealthy as he was shrewd. He acted as the principal resident partner in the allied transatlantic banking and shipping firms of John Fraser & Co., of Charleston, and Fraser, Trenholm & Co., of Liverpool, and this made him the Confederacy's chief fiscal agent abroad. Only Prioleau had the final say when, in the interest of the South, large amounts of cash were to be spent or heavy debts incurred in Britain or on the Continent, and the barometer of his feelings in such matters rose and fell with the success or failure of Southern arms.

The Confederate victory at Bull Run moved Prioleau to an act of interesting generosity. For a charter fee to be reckoned in the future, he placed at the disposal of Anderson and Huse the new iron-hulled screw steamer *Bermuda,* owned by Fraser, Trenholm & Co. This vessel was just off the ways at Stockton-on-Tees; would have as her captain a daring Frenchman, E. L. Tessier; and displacing as she did 1,200 tons, would be large enough to transport to the Confederacy all of the matériel of war that Anderson and Huse had so far purchased.

Both Southern officers welcomed Prioleau's offer, and it was agreed that the *Bermuda* would take on her cargo at Hartlepool, on the northeast coast of England, near the yard of her builder. Anderson awarded Huse the task of seeing to the loading, while he busied himself with certain matters not strictly his business. On Tuesday, August 6, he had heard that North was with Decie at the Isle of Wight, and he wired Decie he would join them on Thursday, the 8th.

Decie met Anderson at Portsmouth on Thursday afternoon and crossed with him to the Isle of Wight by means of a ferrying steamer.

> I was provoked at Decie not being ready to return to the Confederacy [Anderson wrote in his diary], and took him seri-

ously to task for his delay. He replied that he was booked for three races; that North had given him no notice; that he was to have two weeks to get ready after being notified & that under no circumstances could he sail before the 17th. The *America* lay at anchor off Ryde. She sent a boat for us as we landed and I repaired on board of her. Found North and his family in full possession of the cabin, looking absolutely dirty and seedy. It was an outrage to impose himself on the hospitality of Decie, but he seemed to have no shame about the matter. At that time Huse and I were fitting out a fine steamer [the *Bermuda*] to run the blockade and as North was a naval officer and was loafing in England without means and really without an object, I proposed to him on board the yacht to return home in our steamer, telling him that in the event of certain contingencies he might perhaps save the property from capture, as we had determined with the Captain to make fight with any boats that might attempt to stop the vessel, in which case the presence of North on board would at once give a character of nationality to our vessel which would be all important under the circumstances. He became quite indignant at my proposition, saying with much warmth of manner, "I have made up my mind *not to go*," giving as a reason that he did not know what to do with his wife and child.

While on board the *Camilla,* Anderson noticed she was in no condition to race, in spite of what Decie had said. That very morning, he learned, she had collided with another yacht, the *Sissy,* and as a result needed extensive repairs to her stem and head gear. That Decie could talk out of both sides of his mouth became even more apparent somewhat later. Although he agreed to carry back to the Confederacy for Anderson various dispatches and a number of cases of medical supplies, he refused to take aboard a cargo of cartridges lest it might excite "the curiosity of the crew or any casual visitor." The anomalies of the situation received further intensification in an undated letter Lieutenant North wrote Confederate Secretary of the Navy Mallory soon after Anderson's visit, in which he said in part, "I have determined to send the yacht back with dispatches only, as I can see no use in my keeping her over here any longer at only an expense to our Government. I have informed Major Anderson and Mr. Bulloch of my intention, but thus far they both decline sending anything over in her. I have no money, or I certainly would send over a few rifled cannon. . . . I expect to leave for Paris today. Oh, if I only had the money."

Seemingly Anderson had no idea that North planned visiting Paris, and certainly he was not aware that Decie would transport aboard the yacht the three members of the North family as far as Cherbourg—and yet this was what happened. The *Camilla* participated in no race in Britain ever again. She cleared Ryde on August 14 and anchored at Cherbourg on the morning of the 16th. For most of the remainder of the year 1861 the Norths lived in Paris, where they placed their daughter in school. From early 1862 until mid-1864 North busied himself in Scotland with the construction of the large, costly, and ill-fated frigate which, through force of circumstances, he eventually sold at great loss to Denmark. Not until considerably after the close of the Civil War did the Norths return to their home in South Carolina.

Anderson last saw Decie in England at the conclusion of his Isle of Wight visit. On the evening of Thursday, August 8, 1861, they dined together in Ryde at the Royal Victoria Yacht Club, and the next day Anderson informed his diary, "Decie took me in charge last night and kept me in company with his friends until long after midnight. They were a jolly set, many of them being young noblemen, and all of them belonging to the upper ten." Following this gay evening, Anderson journeyed to London, and on August 12 he returned to Liverpool.

That date—August 12—has a special significance in the story of the *America*. It marked the arrival in England aboard a steam packet of a member of the syndicate of New Yorkers responsible for building the yacht more than a decade before. The member in question was that astute man of business, George L. Schuyler, who had driven such a hard bargain with

George Steers and William H. Brown. Now Schuyler held the commission of a colonel in the U.S. Army and he had been sent abroad on a mission for the Union identical with that of Anderson for the Confederacy. Provided with a bankroll of two million U.S. dollars, Schuyler was to buy 100,000 or more small arms and ship them to New York as rapidly as possible. Schuyler bought and shipped, as ordered, but apparently something went wrong. Perhaps the quality of his purchases was not up to snuff, or perhaps the sudden shift of War Secretaries in Lincoln's Cabinet accounted for what happened. Sent to England by Secretary Simon Cameron, Schuyler was recalled after a few months by Secretary Edwin M. Stanton, and other Union purchasing agents were named to replace him.

Meanwhile, Anderson and Huse—with the help of Bulloch—got the *Bermuda* loaded with 500 barrels of gunpowder, 12 Blakely rifled field guns, numerous cases of solid shot and segmented shells, further cases of rifled muskets, and vast quantities of artillery harness, cavalry saddles, blankets, shoes, and bolts of gray woolen cloth for uniforms. The *Bermuda,* flying the British flag, cleared Hartlepool on August 19 and put into Falmouth for coal three days later. Her destination, as given to the authorities, was Havana, Cuba. She crossed the Atlantic without incident and safely ran the blockade into Savannah on September 15.

Anderson, on taking leave of Decie at the Isle of Wight on August 8, had exacted a promise. Before shaping his course for a return to the Confederacy, the yachtsman would touch at Falmouth to pick up dispatches, should any await him. But Decie failed to do this, and Anderston heard nothing from him until August 27, on which day he made this cryptic diary entry: "Received two letters from Decie dated 21st & 22nd of August, at Guernsey, telling me that he would be on his way back to Dixie by the time his letters reached me."

Guernsey, one of the Channel Islands, lies close to Cherbourg, but far from Falmouth. Still unaware that the *Camilla* had transported the Norths to France, Anderson must have been mystified by the course Decie followed. And yet in his diary, Anderson admitted to no mystification, for such was his nature. Only rarely would he confess he did not know everything.

By the late summer of 1861, James Dunwody Bulloch had building in Britain two large war vessels which, as the famed and heavily armed Confederate cruisers *Alabama* and *Florida,* would eventually wreak havoc with Union shipping. The construction was going well and only rarely required Bulloch's presence at the scene. Similarly, Anderson had time on his hands, for now that he had found Caleb Huse entirely trustworthy—and in addition competent and energetic—there was not enough work to occupy them both.

Consequently, Bulloch and Anderson got together, pooled their talents and resources, and schemed another scheme to follow up the *Bermuda* caper. They bought at Greenock, Scotland, the fairly new iron-hulled *Fingal* (named after the Ossianic hero, no doubt), a steamer of about 500 tons with engines developing 120 h.p. They loaded her by forwarding her cargo from London aboard a chartered freighter and then transshipping. The cargo consisted of 15,000 Enfield rifles with cutlass bayonets; 2,000,000 made-up cartridges and an equal number of percussion caps; 3,000 cavalry sabers with scabbards; 500 revolvers in holsters; 4 rifled cannon with traversing carriages and 800 shells; 400 barrels of gunpowder; and a vast number of cases containing uniforms, shoes, mess equipment, tents, stretchers, and medical supplies. Should the *Fingal* reach the Confederacy safely, she would bring in the most valuable shipment of a purely military nature to arrive there so far.

To abet safe arrival, Bulloch commanded the *Fingal* himself, and Anderson acted as his first officer. Aboard, however, were nominal British officers, plus an actual British crew. But the secret buying and loading of the steamer were not as quietly carried on as Bulloch and Anderson thought. Edward Brennan, an intelligence agent employed by the U.S. consul at London, got wind of the affair, drew a reasonably accurate picture of the *Fingal,* and from Scotland sent the drawing—together with his findings—to his consular employer.

F. H. Morse, the consul, received the material at breakfast-time on October 15 at his quarters in London and acted immediately to halt the *Fingal's* departure. But she had already cleared Britain, at 4 A.M., and was well out to sea. The drawing of the vessel was then forwarded to Washington, where on November 7 it reached the desk of Secretary of the Navy Gideon Welles, who in turn sent it to Flag Officer Samuel F. Du Pont, the recently appointed commander of the 75 U.S. warships now comprising the South Atlantic Blockading Squadron.

Communications at sea being what they were in 1861, Du Pont did not learn of the *Fingal* until a couple of weeks after November 7, which was just as well. November 7 was his busy day. It was on that day that his huge fleet stormed and took Port Royal, South Carolina, the natural harbor hitherto considered impregnable by the Confederates, lying as it did with Fort Walker guarding one jamb of the entrance portal and Fort Beauregard the other.

Following November 7, Port Royal became the base of operations for Du Pont's huge squadron, and it lay only 30 miles or so up the coast from Savannah, Georgia. On November 7, the *Fingal,* after coaling at Bermuda, shaped a course for Savannah, with all on board unaware that Port Royal had fallen. For the next six days this state of blessed ignorance persisted; then, on the morning of Wednesday, November 13, the *Fingal* entered Tybee Roads and by early afternoon had run up the Savannah River flying the British flag topped by the Stars and Bars of the Confederacy.

> We dropped anchor abreast of the City near the foot of Whittaker Street [Anderson told his diary]. The whole population of the Town was out to meet me, and as I got into the Slip with the small boat of the *Fingal* I was seized by brawny arms and lifted up on the Dock. Repaired at once to the Telegraph office and communicated with the Secretary of War. I found the people of Savannah frightened to death by the capture of Port

> Royal. Indeed, there was good reason for them to be so, for there was really nothing to prevent the Yankees from following up their success and coming straight to the City. The arrival of the *Fingal* restored confidence to everybody. People seemed to think that because she was an *iron vessel* she was an *iron clad,* and that she could bid defiance to the entire wooden Navy of the United States. Fortunately for us the enemy shared in the delusion of our people and kept their vessels well aloof from the Savannah River.

During Anderson's absence the seat of the Confederate Government had been moved from Montgomery, Alabama, to Richmond, Virginia, and George W. Randolph had succeeded L. P. Walker as Secretary of War. In company with Bulloch, Anderson journeyed by train to Richmond and called on Randolph and Secretary of the Navy Mallory. The travelers reached Richmond on November 18 and remained for several days. Randolph pleased Anderson by awarding him a new assignment much to his liking, for it meant he could live at home. He was to assist General Robert E. Lee, who at this early stage of the war had the duty of supervising the installation of heavy ordnance along the Georgia coast.

Secretary Mallory impressed Anderson as an incompetent who knew little of naval affairs. Although Bulloch, wisely, wished to return immediately to England with the *Fingal* and a cargo of cotton while there was still an excellent chance of running the Savannah blockade, Mallory restrained him. This delayed Bulloch's departure for several months, and when finally he did get back to his important duties at Liverpool, he went as a passenger aboard another vessel out of Wilmington. In addition, the delay proved fatal to the *Fingal.* In 1863, after conversion into a warship, the *Fingal,* by now called *Atlanta,* ventured forth from Savannah to do battle with Union blockaders and suffered capture.

During Anderson's visit to Richmond in November 1861, he made no entry in his diary concerning the yacht *Camilla* or Henry Decie. And yet Decie either was in Richmond at this very same time or had been there shortly before, for his activities were so described in a letter written by Mallory on November 20. Decie had come up to Richmond overland from Jacksonville, Florida, for a brief consultation. The details of Decie's movements at Jacksonville are scant in the extreme, and most of what is known has been gleaned from the muted voice of Confederate Customs records.

Jacksonville, the seat of Duval County, lies about fourteen miles from the Atlantic by survey, but is twice that via the broad and winding St. John's River, which dumps into the sea at Mayport. In 1861, Jacksonville had a population of only a few thousand, yet was important to the Confederacy because of its railroad leading west, its chain of inland waterways stretching both northward to Georgia and southward into central Florida, and its bountiful supply of live oak timber prized for shipbuilding.

Records of Confederate Customs indicate that the *Camilla* first ascended the St. John's to the port of Jacksonville on October 25, 1861. Customs Inspector Thomas Flotard boarded her and was told that she had last cleared Cowes, England. Seemingly, Decie misinformed Flotard, just as he had misinformed the customs authorities at Queenstown on anchoring there in June. No clue has been found to where Decie was or how he had occupied himself during much of the period between writing Anderson from Guernsey on August 22 and his arrival at Jacksonville over two months later. At the outside, barring accident, the voyage should have taken the yacht no more than half this time. The probability is that Decie, for a few delicious weeks, besported himself en route on some tropical isle.

The *Camilla* lay at Jacksonville while Decie visited Richmond. A publication of the Florida Historical Society of many years ago declared that the vessel then became a blockade-runner and made "flying trips to Nassau and Bermuda." Confederate Customs records indicate, however, that if such voyages were made they were limited to two. The yacht was out of the port once in December 1861, returned in early January of the year following, and was then quickly out and in later in January. Never did she pay duty on any cargo she may have carried. But even had she been loaded to the gunnels with dutiable merchandise, she would have been charged nothing, for Decie no doubt had papers proving she belonged to the Confederate Government.

By late January the ever-lengthening cordon of warships forming the Union's South Atlantic Blockading Squadron had extended as far down the coast as the mouth of the St. John's River. Rare was the fast blockade-running steamer that got in or out of Jacksonville, and even rarer the sailing vessel. A man who lived near the river's mouth witnessed the *Camilla*'s last run in and later told the Florida Historical Society the story in these words:

> One moonlight night at Mayport, when the Federal gunboats were just far enough outside for their black hulls to be faintly visible, there came up out of the east on a wholesale sailing breeze a yacht with every stitch of canvas set and drawing. The foam was cut from her bows like a knife would do it and was thrown high over her deck and on her sails. There came a flash and a boom from a gunboat and a shot crossed her bow, followed by more flashes and shots; but on the gallant craft came, spar and rigging untouched, heeling over now and then and righting herself gracefully. She passed inside the bar safely and when she went by the point seemed to be flying. She went up to Jacksonville.

This was the last advantageous use of the *Camilla* as a Confederate vessel. Within a few days, Decie and his British crew left her anchored at Jacksonville and with their personal luggage in hand headed north overland. By February 20 the crew were at Norfolk, Virginia, where they were joined by the British members of the ship's company of the *Fingal,* by now as bottled up at Savannah as was the *Camilla* at Jacksonville. But if Decie himself went to Norfolk, he did not do so directly, for on February 4 Major Edward C. Anderson had other news of him.

Anderson spent that day inspecting the coastal batteries on Jekyl Island, off Brunswick, Georgia, presided over by none other than Charles A. L. Lamar. Lamar appears to have been more efficient as a slave-runner than as an artillery commander. On putting the men of the Jekyl Island batteries through target practice, Anderson found them slow in loading and their aim "abominable."

The next day, while at home in Savannah, Anderson made this entry in his diary:

> On returning last night I learned that Capt Decie, my old shipmate of the Yacht *America*, was in town. Hunted him up at the Pulaski and invited him to take up his quarters at my house. Took him out with me to the Isle of Hope and then to Skidaway. After looking at the Battery, returned to the Isle of Hope and dined there.

Decie remained with Anderson (who was soon jumped in rank from major to colonel in the Confederate Army) through February 7 and then took off for regions temporarily undisclosed. There is no further mention of him in Anderson's diaries for the remainder of the war, nor in Anderson's voluminous correspondence carried on during the eighteen years of vigorous living left to him following the war.

At Norfolk, the sixty-odd British mariners from the *Camilla* and the *Fingal* reported to Major General Benjamin Huger, the Confederate officer commanding. At this stage of hostilities, Norfolk was a flag-of-truce point where communication existed with the Union, as represented by Major John E. Wool, stationed near Norfolk at Fortress Monroe. The people from the *Camilla* and the *Fingal* applied for permission to proceed through Union lines north to New York and from there, as passengers aboard some British vessel, return to England.

In the manner of innumerable military men before, during, and since the Civil War, General Wool seems to have been proficient at passing the buck. Rather than accept the responsibility of deciding the issue himself, he appealed to higher authority in the person of Union Secretary of War Stanton. This worthy, historically renowned for only rarely doing even his intimates a favor, kept the British seamen waiting several days before rejecting their request. If the Britishers got back to England prior to the end of the war, they probably followed Bulloch's example and found berths aboard some blockade-runner out of Wilmington.

As for Henry Edward Decie, he popped up, at the smell of money, in Richmond during the summer of 1863. The money resulted from the heavy and rapid sale of stock in a corporation formed by a group of Richmond bankers and insurance executives called the Virginia Volunteer Navy Company. Through a measure enacted by the Confederate Congress on April 18, the company received authorization to operate privateers against Union shipping and split the proceeds of their depredations with the Government. Vessels belonging to the company would fly the battle flag of the Confederacy, and the officers and men aboard would escape the stigma of piracy by wearing uniforms of the Confederate Navy.

By Confederate law it was all very legal, but by international law questionable. The distinction, however, posed no issue, for the company was without a suitable vessel to put to sea. On hearing of the need, Decie offered to go to England as the company's representative and buy an armed cruiser. He could pick up a fine one, fully outfitted, he declared, for £5,000 cash and the rest in company stock. Only he could buy on such a basis, he contended, for he had numerous friends in nautical circles—friends from the days when he had been a post captain in the Royal Navy.

Until he made this last statement, Decie, who looked to be around 30, had favorably impressed all of the company's executives. But now one of them, aware of the slow rate of promotion in the British Navy and that the rank of post captain stood a mere notch below that of admiral, challenged Decie's claim. Flustered not at all, Decie admitted that while he had overstated his qualifications slightly, he had erred only technically.

For he had once served in the Royal Navy, he insisted, as an acting post captain.

From this point on, the more Decie talked, the less the company listened. Eventually an officer borrowed from the Confederate Navy undertook the company's mission to England, but the war ended before the vessel he found could perform as a privateer. The purchasers of the stock appear to have been the predatory company's only victims. Salesmen for the company were still peddling its worthless shares as late as March 21, 1865. Twelve days after this, on April 2, the heads of the Confederate Government evacuated Richmond and fled south, and on April 9 Lee surrendered to Grant at Appomattox.

Confederate records contain no mention of Henry Edward Decie following his abortive attempt to go to England in the interest of the would-be privateers during the summer of 1863. If, instead, he went back to Florida with the hope of once again reveling at the sight of the yacht *Camilla,* he experienced disappointment. Following adventures of a remarkable sort, the yacht was no longer there, nor did she continue to bear the name Decie had given her.

Apparently by 1864 Decie had somehow returned to England. In its edition for that year, *Hunt's Universal Yacht List* (published in London) carried the brief announcement that Decie had disposed of the *Camilla.* But the editors of the publication, if they knew, failed fairly to inform their readers where, when, or to whom the yacht had been transferred.

Just as Decie's name had never appeared in the yachting press prior to 1860, it did not appear again after 1864. Taking as gospel the assumption that Henry Edward Decie was not the mysterious mariner's real name, nautical historians have spent more than a century fretting over his true identity. Actually it matters little. All that really matters is that for a brief while in the long career of the yacht *America,* the "courteous" yet "careless" man known as Decie sailed her three times across the Atlantic, with interesting objectives.

SIX

"Historic Interest Attaches to This Vessel"

ON THE NIGHT of Tuesday, March 11, 1862, the yacht *America* (no longer called *Camilla*) disappeared from her moorings in the St. John's River off Jacksonville, Florida. Another vessel lying nearby disappeared at the same time. She was the 400-ton *St. Mary's*, an iron-hulled steam packet which before the Civil War had made regular trips between Jacksonville and Savannah.

Also on that Tuesday night, a Confederate warship, building and nearing completion on the stocks at Jacksonville, burned. With the unfinished vessel, seven sawmills burned, as did 4,000,000 feet of lumber, two iron foundries, and the railroad depot.

As the flames lit up the town, the few hundred Confederate infantrymen quartered there left hurriedly. They belonged to the Third Florida Regiment, and after withdrawing, most of them pitched their tents about 15 miles to the west of Jacksonville at a spot subsequently called Camp Milton.

All of this activity, destructive and otherwise, followed hard on a message telegraphed at sundown from a signal post at Mayport, near the mouth of the St. John's. The message said that at flood tide a flotilla of Union ships had steamed in off the Atlantic, crossed the bar, located the channel expertly, and swiftly proceeded up the river. Most of the ships bristled with cannon, and while each seemed to have a full complement of sailors, the decks of some were also crowded with blue-uniformed troops.

The message proved remarkably accurate. The invaders' lead vessels were the 500-ton gunboats *Ottawa, Pembina,* and *Seneca,* all launched less than six months before and each carrying some combination of heavy-caliber Dahlgren smoothbores, 20-pounder Parrott rifles, or 24-pounder howitzers. Following were the *Isaac Smith,* a screw steamer of 450 tons equally well armed; the *Ellen,* a side-wheeler of light draft built originally as a ferry; and the *Darlington,* another side-wheeler of light draft. Most of the soldiers were aboard the side-wheelers. They consisted of six companies of the Fourth New Hampshire Regiment of Volunteers.

These oncoming vessels represented part of a wing of Flag Officer Samuel F. Du Pont's South Atlantic Blockading Squadron. Their mission, as spelled out in Du Pont's orders, was to explore the St. John's at least as far as Jacksonville and reduce its defensive and offensive potentials. If fortifications guarded the banks of the river, they were to be destroyed. If Jacksonville proved to be a haven for blockade-runners, its citizenry should be taught the wisdom of extending hospitality to more acceptable guests. Should Jacksonville serve as a center for forwarding north troops or supplies for the Confederate Army, it should be warned that such conduct, if continued, would result in its erasure from the map.

Heading the expedition, aboard the lead gunboat *Ottawa,* was Lieutenant Commanding Thomas Holdup Stevens. At 42, after twenty-five years in the Navy, Stevens looked upon the mission as routine, for at this juncture he saw nothing in it likely to win plaudits from Washington. Yet in making such an estimate Stevens proved himself as incompetent a prophet as he was competent as a naval officer. Hereafter he would advance in rank and end up a rear admiral.

Accompanying, if not actually sparking, Steven's promotion

was the interest he would soon exhibit in the *America.* As he entered the St. John's River, however, it is doubtful that he even knew the yacht was in Florida or had ever been there. More pressing matters concerned him. With the coming of night, he ordered the six vessels of his flotilla to drop anchor, for the ascent of the winding stream was too risky to attempt in the dark.

At dawn the steamers were off again. Almost immediately a lookout sighted gun emplacements atop St. John's Bluff on the south bank of the river. When a few invitational shells fired at the emplacement elicited no response, a landing party climbed up and found deserted eight cannon and numerous cases of ammunition. The cannon carried markings indicating their nativity; they had been cast and bored in England during the year preceding, 1861.

Stevens held up the procession long enough for these treasures to be hauled down from the bluff and aboard one of his vessels, and then got under way once more. Jacksonville, reached at noon, was barely visible through a haze of smoke. But when a momentary breeze whisked the smoke away from the shoreline, those aboard the Union ships made out the figure of a lone man who, they discovered, was Frederick Lueders, the local sheriff. Years later, in an article contributed to the Jacksonville *Industrial Record,* Sheriff Lueders told the story of what happened:

> As I was standing on the river bank at the foot of Laura Street, I saw gunboats come steaming up the river and drop anchor. I was getting pretty well scared, when the thought flashed through my head, "If they bombard Jacksonville, it will be nothing short of murder." I happened to have a stick in my hand, so I took out my handkerchief, tied it to the stick, and waved it vigorously over my head. The commander of the fleet saw the peace signal and with his aides came ashore. I told him the existing circumstances and begged him not to open fire. He said he would not, and for me to go on board. After I explained that I was the only law officer in the town, he requested me to

sign the surrender papers, which I did. Upon my return I found to my surprise that troops had been landed and pickets were out.

The mayor of Jacksonville and a local judge soon joined Sheriff Lueders at the waterfront. The three confirmed an assumption Stevens had already made—that Southern troops, on evacuating the town, had set fire to Confederate property to prevent its use by the Union. Stevens deplored the destruction, warning that any further act of sabotage would result in the seizure of hostages.

Perhaps for fear Stevens would find out anyway and hold them accountable, the Jacksonville officials told him of the disappearance the night before of the *St. Mary's* and the *America* from their anchorage off the town. While none of the three admitted witnessing the hurried departure of the vessels, all voiced the reasonable belief that the steamer had towed the yacht and that the course taken had been upstream rather than down, lest the flight run counter to the approaching gunboats.

Stevens remained in Florida about a month. The *America* appears to have been so much on his mind that he spent, at the outset of his stay, a large portion of his time hunting her, and then, after finding her, additional time extricating her from a sorry predicament. Instead of censuring Stevens for his preoccupation with the yacht, Flag Officer Du Pont, from the Union base established at Port Royal, South Carolina, urged him on and authorized him to turn over the job of subjugating Jacksonville and the surrounding area to the Union Army. For this purpose, Brigadier General Horatio G. Wright and several companies of Pennsylvania troops soon joined the New Hampshire soldiers already occupying the town.

The subsequent exchange of letters between Du Pont and Stevens concerning the *America,* although at first prosaic, eventually took on a remarkable tone. At times the writers showed themselves almost boyish in their enthusiasm for the quest engaging Stevens, and while in all probability neither officer had ever seen the yacht in her racing days, both were familiar with her triumph over the Royal Yacht Squadron nearly eleven years before and admired her for it. In the middle of a great Civil War, the story of one of its offshoots—that of a small, but intense struggle—emerged.

The St. John's is a contrary stream in that, unlike most major American rivers, the general direction of its flow is north. Rising in southern Florida, it obstinately persists in its northerly course for around 250 miles until at Jacksonville it turns east to reach the Atlantic. For the first two-thirds or so of its length, the river is only occasionally deep and narrow, since it often merges its identity with the frequent broad and shallow lakes through which it passes. From a point, however, considerably above the town of Palatka (about 100 miles from the sea) it is readily navigable. At this juncture it is fed by a creek flowing out of a lake. While today that body of water is called Crescent Lake, during the Civil War it was known as Dunn's Lake. The creek, however, still bears its old name—Dunn's Creek—and it was in this creek that Lieutenant Commanding Stevens eventually found the *America.*

On March 17, 1862, while aboard the gunboat *Ottawa* at Jacksonville, Stevens wrote Du Pont, giving the first intimation that he had obtained a clue to the yacht's whereabouts.

> Since my last communication I have made a reconnaissance as far as Palatka [Stevens said]. I go up this evening in the *Ellen* with the two armed boats from the *Wabash,* in company with the *Darlington,* to capture, if possible, the yacht *America* and steamer *St. Mary's.* When the objects in view have been accomplished, I shall make a full report.

The *Wabash,* a 3,200-ton frigate, was Du Pont's flagship. On undertaking the Florida mission, Stevens had borrowed two of her boats—both equipped with swivel guns—anticipating he might need them for exploring shallow streams.

On March 28, Stevens again wrote Du Pont from Jacksonville, and the pertinent portions of his letter read:

I returned this morning with the launch and first cutter of the *Wabash* and the steamers *Darlington* and *Ellen* from Dunn's Creek with the yacht *America,* which, after a week's hard labor and the valuable assistance of Lieutenant [John] Irwin, Acting Master [William] Budd, and First Assistant Engineer [William W.] Dungan, I succeeded in raising and bringing to this place, where I shall keep her awaiting your further instructions.

She is without ground tackle or sails and almost everything else but her lower masts, bowsprit, gaffs and some light spars. I propose to go to Haw Creek and raise the steamer *St. Mary's,* in which I have no doubt we shall succeed.

Haw Creek flowed into Dunn's Lake at a point some 15 to 20 miles south of where Stevens had recovered the sunken *America* from Dunn's Creek. With his letter, Stevens enclosed a copy of a proclamation he had posted on March 27 at Orange Mills, an establishment for grinding grain, located on the St. John's River somewhat below both Palatka and Dunn's Creek and owned by an avowed enemy of the Union, Dr. R. G. Mays. In the proclamation, Stevens accused Mays of having "maltreated and incarcerated" a Palatka resident with Union sympathies named De Costa for "holding intercourse with persons belonging to the naval forces of the United States," and warned Mays that unless De Costa was "delivered in Jacksonville by March 30," Orange Mills would be shelled. It had been De Costa, apparently, who had tipped Stevens off to the general area in which he would find the *America* and the *St. Mary's.* When Dr. Mays failed to produce De Costa by the deadline date, Stevens was as good as his word. He turned the guns of one of his vessels on Orange Mills and destroyed its buildings.

On April 3, when next in Jacksonville, Stevens wrote a chatty letter to his friend and fellow naval officer, Commander Percival Drayton, who was serving elsewhere on the Southern coast. After telling Drayton about finding the *America,* he expressed this wish: "I hope the Flag Officer will conclude to give the good people of New York once again a sight of this beautiful vessel."

Seemingly such an idea had already occurred to Du Pont, for in a letter of praise sent Stevens on April 5 he said:

> I have not had an opportunity to write you since the receipt of your communication of the 28th ultimo, informing me of your recovery of the yacht *America.*
>
> I beg you to receive my commendations and congratulations on this interesting service, in the performance of which you have shown so much untiring determination and skill. I have received from Lieutenant Irwin, of whom you have spoken so favorably in your report, a full account of the event. Please convey my thanks to Acting Master Budd and First Assistant Engineer Dungan, whose valuable assistance is also referred to by you.
>
> The historic interest which attaches to this vessel and the incidents attending her career up to the time of your remarkable capture and recovery of her, make me very anxious to get her safely to Port Royal, where I propose to refit her and send her North. You will therefore use your best judgment in getting her towed up.

In a postscript, Du Pont informed Stevens of an order from Washington he had "this moment received." The Union was to withdraw from Jacksonville and the surrounding area; greater need existed elsewhere for the vessels and personnel deployed there. The news disappointed Stevens, since it meant he could not follow through with his plans for recovering the *St. Mary's* from where she lay scuttled in Haw Creek.

Later in the war, the Confederates raised the steamer, and she ran the blockade to Nassau with a load of cotton. On her return in February 1864, the Union gunboat *Norwich* chased her up the St. John's, and her crew, rather than permit her capture, scuttled her in McGirt's Creek, about 15 miles above Jacksonville. Union sailors found her, but were so harassed by snipers they abandoned their attempts to raise her. Instead, they hurriedly lowered and set off underwater explosives and on February 9 reported her destroyed.

The report was erroneous. At the end of the war, the owners of the *St. Mary's* raised her, scraped the rust from her iron hull, and found her nearly as good as before. Renamed *Nick King,* she was placed on her old Savannah and Jacksonville packet run. In April 1870, when Robert E. Lee and his daughter Agnes visited Florida, they took passage aboard her. Host to the Lees was Colonel Robert G. Cole, who during the war had been chief commissary of the Army of Northern Virginia and was now a grower of citrus products he had given the name "grapefruit" because they grew in clusters. Cole lived in a hamlet on the St. John's called after a grain-grinding establishment which had once stood there, Orange Mills. Matters had come full circle.

Stevens, after receiving Du Pont's letter of April 5, 1862, did not leave the St. John's immediately, for he felt responsible for those Southerners who had befriended Union personnel and might suffer in consequence. Some days later, however, Stevens felt free to go, on the appearance in the river of a Union gunboat commanded by Lieutenant Daniel Ammen, who had orders to remain there as long as necessary on just such police duty.

Before the war, Ammen had been a close friend of Edward Clifford Anderson, and in February, 1861, Anderson had visited him at his home in Baltimore. Now Ammen saw the *America* as Stevens, headed for Du Pont's base at Port Royal, towed her out to sea from the mouth of the St. John's in the wake of his gunboat *Ottawa.* Because of the yacht's fame as a racer, Ammen doubtlessly regarded her keenly. Even so, his interest would have been all the keener had he known that less than a year before, while called *Camilla,* she had transported his friend Anderson—a man now technically his enemy through the fortunes of war—from Savannah, Georgia, to Queenstown, Ireland.

On April 23, a few days after his safe arrival at Port Royal with the *America* in tow, Stevens wrote Du Pont this informal account of his adventures in Florida during the month preceding:

As you intimated it would be interesting to know more of the circumstances connected with the recovery of the yacht *America* than was contained in my official report, I have to inform you that the day after the occupation of Jacksonville I proceeded up the river as far as Palatka, and there met a person who informed me in general terms as to her whereabouts and that of the steamer *St. Mary's*. On my way down on board the *Ellen* a boat was discovered with two persons in it, to which we gave chase, when as we neared the shore the boat was abandoned. Upon searching the boat a letter was discovered from a Mr. Hemming, the person who was employed to sink the yacht and the steamer, giving all the information desired. I reached Jacksonville the same evening, and the next morning I started in the *Darlington*, with the *Ellen* and the launches of the *Wabash*, for Dunn's Creek, where I found the yacht sunk in about 3 fathoms of water, only her port rail being above water. Leaving the *Ellen* to protect her from any further injury, I proceeded on in the *Darlington*, with the two boats of the *Wabash*, through Dunn's Lake into Haw Creek, and there found the *St. Mary's*, a fine and valuable steamer, also sunk.

As we had no suitable purchases to raise the vessels, I returned to Jacksonville in the *Darlington* for them, leaving the *Ellen*, with the boats named, alongside of the yacht to make preparations for raising her. Finally, after procuring such imperfect means as I could find, and after a week's hard and laborious effort on the part of all the command, our efforts were successful in raising the *America*, and I have to report her safe arrival in this place, where she was towed by the *Ottawa*, and where she awaits your orders.

The *America* was brought to Jacksonville by a Lord Dacy, and, I am well informed, was sold to the Confederate Government some four months ago (at which time she ran the blockade) for the sum of $60,000. It is asserted and generally believed she was bought by the rebels for the purpose of carrying Slidell and Mason to England.

The "Mr. Hemming" credited by Stevens with scuttling the *America* and the *St. Mary's* must have been Charles C. Hemming, the adventurous son of Colonel J. C. Hemming. The father had come to Florida from England many years before, had fought in the Seminole wars, and had reared a large family. At the outbreak of the Civil War, young Charles, then seventeen, joined the Jacksonville Light Infantry, which by March 1862 had been mustered into the Confederate Army as Company "A" of the Third Florida Regiment.

As the Union gunboats entered the St. John's, it had been this regiment that disappeared from Jacksonville coincident with the disappearance of the *America* and the *St. Mary's.* But young Hemming undoubtedly had help in the upriver tow, for acting alone he could not possibly have fired the steamer's boilers, managed her helm, and managed as well the trailing yacht.

Later in the war, Hemming suffered capture during a battle in Tennessee, but escaped from a Union prison camp and fled to Canada. There he joined a band of other Confederate expatriates and made guerrilla sorties across the border into New York State. On one such, when hotly pursued by Union soldiers, he found sanctuary in the Fredonia, New York, home of Miss Mary Cumming, a woman of middle age.

During the final weeks of the war, Hemming took passage on a steamer from Halifax, Nova Scotia, to Havana, Cuba, and from Havana returned to Jacksonville via a rowboat lowered at sea from a blockade-runner. After the war, Miss Cumming visited Florida and received her reward; she married young Hemming's father, by then a widower.

Also after the war, Hemming went west, founded a town in Texas, and from there moved to Colorado Springs, Colorado, where he ended his business career a bank president. In 1899, at a cost of $20,000, he presented Jacksonville with a 62-foot-high Confederate monument, fittingly erected in Hemming Park. In 1906, John W. Headley, a Kentuckian who had been with Hemming in Canada, wrote a book about his Civil War experiences. In it he described Hemming as an "accomplished boatman"—and so he must have been.

Certain statements made by Stevens in his informal letter to Du Pont of April 23, 1862, are puzzling. Did he actually believe the Confederate Government had bought the *America* for $60,000 four months before—in other words, around Christmas, 1861—or was he merely passing along misinformation he had picked up, feeling sure Du Pont would recognize its falsity? Similarly, did he really believe the yacht had been purchased to carry Slidell and Mason to England?

Stevens could be given the benefit of the doubt but for another letter he wrote eleven years later, by which time he was a commodore, stationed at Norfolk. In the weekly *Army and Navy Journal* for June 7, 1873, appeared brief mention of the *America,* and Stevens contributed amplifying material published in the "Correspondence" column of the *Journal's* next issue. He told of finding the *America* in a creek off the St. John's and then flatly stated that the yacht had been "purchased by the Confederate Government for the purpose of taking Messrs. Slidell and Mason as its representatives to Europe, the price paid for her being $60,000 in gold. Our unexpected entrance into the river thwarted this intention."

John Slidell, of Louisiana, and James Mason, of Virginia, were appointed Confederate commissioners to France and England respectively (with authority over the commissioners already abroad) on August 24, 1861. At this time the yacht *America,* with Decie in command, was on the other side of the Atlantic from the Confederacy.

The Confederate Navy Department arranged for Slidell and Mason to proceed to Britain aboard one of its armed vessels, the *Nashville,* and in September the commissioners traveled to Charleston, South Carolina, where the *Nashville* awaited them.

Neither commissioner, however, liked the look of the *Nashville.* They feared she drew so much water she might have difficulty running the blockade out of Charleston. So they arranged instead to charter for $10,000 the light-draft, iron-hulled blockade-running steamer *Theodora,* owned in Charleston, to transport them as far as Cuba.

Mason (together with his secretary James Macfarland), and Slidell (together with his wife, their two daughters, and his secretary George Eustis) boarded the *Theodora* at 1 A.M. October 12 and got out of Charleston without difficulty. Also without difficulty, the *Theodora* landed them four days later at Cardenas, Cuba, and by the end of the month was back at Charleston.

Meanwhile, on October 25, Henry Decie returned with the *America* to the Confederacy, entered the St. John's River for the first time, and sailed up to Jacksonville.

In Cuba, the Mason and Slidell parties traveled overland from Cardenas to Havana. On November 7 they took passage to England aboard the British royal mail packet *Trent*. The next day, Captain Charles Wilkes, commanding the 12-gun U.S. warship *San Jacinto,* halted the *Trent* in the Bahama Channel, sent Marines aboard, and by force of arms removed Mason and Slidell and their secretaries. Then the *San Jacinto* steamed to Boston, where the four Confederates were imprisoned at Fort Warren.

During these early November days, Lieutenant Commanding Stevens and his gunboat *Ottawa* were engaged in the siege that resulted in the capture of Port Royal. But the siege lasted for less than a week, and the vessels participating soon regularly received mail and newspapers. Throughout the next several months, anyone who read the papers—on either side of the Atlantic—could not help but learn virtually every detail of the Mason and Slidell "Trent Affair," for it came near to causing war between England and the United States. England, in fact, in anticipation of such a struggle, sent 8,000 troops to Nova Scotia, and hostilities were averted largely through the skillful diplomatic actions of two nonprofessional diplomats, Abraham Lincoln and Queen Victoria's beloved Prince Consort Albert, who was fatally ill at the time. On January 1, 1862, in accordance with an agreement arrived at between the two countries, a tug carried Mason, Slidell, and their secretaries from Fort Warren to Provincetown, Massachusetts—at the tip of Cape Cod—where they were released. The four Confederates then boarded the waiting British warship *Rinaldo,* and on January

29, after a stopover at Bermuda, they completed their interrupted journey to England.

This latter date, a Tuesday, was exactly six weeks before the Tuesday, March 11, 1862, on which Lieutenant Commanding Stevens entered the St. John's River—an entry causing the yacht *America* to take flight upstream. Thus the appearance of Stevens in the river could have had nothing to do with thwarting the means chosen by Mason and Slidell for going abroad, for they had long since arrived there. Why Stevens told the erroneous story—at least twice—is difficult to fathom. If he believed it, he displayed woeful ignorance of current history. If he did not, it might be thought that he proved himself guilty of attempting to attach unearned importance to his recovery of the yacht *America*—a feat already important enough.

Toward the end of April, after Stevens had towed the *America* to Port Royal, Du Pont asked the Navy Department in Washington what disposition to make of her. On May 17, having received no reply, he wrote again, this time to John Lenthall, of the Bureau of Construction and Repair. "I find I can make her very useful here as a blockading vessel," Du Pont declared. "May I ask the Bureau to allow her a suit of sails, and enclose a draft of the same; also the card of the sailmaker who made her original set, though I presume they can be made in the yards as well."

While there is no record of where the sails came from, the *America* soon had them, and all other equipment to outfit her as a U.S. Navy vessel, including three guns, two mounted amidships and one forward. Acting Master Jonathan Baker took command of her. Formerly an officer in the merchant service, Baker, a volunteer, had entered the Navy as a mate the November before and on exhibiting great proficiency had been rapidly promoted.

For a trial period of a month, Baker and his crew of nine men sailed the yacht as a dispatch boat out of Du Pont's headquarters at Port Royal. She delivered orders, mail, and express packages to the fifty-odd vessels of the South Atlantic Blockading Squadron stretched along the coasts of South Carolina and Georgia and along the east coast of Florida. Then, having proved herself in terms of seaworthiness, speed, and maneuverability, and with her crew tripled to 27, she became a member of the unit of the dozen or so blockaders patrolling the four main channels and the numerous inlets of the 15-mile-wide estuary leading to Charleston.

Because of her light draft, the *America* was assigned a station near the northeastern end of the blockading line—an area of the sea called Rattlesnake Shoal. Here the depth of water was never certain, for the bottom shifted and twisted at the fickle commands of storm and tide. Only seasoned Charleston pilots could make an educated guess as to whether a keel would clear or strike, and the pilots employed aboard the more successful vessels running the blockade were, of course, of just that stripe.

The *America* had hardly taken up her station before she saw action and found herself mentioned in dispatches. On July 24, the "Senior Officer Present" off Charleston (and such Senior Officers changed often) wrote Du Pont:

> I regret to state that a rather large three-masted propeller succeeded in running the blockade this morning. She was seen about midnight inside the *America,* between Rattlesnake Shoal and DeWees Inlet, going slowly. The *America* fired three shots at her, when she quickened her speed and was soon out of sight. We chased her for some time, the wind being very light, and then anchored on account of the shoalness of the water. At daylight, we saw the steamer standing in, as appeared to us, by Maffitt's Channel.

A few weeks later the *America* had another disappointing encounter with a blockade-runner on virtually the same stretch of water. Du Pont, who had been made a rear admiral on July 30, consolidated the accounts of the commanding officers of the several blockading vessels involved and on September 2 passed along his summary to Gideon Welles, the Secretary of the Navy:

I regret to report the escape of a steamer from Charleston on the night of the 28th ultimo through Maffitt's Channel. At 8 o'clock in the evening Commander Mullany of the *Bienville* sent his launch to guard the entrance to the channel, in charge of Acting Master Rogers. Near 10 o'clock Rogers saw a steam propeller passing close along the beach, moving silently and swiftly. He immediately fired a rocket and burned a blue light—the signals agreed upon—and the *Bienville* at once slipped her cable, alarmed the rest of the fleet, and gave chase, but was unable to see anything of the escaping vessel. Shortly afterwards guns were fired from the *America,* which, with the *Flag,* guarded the N. E. entrance to Maffitt's Channel, but on the *Bienville* reaching them the steamer had succeeded, in the darkness, in escaping. Acting Master Rogers, in charge of the launch, reports that though the steamer passed within 300 yards of him, yet when the land behind was higher than the hull, he could see nothing of her. I refer to this particularly that the Department may be apprised of one of the great difficulties of the blockade of Charleston.

On September 3, the day after Du Pont wrote this report, the Charleston blockaders nabbed a prize of trifling value—the *John Thompson,* a down-at-the-heel sloop of but 6 tons carrying a meager cargo and manned only by her owner, Henry Cushman, and a boy, John Katzenberger. Blockader officers pronounced the sloop unseaworthy and ordered her cargo and crew of two sent to Port Royal aboard the *America.* Apparently young Katzenberger was so delighted at the prospect of going for a sail on the famous yacht that he answered questions readily concerning other violators of the Charleston blockade—mariners of greater financial stature and certainly of more maturity.

The *America* deposited the two prisoners and their seized goods at Port Royal and returned to her station off Charleston without notable incident. Soon she made a worthwhile capture all on her own. The day following, Jonathan Baker, in a report sent direct to Du Pont, wrote:

> On Monday night, October 13, 1862, at 11 P.M., while lying at anchor off the mouth of DeWees Inlet in 4 fathoms of water, wind west, weather cloudy, I discovered a sail trying to run the blockade out from Charleston. I commenced firing, and sent a boat with six men in charge of Acting Master's Mate G. H. Wood to cut him off from the shore. After firing three shots at him he came to. I boarded and found the vessel to be the schooner, *David Crockett,* from Charleston for Bermuda, with cargo. The crew consisted of six men and two passengers, whom I sent on board of the U. S. *Flag,* Commander J. H. Strong, which came to me after I commenced firing.

While the captured schooner, on inspection, proved not to be worth much, her cargo had considerable value. It consisted of 175 barrels of spirits of turpentine and 10 barrels of rosin—products plentiful in the pine country of the South, but in short supply in the North and in Britain. As with all prize cases, the legitimacy of the capture would be, in time, passed upon by a judge of some U.S. District Court; the vessel and her cargo would be sold; and a portion of the proceeds of the sale would be divided among the Navy personnel responsible for the capture in accordance with the rank and pay scale of each participant. Although this system provided incentive virtues, it also produced evils. Too often officers commanding blockaders, being human, claimed for their vessels, themselves, and the men under them feats of derring-do considerably magnified.

On October 26, less than two weeks after the *America* seized the *David Crockett,* Du Pont ordered Jonathan Baker to sail the yacht north for a complete overhaul and refitting at the New York Navy Yard. When she had been gone for nearly two months, Du Pont wrote a private letter to his friend, Gustavus Vasa Fox, Assistant Secretary of the Navy, complaining about the delay. "Oh, those yards!" he lamented. "Please think of the *America;* they miss her much inside the Rattlesnake." Perhaps Fox took action. In any event, Acting Master Baker, with the *America* in excellent trim, arrived aboard her at Port Royal on January 3—the year was now 1863—and Du Pont ordered the yacht and her commander to return to their accustomed blockading station off Charleston.

The next day, the U.S.S. *Quaker City* and the U.S.S. *Memphis* found themselves concerned with another yacht, the *Mercury*. They captured her attempting to run the blockade out of Charleston, possibly through the connivance of her master, Arnold G. Harris, before the war a petty officer in the U.S. Navy. Aboard was a lone passenger who called himself George Sharrer, but turned out to be Reid Sanders, a major in the Confederate Army on a mission to Europe, where he was to meet his father, George Nicholas Sanders—the same George Nicholas Sanders who had been in the company of Henry Decie at Montgomery, Alabama, nearly two years before. Papers in the possession of Major Sanders disclosed that the Confederacy planned to contract with the elder Sanders for a line of fast dispatch boats between Southern ports and Halifax, Nova Scotia. In the view of the captors of Major Sanders, the scheme seemed totally infeasible—dreamed up by George Nicholas Sanders solely for his own enrichment—and in disrupting it the officers of the *Quaker City* and the *Memphis* felt they were doing the Confederacy an inadvertent favor.

Before dawn on the morning of January 29, the *America* played a modest part in the capture of a fine screw steamer of 828 tons, the *Princess Royal,* when that iron-hulled vessel attempted to run the blockade. The offender, laden with a valuable cargo for the Confederate Navy consisting of marine engines, rifled Whitworth cannon, small arms, and ammunition, was commanded by Captain Joseph Lawson, an Englishman. At least twice in the past the *Princess Royal* had slipped by guarding Union vessels, into and out of Beaufort, South Carolina, shortly before that port suffered seizure back in the fall of 1861.

Now, nearly a year and a half later, on trying at Charleston, the steamer attracted the attention of the watch aboard the blockading schooner *Blunt,* who threw up a rocket giving the alarm. The gunboat *Unadilla* rushed for the steamer and when within range began firing. Although none of the shells found their target, the *Princess Royal* abruptly veered off course, ran for the land, and grounded, and her captain, pilot, supercargo, and passengers escaped ashore by means of her boats.

Other vessels of the blockading squadron, including the *America,* soon reached the stranded vessel, and their crews boarded her. The men remaining on the *Princess Royal,* instead of making any show of resistance, assisted the Union sailors in doing all possible to lighten her and prevent her breaking up. Winches, lines, and kedge anchors came into play, and with aid provided by the tide she was soon hauled off.

On that very same January 29 the hull of the new U.S. gunboat *Kansas* slid down the ways at Philadelphia. Soon afterward, manned by a prize crew, the *Princess Royal* arrived there for adjudication by the U.S, District Court. On March 18 the Navy bought her in for $112,000, and some of the ordnance and one of the marine engines she had carried as cargo went, respectively, for arming and providing motive power for the *Kansas.* As for the rest of the ordnance, it was mounted aboard the *Princess Royal* herself. On May 29 she was provided with appropriate flags and commissioned the 7-gun U.S.S. *Princess Royal,* and so named she served the Union for the remaining two years of the war.

Meanwhile, in mid-March 1863, the *America* had an experience in at least one respect similar to her encounter with the *Princess Royal,* and in a letter dated March 21 Du Pont told Secretary of the Navy Welles about it:

> I have the honor to report to the Department that about midnight of the 18th instant the English iron steamer *Georgiana* attempted to run into Charleston through Maffitt's Channel.
>
> The alarm had been given by the U.S. yacht *America,* Acting Master J. Baker, who also fired into her, and the U.S.S. *Wissahickon,* Lieutenant-Commander J. L. Davis, soon after perceiving her, opened so heavy a fire upon her that her commander hailed to say that he surrendered. Upon this the *Wissahickon* ceased firing, but the captain of the ship, taking advantage

thereof, pointed his vessel toward the shore, which was quite near, and succeeded in running her aground, and, with all on board of her, escaped on the land side.

Captain Davis being of opinion that the vessel could not be saved, determined to destroy her, and set her on fire.

The cargo was a very valuable one, and, according to some statements, the vessel itself was pierced for fourteen guns, but as I have not received any report as yet from Lieutenant-Commander Davis, I am not certain that this was the case. I shall be able to give further particulars by the next mail.

Before Davis could closely examine the burning *Georgiana*, she blew up, and it is probable Du Pont was never able to enlighten Secretary Welles on the point raised. Du Pont did receive, however, a subsequent report from Captain Thomas Turner, the Senior Officer Present off Charleston, which contained this significant paragraph:

> From all I can ascertain, the *Georgiana* was sent into Charleston to receive her officers, to be fitted out as a rebel cruiser there. She had 140 men on board, with an armament of guns and gun carriages in her hold, commanded by a retired British naval officer.

Since Annapolis, Maryland, lay dangerously close to the Confederacy, the Naval Academy, early in the war, had been removed for year-round operation to Newport, Rhode Island, where for a long while it had maintained facilities for the summer training of midshipmen. Such training included practice cruises aboard schoolships, and from an order Secretary Welles sent Du Pont on March 25 it became apparent that the Academy's small fleet of vessels would soon experience expansion. Du Pont's order read: "You will send the U.S. yacht *America* to Newport, R.I., between the 10th and 20th of May next, for the purposes of the Naval Academy."

This gave the *America* only a few weeks in which to rack up further honors as a blockading vessel. She began doing so almost immediately when, on March 31, in collaboration with the

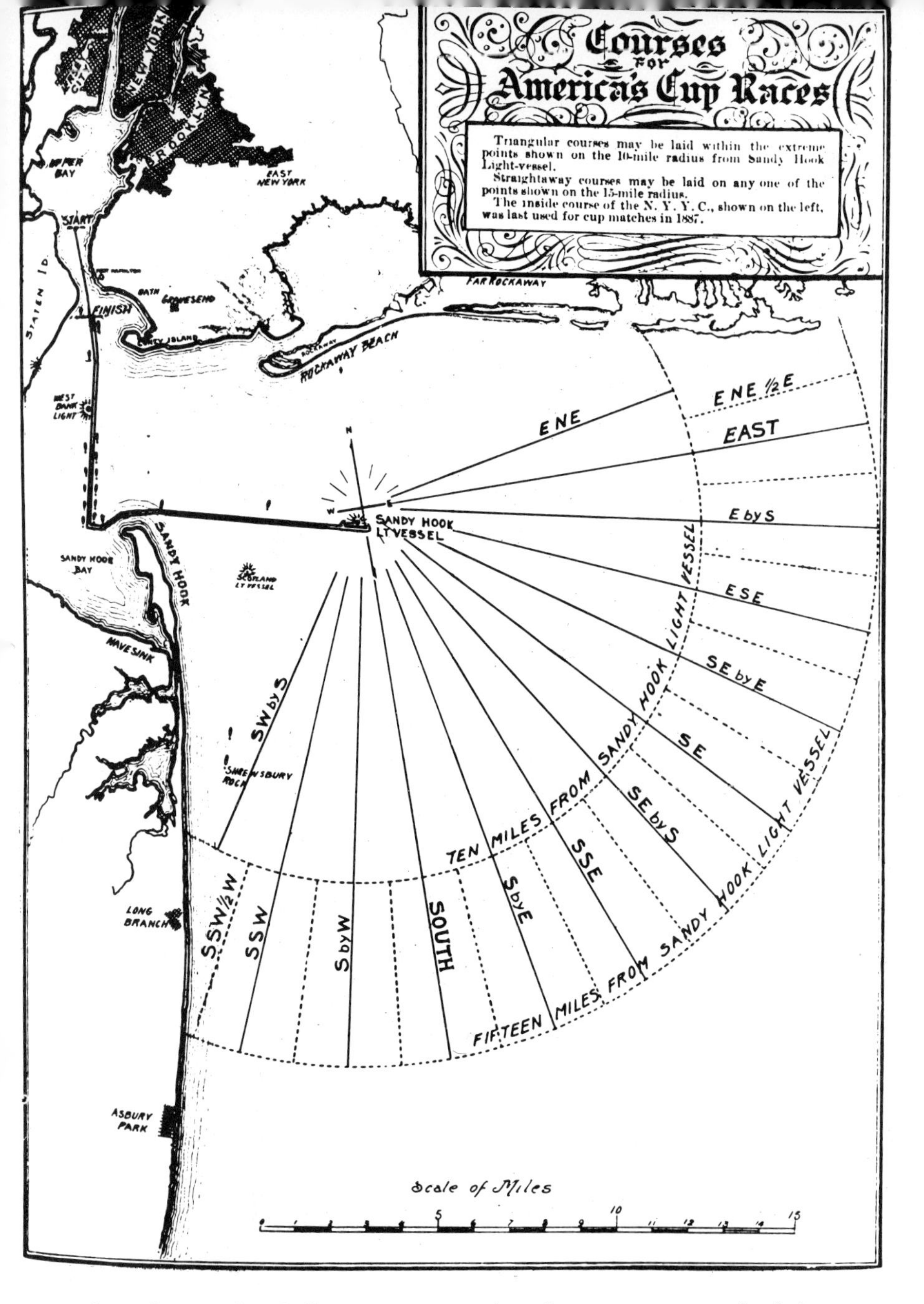

Through 1887 the challenge races started in the Upper Bay north of the Narrows, proceeded south to a point west of Sandy Hook, then east to Sandy Hook Light Vessel, and returned over the same course. After 1887 and until 1930, all America's Cup races started at Sandy Hook Light Vessel and proceeded out to sea either on an out-and-back course or on a course forming an equilateral triangle and ended at Sandy Hook Light Vessel. From *The Lawson History of the America's Cup.*

Gazaway Bugg Lamar, wealthy New York banker, took flight to his native Georgia following the outbreak of the Civil War and operated a fleet of blockade runners. After the war, Ben Butler extricated Lamar from his multitudinous troubles with the U.S. Government, and as a return favor Lamar claimed ownership of the *America,* then at the Naval Academy. In 1873, his fabricated contention had a distinct bearing on the sale of the famous yacht at a fraction of her value to John Cassels, who had been Provost Marshal on the staff of General Ben Butler during the Civil War. By frightening off all other potential buyers, Cassels got the yacht dirt cheap for his master. Portrait of Gazaway Bugg Lamar courtesy of *Georgia Historical Quarterly.* Portrait of John Cassels from *Butler's Book,* Boston, 1892.

Benjamin Franklin Butler—controversial General in the Union Army during the Civil War, Congressman from Massachusetts, Governor of Massachusetts, scheming politician, and tricky lawyer—zestfully raced the *America* and cruised aboard her for nearly 20 years. This Mathew B. Brady photograph of Butler, the negative of which is in the Library of Congress, shows him in a rare pose. Sensitive about the permanent droop afflicting his left eyelid (which became the more marked the older he grew), he usually sat for a camera only in right profile.

This engraving is the frontispiece to Butler's autobiography, *Butler's Book*, published in Boston in 1892.

The *America,* while sailed by Ben Butler, never flew the burgee of the New York Yacht Club. Following Butler's death, she came into the possession of his grandson, Butler Ames, who on election to the Club provided her with a proper pennant. This photograph of the *America* was taken off Newport in August 1901 by Frank Child. The *America* had just raced the *Corona,* the New York Yacht Club flagship, from Vineyard Haven and for a vessel of her age had made a surprisingly good showing. Courtesy of The Mariners Museum, Newport News, Virginia.

Long neglected, the *America* in 1921 came close to being sold for conversion into a lowly trading vessel. A group of dedicated yachtsmen, headed by Charles Francis Adams, the treasurer of Harvard, formed themselves into the America Restoration Fund Committee, bought her, and put her in sufficiently good shape for towing to Annapolis, where, after an absence of 48 years, she was returned to the Naval Academy. This picture, taken aboard the *America,* shows Admiral Henry Braid Wilson, Superintendent of the Academy, on the point of "buying" her from Adams for $1, with other Naval officers and Academy midshipmen standing by. U.S. Naval Academy photo.

Off the forward end of the *America*'s cockpit, this hatch provided entrance to a companionway leading to the main saloon.

Aft, sunk in the deck of the *America,* was a roomy cockpit containing this **horseshoe-shaped seat.**

Below: Aft of the *America*'s mainmast, this skylight provided ventilation and light. Photographs courtesy of The Mariners Museum, Newport News, Va.

The *America,* during her second sojourn at the Naval Academy, had a long and nearly unbroken rest of 20 years, dating from 1921. Sailed only rarely at first, later she functioned merely as an object of interest to Academy visitors, many of whom trooped aboard her at her moorings, where she is shown here in this 1938 photograph. Eventually rot set in, and finally it became imperative that she be given extensive repair. However, money for the undertaking was not appropriated until 1941, at which time she was hauled out and stripped at a private boatyard near the Academy. Courtesy of The Mariners Museum, Newport News, Va.

In 1941, hauled out at the Annapolis **Yacht** Yard, the establishment of a private contractor, the *America* was put in frame preparatory to undergoing repairs vitally needed. Following the bombing of Pearl Harbor, when the Annapolis Yacht Yard abruptly converted to war work, all efforts to rehabilitate her stopped. U.S. Naval Academy photos.

7-gun U.S.S. *Memphis,* she made a capture. In his account of the event, dated that same day, the commanding officer of the *Memphis* wrote:

> I have the honor to report that a topsail schooner was discovered this morning beating up for the shore, to the southward of Bull's Bay Shoal. Got under way and stood for her as far as practicable [the *Memphis* drew 15½ feet of water], and then despatched our boats after her under Acting Ensign Magone, who succeeded in boarding her as she was endeavoring to escape by the regular channel seaward. She had thus passed around the shoal. The *America* was guarding the channel outside, and brought her to by a shot. She proved to be the *Antelope,* under English colors, with regular clearance from London for Nassau. She has a cargo of salt. Enclosed I send her papers. The captain admits his intention of breaking the blockade.

This capture fetched in prize money for the officers and men participating $2,775, which was all it was worth in the North, where salt was cheap and plentiful. In the South, however, the *Antelope*'s cargo alone would have sold for many multiples of the amount, in gold, for salt was used there not merely as a seasoning, but in vast quantities as a meat preservative and during the war was the scarcest of all commodities—so scarce that large vats of sea water were distilled to obtain a few ounces.

The *America*'s last blockade-running antagonist was one of the more famous of the breed. Owned by the Confederate Government, she bore the name *Leopard* when acquired in early 1862, but less than a year later she was rechristened *Stonewall Jackson* in honor of the Southern hero. A fast side-wheel steamer of 862 tons, with an iron hull, she successfully ran the blockade off Charleston five times in 1862 and three times more in early 1863, going in with guns and other military necessities and coming out with her hold crammed full and her deck piled high with baled cotton, the Confederacy's only currency negotiable abroad. Her master, an adventurer who called himself

"Captain Black," boasted that he kept a regular schedule between Charleston and Nassau—and so he did until the night of April 11.

An account of what happened that night was sent Du Pont the day following by Captain J. F. Green, commanding a wing of the blockading fleet off Charleston.

> I have respectfully to report [Green wrote] that last night, between 11 and 12 o'clock, a steamer, bound in, succeeded in passing the steamers *Flag* and *Huron* and schooners *America* and *Blunt*, stationed in and off the Rattlesnake Shoal. Each of the blockading vessels named fired at her repeatedly, and at daylight this morning the steamer was discovered abandoned, on fire, and fast aground about one-half of a mile from the beach and 1½ miles from the Beach Inlet batteries. She was probably struck and set on fire by the shells fired at her, and is apparently a complete wreck.

The Southern version of the occurrence, as reported to the Confederate Adjutant General by Captain Charles T. Haskell, Jr., who commanded the Beach Inlet batteries, said:

> The steamer *Stonewall Jackson*, just from Nassau, was fired into last night and chased ashore by the abolitionists. She was set on fire at daylight by her captain and will prove a total loss. Her passengers, officers and crew are now at this post, 54 in number. It is a pity she was fired, as she was under the protection of my battery.

Du Pont, having no access to the Confederate report, remained unaware of the identity of the destroyed steamer until some days later he read of the incident in a captured Southern newspaper. This story, dated at Charleston on April 12, declared:

> Last night the steamer *Stonewall Jackson*, formerly the *Leopard*, while attempting to run into this harbor was hotly chased by a half dozen blockaders, which fired at her, and she received several shots through her hull. Captain Black, finding it impossible to escape, ran the steamer on the beach and burned

her. The crew and passengers took to the boats. Very little was saved excepting the mails and the passengers' effects. The steamer burned to the water's edge in sight of the Yankees. Her cargo consisted of several pieces of field artillery, 200 barrels of saltpeter [nitrate of potassium, a component of gunpowder], 40,000 pairs of army shoes, and a large assortment of other military supplies.

Du Pont, from his list of the more elusive and persistent violators of the blockade, could now happily strike off the name *Stonewall Jackson,* alias *Leopard.* At virtually the same time, however, he was forced by the edicts of Secretary of the Navy Welles to remove from his roster of Charleston blockaders two of the vessels in part responsible for the end of the *Stonewall Jackson*—the *America* and the 121-ton schooner *G. W. Blunt.*

On May 1, Du Pont, while aboard his Flagship *Wabash* at Port Royal, wrote the Senior Officer Present off Charleston, "Enclosed is an order to Acting Master Baker to proceed at once with the yacht *America* to Newport. This is done in accordance with a peremptory order of the Navy Department." And three days later the *America* sailed.

Then, on May 12, Du Pont sent the following letter to Secretary of the Navy Welles:

> I deem it my duty to inform the Department that the infractions of the blockade off Charleston are increasing in consequence of an increase of the number of steamers engaged in violating it, of greater speed and less draft of water.
>
> I have no reason to doubt the vigilance of the officers off that port, but the whole number of vessels which I am able to place there is not by any means sufficient to keep out the blockade runners.
>
> The withdrawal of the *America* and the necessity of sending the *Blunt* north have been seriously felt, as those two vessels from their draft were able to take up effective positions which the other ships could not assume.

On June 15, Du Pont got the *G. W. Blunt* back, but it is doubtful that he ever saw the *America* again. Since early in

1863 he and Welles had engaged in numerous squabbles over policy, with the cumulative result that on July 6 Welles removed him from command of the South Atlantic Blockading Squadron and installed in his stead Rear Admiral John A. Dahlgren. A member of the prominent Du Pont de Nemours family of Delaware, Du Pont sat out most of the rest of the war at his home near Wilmington. Two months after the fall of the Confederacy he died, aged 61. In 1882, by Congressional action, an area in Washington at the intersection of Connecticut and Massachusetts Avenues received, as a tribute to Du Pont considerably overdue, the name Du Pont Circle.

After parting with the blockading fleet off Charleston on May 4, 1863, the *America*, while on her way to Newport, Rhode Island, stopped off at New York to transact a piece of important unfinished business. Although the yacht had served as a vessel of the U.S. Navy for more than a year, she was yet to belong to the Navy—legally.

The matter was attended to on May 19 in proceedings held before a judge of the U.S. District Court. The judge properly "condemned" the *America* as a prize; she was offered for sale; and immediately she was "bought in" by the Navy Department for $700. This sum, no indication of the yacht's true value, was arrived at arbitrarily merely to comply with the law. Just as readily, the amount could have been much more or something less, for the Navy merely transferred the money from one of its pockets to another. The unrealistic figure indicates that Lieutenant Commanding Thomas H. Stevens and the officers and men under him responsible for locating the *America* and raising her from the waters of Dunn's Creek had patriotically signed a waiver relinquishing all claim to prize money.

As a matter of routine, copies of the findings of the U.S. District Court at New York concerning the *America* should have been sent to Washington. But in 1876, when sought by a Congressional committee investigating the Navy Department, no copy could be found at departmental headquarters, and just as mysteriously the original papers had disappeared from the files of the court. Nearly a half century later, however, the bulk of the information contained in the papers turned up in time for use by historians on the staff of the Navy Department who were compiling the *Official Records of the Union and Confederate Navies in the War of the Rebellion,* a gigantic work of thirty-one volumes, the last of which (exclusive of a cumulative index) achieved publication in 1921. All that was missing was the waiver. This caused the Navy's historians to say in one breath that the Navy had legally purchased the *America,* and in the next that the Navy had never had clear title to her. Obviously certain shenanigans had occurred, the cloudy nature of which will be explored later, at a proper place in this narrative.

After the May 19 court proceedings, the *America* ran to Newport, where Acting Master Jonathan Baker turned her over to the Naval Academy. Baker subsequently transferred from the South Atlantic Blockading Squadron to its counterpart off the coasts of North Carolina and Virginia, the North Atlantic Blockading Squadron, and served with distinction until the end of the war. Rewarded with a long leave on half-pay, he then got an honorable discharge from the Navy on May 24, 1868.

At Newport, the *America* received as her commanding officer Theodore F. Kane, a 24-year-old Lieutenant who, after service on the West Coast of Africa Station, had only recently won the appointment of Assistant to the Commandant of Midshipmen at the Naval Academy. The yacht's official designation was that of tender to the practice ship *Marion,* a sailing sloop-of-war of 596 tons, built a quarter-century before and presided over by Lieutenant Commander E. Orville Matthews. Actually, however, the yacht proved to be as much a practice ship as the *Marion,* and as time went on many midshipmen preferred assignment aboard her on account of her beauty, fame, and superior speed.

On a Naval Academy break-in cruise, the *America,* in company with the *Marion,* cleared Newport soon after her arrival there for a leisurely sail back to New York. Lieutenant Kane had aboard twelve midshipmen, while Lieutenant Commander Matthews carried on the *Marion* officer-aspirants to the number of twenty-five. Barely had the two vessels dropped anchor off the New York Navy Yard on June 14 when the youngsters comprising their crews quickly matured. One day they were trainees for war, the next, participants.

This rapid transition came about as a result of the fantastic activities of a young Confederate naval officer, Lieutenant Charles William Read, known to Lieutenant Kane. Indeed, the two had studied at Annapolis together, although not in the same class. Kane had graduated in '59, Read in '60. With the outbreak of the Civil War, Kane, a New Yorker, naturally remained in the Union Navy, while Read, a Mississippian, just as naturally resigned and threw in his lot with the South.

During the first year and a half of the war, Read won a reputation as a Confederate daredevil for his wholesale disruption of Union activity on the Mississippi River. As a result, he was chosen as first officer by John Newland Maffitt, who commanded the feared commerce-destroying *Florida,* a 6-gun cruiser built for the Confederacy in Britain under the aegis of James Dunwody Bulloch.

Maffitt roved the high seas of the South Atlantic, capturing and burning or bonding one fat Union merchantman after another. Then, on May 6, 1863, after bringing to heel the *Clarence,* a swift 250-ton brig out of Baltimore engaged in the fruit trade with South America, Maffitt decided to make of this prize an auxiliary cruiser and thus do the Union double damage.

Charles Read, with a force consisting of one other officer, three petty officers, and twenty sailors, took command of the *Clarence* and received orders from Maffitt to sail north and inflict on the Union as much injury as possible. For armament, Maffitt equipped the *Clarence* with all he could afford—one gun, a howitzer—and informed Read and his men that should they wish to fire anything else they would have to depend on their pistols and muskets.

Never has a force so small and so poorly armed hit an enemy

harder. During the next five weeks, above the latitude of Norfolk, Virginia, Read and his men captured and then burned or bonded eighteen commercial vessels owned in the North. Shippers, ship owners, their bankers and insurers deluged Secretary of the Navy Welles with telegrams, and he in turn wired commands ordering out every available Navy craft, plus 33 specially chartered steamers, to speed off in search of the *Clarence*. Yet soon after he had done so, he was forced to send revised orders. For meanwhile he had learned that Read, on June 12, had captured the bark *Tacony* out of Philadelphia, set her crew aboard another prize, burned the *Clarence,* and gone flying away with the *Tacony*.

It was at this stage of the game—in the early evening of June 14—that the *America* and the *Marion,* sailed by midshipmen, reported at the New York Navy Yard. Hiram Paulding, its harried Commandant, wired Welles: "The yacht *America* is here. May I send her in pursuit of the *Tacony*? Also the *Marion* is here. May I send her?"

Within an hour Welles telegraphed back: "Your dispatch with regard to the *America* and *Marion* received and approved. Send them off at once. The *Tacony* was in ballast and must be short of provisions. She has no cannon, the pirates having left the only one they had on board the *Clarence* when she was abandoned and burned."

Throughout the night, the two Naval Academy vessels took on supplies, and early the next morning Paulding handed orders to their commanders. Those for Lieutenant Kane read:

> You will proceed to sea in the U.S. schooner yacht *America,* under your command, keeping a safe distance from the land, examining all vessels that you may fall in with, and obtain what information you can of the pirate *Tacony*. Be governed by the information you may obtain in shaping your course, and in the absence of information that may guide you, steer to the southward when you arrive off the capes of Delaware, sighting the coast of North Carolina, crossing the Gulf Stream in or near the latitude of Cape Hatteras, there traversing as it may suit your

judgment, arriving in New York in ten days from the time of your departure.

And the orders given Lieutenant Commander Matthews, while otherwise similarly worded, directed him to proceed to sea with the U.S. ship *Marion* and "traverse between Sandy Hook and the outer edge of the Gulf Stream, in the track of vessels approaching New York. If the wind is favorable, look in about Montauk [the easternmost point on Long Island] and that part of the coast."

The *Marion* returned after but six days at sea, during which she had encountered storm after storm and had been three times struck by lightning.

> The last stroke brought about half of the main conductor on deck [Matthews reported]. With nearly all of the midshipmen seasick, I concluded to stand to the westward in hopes of finding better weather, but during the 18th the weather not improving and on the 19th getting the wind fresh from the E.S.E. with every prospect of easterly weather, and the ship not being in a fit condition for beating in seaway, I wore ship and ran inside Sandy Hook, where I anchored. During the cruise we have neither seen nor heard of anything piratical.

The *America,* on the other hand, remained at sea her allotted time, covered virtually all of the much longer course assigned her, and in spite of extensive storm damage performed her every duty. Lieutenant Kane's account of the cruise, handed Commandant Paulding on June 25, read:

> I have the honor to report the return of the *America* to this port, after an unsuccessful search for the privateer *Tacony.* In obedience to your orders, we left the navy yard on June 15 and shaped our course southward. We have during the cruise sighted the coasts of New Jersey, Delaware and Virginia, and have overhauled and boarded all square-rigged vessels we have met with and have spoken all fore-and-afters, but have not had the good fortune to learn anything of the whereabouts of the privateers.
>
> We have been very unfortunate in regard to weather. For the

first five days of the cruise we encountered storms, fog and easterly winds, and the remaining days we met with light southerly airs and calms. On the afternoon of the third day the shackle of the jib stay carried away at the cutwater, and, as there was quite a heavy sea running at the time, with a strong N.E. wind, I had some fears for our foremast. Secured the stay with a tackle to the stem. The next day our bobstay went, which we also secured temporarily.

Being in this crippled condition, and fearing we might encounter more heavy weather, I deemed it not prudent to venture far to the eastward, so, after gaining the latitude of the capes of the Chesapeake, we turned to the northward, stretching more out to the eastward than on our downward run.

Enclosed you will find a list of the vessels boarded and spoken during the cruise.

The list was impressive. Had it been even longer, however, it could hardly have aided in the capture of the *Tacony,* for the *Tacony* was no more. Continuing his game of hop, skip, and jump, Read, after capturing the *Archer,* a fishing schooner of 90 tons, had transferred his crew to that vessel, sent the fishermen aboard still another prize, burned the *Tacony,* and kept along on his way farther north.

On the sunny afternoon of June 26, Read boldly sailed the *Archer* into the harbor of Portland, Maine, and dropped anchor near a United States fort where the revenue cutter *Caleb Cushing,* a sailing vessel armed with a pivot gun, lay tied up at the dock. More than a year later, near the end of a long report sent Mallory, Secretary of the Confederate Navy, Read told what happened next:

At 1:30 A.M. we boarded the cutter *Caleb Cushing* and captured her, without noise or resistance. The wind was now very light, the tide was running in, and before we could get from under the guns of the forts day dawned.

At 10 A.M., when off the harbor, two large steamers were discovered coming out. The cutter was cleared for action, and as soon as the leading steamer was in range we opened fire upon her. After firing five rounds from the pivot gun I was mortified to find that all projectiles were expended. From the movements of the enemy's steamers it was evident that they intended to attack us simultaneously on each side and endeavor to clear our deck with their sharpshooters. It was plain that we could offer but an ineffectual resistance, and therefore I directed the cutter to be set on fire and the crew to take to the boats. At 11:30 I surrendered myself and crew to the steamer *Forest City*. At 12 o'clock the cutter blew up.

Read's rampage, although destructive of property to the tune of perhaps a million dollars, had cost not one drop of blood. Imprisoned at Fort Warren, Boston, until October, 1864, Read was then exchanged in Virginia for a Union officer of equivalent rank held by the Confederates. After the war, Read became harbor master of the Port of New Orleans and died in 1890 when not quite fifty.

In June, a few months before Read's exchange, the principal speaker at the Naval Academy's graduation ceremonies for the class of '64 was a gentleman who knew the yacht *America* of old, and he must have looked upon her with fond and nostalgic interest as she lay anchored at Newport. The gentleman, Colonel James A. Hamilton, still sprightly at 76, had not seen the yacht since, as a member of the syndicate responsible for her building, he had gone abroad to watch her gratifying performances off the Isle of Wight.

In a way, Colonel Hamilton seemed a curious choice for orator before an assembly of the Union's potential fighting men, in the midst of the Civil War, considering its issues. Before the war Hamilton had supported slavery, arguing that the institution received shelter under the Constitution. Once spilled blood colored his thinking, however, he accepted emancipation as a needed military measure.

In the main, Hamilton's talk at Newport avoided controversy. He admonished the graduating midshipmen to abide by the homely virtues of cleanliness, abstinence from tobacco and alcohol, honesty, modesty, and obedience to higher authority.

His only novel utterance was that a state had no more right to secede from the Union than had the Union to expel a state. Lest his valuable remarks be lost to posterity, Hamilton had them printed in a 28-page pamphlet which he distributed among his friends.

During the summer of 1864, the *America* and her sister vessels belonging to the Naval Academy served not merely as schoolships, but as sentinels at the entrance to Long Island Sound. Stationed at Gardiner's Bay, they patrolled between that point and New London, Connecticut. Twice they received alerts that some Confederate cruiser, having presumably borrowed a leaf from Charles Read's manual, hovered off the New England coast bent on destruction. In quick response to one such alarm, the *America* raced more than a hundred miles to the northeast and rounded Martha's Vineyard, only to sight no marauder.

In November—the last November of the Civil War—the *America* was laid up for the winter at Newport. The handwriting on the wall—penned there in large measure in the vigorous script of General William Tecumseh "War Is Hell" Sherman—said that the Confederacy, after battling bravely for nearly four years, was nearing the end of its resources in terms of both men and matériel. Sherman took and burned Atlanta, Georgia, in early November 1864, and on the 15th of the month, with 62,000 troops, began his famous march from Atlanta to the sea.

The sea, in this case, meant Savannah. Confederate General William J. Hardee evacuated Savannah and retreated into South Carolina on December 21, and with Hardee and his army of 15,000 went Colonel Edward Clifford Anderson. Sherman entered the undefended town the next day and for his headquarters there first considered using a wing of the Pulaski House—the hotel at which Anderson had first met Henry Decie back in 1861.

Sherman followed in other of Decie's footsteps. The man who at the start of the war had played host to the yachtsman, as well as to William Howard Russell and the newspaperman's two traveling companions, now near the close of the war sought out and made overtures toward the new celebrity.

> I dispatched an officer to look around for a livery stable that could accommodate our horses [Sherman wrote in his *Memoirs*]. While waiting, an English gentleman, Mr. Charles Green, came and said that he had a fine house, completely furnished, for which he had no use, and offered it as headquarters. At first I felt strongly disinclined to make use of any private dwelling, lest complaints should arise of damage and loss of furniture, and so expressed myself to Mr. Green; but, after riding about the city, and finding his house so spacious, so convenient, with large yard and stabling, I accepted his offer, and occupied that house during our stay in Savannah. He only reserved for himself the use of a couple of rooms above the dining-room, and we had all else, and a most excellent house it was in all respects.

Sherman might not have felt so comfortable in the mansion had he known more of the history of his genial host. In July 1861, Green, utilizing his British passport, had sailed to England via New York after assuring Union authorities he had terminated his business in Savannah. Instead, partly out of sympathy for the Confederacy, but principally further to enrich himself, Green bought in England huge amounts of civilian goods for shipment back across the Atlantic by blockade-runners. Then, following his purchases by what he considered safer means for his own precious carcass, he journeyed to Canada, and on November 6, at Detroit, Michigan, suffered arrest just as he was making arrangements for slipping back south. The caper cost him three months' confinement in a cell at Fort Warren, Boston, and how much more, in gold, for a safe-conduct pass returning him to the Confederacy remains uncertain.

Green, splendid opportunist though he was, had his superior in the breed at Savannah in the person of Gazaway Bugg Lamar. This worthy, on resigning as president of the Bank of the Republic in New York City at the start of the war, sold his stock in the bank and converted the proceeds into other securities, which he cached away in a safety deposit vault in the Banc de Peuple at Montreal.

Early in the war, Lamar acted both as president of the Bank of Commerce at Savannah and as paymaster of Georgia troops stationed in the area, for the mere handling of money had for him enormous appeal. In June 1863, he formed and headed the Importing & Exporting Company of Georgia, a shipping concern which soon had in operation five large and fast blockade-running steamers. While these vessels earned for Lamar huge sums, he remained unsatisfied and constantly contested a Confederate regulation requiring that space aboard them be reserved for Government cargo.

While living in New York, Lamar had known Fernando Wood, then the Mayor, who later became a Congressman. In October 1863, Lamar sent Wood a secret message suggesting that he bribe the commanders of certain Union blockaders to permit the ready passage of Importing & Exporting Company vessels, and that thus between them they could make a fortune. Intercepted and widely published, the proposal embarrassed Wood, who was far too upright to soil his hands with such a scheme, and disgusted all honorable Southerners. Had Lamar been a man not so highly placed, one Georgia newspaper proclaimed, he would have stood "a first-class chance of being shot or hung."

Immediately after General Sherman and his hordes occupied Savannah, Lamar bowed and scraped before the conquerors. On January 6, 1865, he renounced the Confederacy and took the oath of allegiance to the Union. This permitted him to engage in business and to buy and sell property, and he immediately plunged into a variety of lucrative deals involving cotton.

In another area of the struggle, the profiteer's son, Charles A. L. Lamar, continued fighting in defense of his misguided convictions. On April 16—a week after Lee's surrender in Virginia—the former owner of the slave yacht *Wanderer* fell mortally wounded in a battle near Columbus, Georgia. Following his burial at Savannah, a local diarist wrote: "Poor Charley Lamar was interred as he had lived in the midst of storm and tempest."

Also in April 1865, Gazaway Bugg Lamar, along with other prominent Southerners, found himself charged with implication in the assassination of Abraham Lincoln and thrown into the Old Capitol Prison at Washington, where he remained until late in July. After his release, he vainly instituted suit for false imprisonment against the War Department official who had ordered his arrest.

Hard on the occupation of Savannah, agents of the U.S. Treasury arrived there and took possession of all the cotton found—31,000 bales, according to General Sherman—and it was shipped to New York and sold. Lamar laid claim to the proceeds realized from the sale of more than a thousand bales, and the Importing & Exporting Company of Georgia filed a similar claim. On December 27, 1865, a military tribunal convicted Lamar of attempting to collect twice on the same cotton, fined him $25,000, and sentenced him to three years in prison. But the fine was somehow remitted and the sentence revoked.

Several years later, Lamar reactivated his suits, filing one against the Treasury in the U.S. Court of Claims in Massachusetts and another in New York. On June 2, 1873, he won an award of nearly $580,000 in Massachusetts, and a similar victory in New York brought his total winnings up past the million mark. On August 2 the Treasury sought reversals in the U.S. Supreme Court, but that lofty tribunal refused to disturb the findings of the lower courts.

The lawyer chiefly responsible for Lamar's eventual financial triumphs was Benjamin Franklin Butler, later owner of the yacht *America* and one of the most colorful and controversial characters ever to lumber across the American scene. Born in New Hampshire in 1818, Butler grew up in Lowell, Massachusetts. His father, John, roved the West Indies and died there when Butler was barely out of infancy. During his adult years, Butler described his father's rovings as those of a trader and attributed his death to yellow fever. A different story gained circulation, however, that the father had been a pirate and had died a proper death, hanged from a yardarm.

In Lowell, Butler's widowed mother ran a boarding house for mill workers and out of her small profits put her son through college. He was a quick and brilliant student and after graduation and two years of clerking in an attorney's office gained admission to the Massachusetts bar. He was immediately successful as a criminal lawyer, but the slender rewards of such a practice soon palled on him, and he turned to the handling of intricate financial matters and to the pursuit of another endeavor for which he possessed a natural affinity—politics.

Butler was the friend of both Capital and Labor, as well as of the Protestant, the Catholic, and the Jew—indeed, of anyone who had a vote. He switched parties as readily and with as little conscience as another politician might change clothes. Before the Civil War he was successively elected to the Massachusetts House of Representatives and, to the Senate, and during the Democratic convention of 1860 he proposed for nomination as that party's candidate for President of the United States a Southerner named Jefferson Davis.

A year later Butler raised and equipped a brigade of Massachusetts volunteers eager to march south and fight his erstwhile friend Davis and the Confederacy he headed. Butler's men elected him their brigadier general, and after he quelled a riot in Maryland, Lincoln commissioned him a major general. As such, in 1862, Butler commanded Union troops in occupied New Orleans, where he was accused of condoning plunder, provided he received his share. Some accounts have it that amid the booty he sent back to Massachusetts were several hundred bells—church bells, plantation bells, and ship bells—and the silver spoons from the New Orleans mansion he used as his headquarters. For the balance of his life he was known to many Southerners as "Spoons" Butler.

In 1863, while serving in Virginia, Butler incurred the wrath of General U.S. Grant when he got several thousand Union troops bottled up by a vastly inferior Confederate force. And yet a few years later, when Grant became President, he relied upon Butler, in preference to several others of his close advisers, in making important executive decisions.

Not so in the case of Butler and Admiral David D. Porter. In December 1864, when Porter commanded the North Atlantic Blockading Squadron, he proposed taking Wilmington, North Carolina, the port most offensive to the Union as a haven of blockade-runners. The plan included the use of Butler and his troops, and once the assault was launched, Butler failed miserably in pressing his end. During January 1865, Porter tried again—with a replacement for Butler—and Wilmington fell. Thereafter, Porter, who immediately following the Civil War served for four years as Superintendent of the Naval Academy, could not stand the sight of the Massachusetts politician.

A Democrat before the war, Butler found it advantageous to become a Republican afterward, since he aspired to run for Congress. The remaining obstacle was that the well-entrenched Republican Congressman from Butler's Lowell district had no intention of retiring. So Butler, who owned a tract of undeveloped land about forty miles from Lowell, at Ipswich Bay, on Cape Ann, in the Essex district, ran for Congress from there, although he was not a bona-fide resident, and won the election. Later he built an elaborate home on the shores of Ipswich Bay—complete with a yacht anchorage—and continually represented the Essex district in Congress until 1875.

Owning a yacht anchorage, Butler naturally needed a yacht. He bought two, but neither suited him, for they were insufficiently impressive for a lawyer and legislator of his stature. Naturally he knew of the *America,* just as millions throughout America knew of the *America,* but it is doubtful that until 1873 he made any strenuous effort to euchre the yacht away from the Naval Academy. A casual attempt, yes, and when that resulted in failure, he wisely bided his time.

The right moment came in 1873, coincident with Butler's

representation of Gazaway Bugg Lamar. By seeking for Lamar (successfully, as matters turned out) more than a million dollars in cotton-claim awards, surely Butler conferred upon him a favor, and since turnabout constituted fair play, it then behooved Lamar to make an all-out effort to satisfy Butler's heart's desire. How the trick was turned becomes a matter for later elucidation.

SEVEN

"The Yacht America *Is Advertised to Be Sold"*

IN THE LATE SUMMER of 1865, following the close of the Civil War, the Naval Academy returned to its permanent home at Annapolis after a four-year absence. With the Academy's small fleet of schoolships and practice vessels came the yacht *America,* sailed by First Classman Willard Herbert Brownson, from upstate New York. In after years, Brownson taught math at the Academy, was later its Superintendent, and during the Spanish-American War, while commanding the cruiser *Yankee,* seized a part of Cuba still of enormous importance to the United States—Guantanamo.

James Douglas Jerrold Kelley, a native of New York City, was the last candidate for admission to the Naval Academy to receive his appointment direct from President Lincoln. Duly graduated and commissioned, he rose to the rank of Commander and was retired for "incapacities incident to service." Kelley wrote extensively on naval subjects and yachting and served as a fleet commander of the New York Yacht Club. In one of his books, published in 1884, he spoke of a summer cruise aboard the *America* soon after the Civil War, saying:

> I know in my early service days we gloried in her as in no other thing which floated . . . and looking back I can recall many

a night when the peace and quiet . . . would be broken by the chorus of a hundred boyish voices singing:

> Where did she come from? New York town!
> Who was her skipper? Old Dick Brown!

And how heartily and with what faith we roared the rude old ballad, for there she was in all her beauty alongside of us, a tender to that little squadron which included those dear old dead and gone ships, all ancient sloops and frigates, the *Marion*, *Macedonian* and *Savannah*, wherein the middle-aged lieutenants of today were taught to hand, reef and steer and to keep an anchor watch.

George Dewey, the Vermonter who, as Admiral Dewey, became the "Hero of Manila Bay" during the Spanish-American War, was graduated from the Naval Academy in 1858. While serving with Farragut in 1862, he distinguished himself in the taking of New Orleans, and in 1867 he received his first shore assignment, as an administrative officer at Annapolis. In the course of that year and the next, as part of his duties, he had charge of the *America* and when weather permitted gave successive crews of midshipmen pointers on sailing.

Lieutenant Commander Montgomery Sicard, who had also served with Farragut at New Orleans, and who later assisted Admiral Porter in taking Wilmington, came to the Naval Academy in 1868 as head of the Ordnance Department. In his free time, Sicard gave Dewey a hand showing midshipmen how to handle the *America*.

Lieutenant Commander Richard Worsam Meade, the third of his name, was the son of Captain Richard Worsam Meade, U.S.N.; the grandson of Richard Worsam Meade, who had been navy agent at Cadiz, Spain; and the nephew of George Gordon Meade, the Union general who distinguished himself by stopping the Confederates at Gettysburg in July 1863. Lieutenant Commander Meade married Rebecca, the daughter of Admiral Hiram Paulding, in June 1865—two months after the close of the Civil War—and that fall he brought his bride to the Naval

Academy, where he had been appointed head of the Seamanship Department. He, too, sailed the *America* and gave instruction in her sailing, and some years later, in collaboration with Sicard, he wrote an ordnance manual the Navy adopted and published.

All told, the *America* served the Navy handsomely, and the Navy, somewhat belatedly, moved to repay her. In 1869, Admiral Porter, who had introduced the honor system at the Academy, finished his tour of duty as Superintendent there and was then asked by President Grant, recently inaugurated, to act as adviser to incoming Secretary of the Navy Adolph Borie, a Grant appointee who admittedly knew little of naval affairs. Porter gladly accepted the assignment and during the next several months virtually ran the Department. In this time he launched an extensive and needed program of repairing and refitting vessels damaged or worn by war service and placed the *America's* name on the list.

In December 1869, at the Washington Navy Yard, work done on the yacht cost the government $3,048.99, and in May 1870, at the New York Navy Yard, she ran up an additional bill, more than three times as large, of $10,342.45. Both in Washington and in New York the repairs came under the general supervision of Richard Worsam Meade, who by 1870 had progressed in rank from lieutenant commander to commander.

While Admiral Porter controlled the Navy Department, with Secretary Borie sitting twiddling his thumbs and wishing he had never accepted the post in Grant's Cabinet, General Ben Butler, by now a Congressman, launched his first attempt to acquire the *America.* He simply strode into Navy headquarters and announced his wants (so the story goes), and looked at first surprised and then annoyed, like a disgruntled charge customer of a department store, when no one offered to wrap the yacht up and hand her to him. Instead, Admiral Porter, a man noted for his courtesy, acted out of character. He rose from his desk and without saying a word showed Butler the door.

It is as well that the Navy spent the money it did, at the time it did, putting the *America* in shape. For soon the yacht would be called upon to serve as one of the defenders in the first challenge race for the trophy she had won nearly two decades before, the America's Cup. The challenge came from a wealthy Englishman, James Ashbury, who allegedly had taken up yachting to improve his social status.

The founder of Ashbury's fortune was his father, a wheelwright who had invented an underpinning that contributed to the comfort of passenger coaches on British railroads. Born and reared in the industrial city of Manchester, Ashbury, once he inherited his father's wealth, found for himself a more fashionable address in London and joined several yacht clubs, including the Royal Thames. Over the years he owned and raced a succession of yachts, one of which, the *Cambria,* a deep-keel schooner of 248 tons (New York measurement), happened to beat, in a race around the Isle of Wight in 1868, the *Sappho,* an American schooner just arrived in England from New York. Before the race the *Sappho* had not had time to discharge the several tons of extra ballast she had taken aboard in order to cross the Atlantic safely, and in her trial with the *Cambria* she was consequently not up to her best.

The hollow victory so inflated Ashbury's ego that he immediately wrote the New York Yacht Club challenging for the America's Cup. This first letter, together with others, demonstrated his ignorance of the terms under which the Club held the Cup and was permitted to offer it as a challenge trophy. Ashbury seemed to think, for instance, that in order to compete for the America's Cup he would have to wager a cup of equal value and that the contest would consist of "the best two out of three races around Long Island." Lastly, he persisted in calling the trophy the "Queen's Cup," but this was an error so often made that no one bothered to correct him.

For their part, the members of the New York Yacht Club's

race committee showed themselves capable of misinterpreting the spirit, if not the actual wording, of the Deed of Gift under which the Club kept the Cup. The committee contended that since the *America* had won her Cup in a contest involving numerous rivals, there was nothing improper about the *Cambria* trying for the trophy in a race just as thickly populated. And so finally when the *Cambria* did try—on August 8, 1870, after negotiating for the privilege for nearly two years—she found herself in the company of twenty-two other entries, seventeen of which started.

But vital differences distinguished the 1851 Isle of Wight affair from the race off New York nearly two decades later. In the former, the multitude of yachts entered belonged to a variety of clubs, and each attempted to achieve victory on her own. In the latter, all the participating yachts, excepting the *Cambria,* flew the colors of the New York Yacht Club. While the 1851 race had been yacht against yacht, the race of 1870 produced the effect of pitting the lone foreign challenger against a domestic fleet. Thankfully it can be said of the New York Yacht Club's race committee that, since 1870, this deviation—seeming or otherwise—from the true channel of sportsmanship has not been repeated. Now, for nearly a century, in each of the numerous tries to wrest the America's Cup away from America, the fate of the famous trophy has been decided by the swift movements of but one defending vessel per race.

By 1870 the New York Yacht Club had moved from its original clubhouse at Elysian Fields, Hoboken, and occupied a much more imposing residence at Clifton, on the shore of Staten Island, overlooking the Upper Bay of New York Harbor. The new clubhouse was a large Victorian structure of two stories, boasting a wide veranda, gingerbread in abundance, a cupola on top, and a lawn sloping down to a yacht anchorage.

For the purposes of the 1870 race, the Navy vested temporary title to the *America* in a member of the New York Yacht Club so that the yacht, the cause of it all, might participate.

Aboard was a carefully picked crew of midshipmen under the watchful eye of Commander Richard Worsam Meade, but Meade did not give orders. The man at the tiller who performed that vital function was a professional racing skipper—Charlie Brown, the son of "Old Dick" Brown, who had guided the *America* to her Isle of Wight victory.

Although August 8, the day of the race, was a Monday, so intense was public interest that many New York banks and brokerage offices closed, and trading on the Stock Exchange fell off sharply. The race course led from a start in the Upper Bay directly in front of the New York Yacht Club's clubhouse south through the Narrows separating Staten Island from Brooklyn; then southwest to and around a buoy marking Southwest Spit, a point of land off the New Jersey coast; then east to and around the Sandy Hook lightship anchored far out in Lower New York Bay; then by the same route back to the point of starting—a distance all told of 38 nautical miles.

Perhaps the best account of the race was written by Commander J. D. Jerrold Kelley, who while still in the Navy occasionally covered important yachting events for the New York *Herald*, and after retirement became a regular member of the *Herald's* staff. The salient features of Kelley's story of the first defense of the America's Cup follows:

> Throughout the country there was the greatest interest manifested in the result—the public prayer being for any yacht to beat the representative of the Royal Thames Club, but best of all that it might be the *America*. The course and conditions were those of the New York Yacht Club, and were admirably carried out.
>
> The flagboat was anchored abreast of the clubhouse, about midchannel, and the yachts were directed to anchor on an east and west line, a short distance to the northward. In taking position in line each yacht was allowed to select its own place, in the order of arrival at the anchorage.
>
> The day opened overcast and gloomy, and soon after daybreak heavy rain clouds brooded threateningly over the bay; but by

nine o'clock the sky shone bright and clear, and a brisk and cheery southerly breeze bravely blew landward.

It was emphatically a holiday. For the fair fame of the country was at stake, and all classes of our citizens were assembled to greet the foreign yacht which had pluckily sailed 3,000 miles of stormy sea to redeem a national defeat. Excursion boats overshadowed every ripple of water not occupied by contestants, and in odd mixture there were assembled men-of-war, traders, fruiters and pleasure boats. By 11 o'clock the gateway of the port was so blocked with vessels that it was impossible to get a view through the Narrows, of the horizon seaward or of the blue Monmouth hills beyond; while on either hand not only were the banks crowded with a cheering multitude, but Forts Hamilton and Lafayette to the eastward, and Forts Wadsworth and Tompkins to the westward, had their ramparts packed with thousands. At 11 o'clock the *Middletown* [the judges' boat] steamed down the line flying the burgee of the Club and it was evident that preparations were being made to start.

The line was beautifully formed, the yachts being separated by an even distance of 50 yards, with their heads riding to the ebb. There were in all 18 starters and of these the *Alarm* was at the extreme eastern end of the line, with *Widgeon* next, and then the *Silvie, Magic, Dauntless, Tarolinta, Halcyon, Madgie, Idler, Rambler, Phantom, Fleetwing, Madeleine, Calypso, America, Tidal Wave, Cambria*, and finally the *Alice*, which held the extreme western end. Choice of position had been granted the *Cambria*, and Mr. Ashbury had taken that near the clubhouse.

Public interest was mainly centered in the *Dauntless, America*, and *Cambria*, and before the start every steamer and passing sailing-craft accorded them the honors of a salute—too vociferous, too partisan, perhaps, at times, but still kindly meant, for the roughest of men are subdued by the influence of such a scene as this.

At 26 minutes past 11, on the very last of the ebb, and with a fresh wind, the starting-gun roared its orders to make sail and slip, and in a moment the yachts had spread their canvas, flattened their jibs, and then almost simultaneously turned seaward, the *Magic* [a centerboard schooner of 92 tons], one of the smallest of the squadron, leading. The windward boats had the best of it, and as they flew towards the Hook, they quickly left the others behind; among these was the *Cambria*, for she had been nearly the last to get away.

Off the lower quarantine the *America*, a short half-mile astern of the *Magic*, was rushing for a commanding position. Few of the yachts carried their gaff-topsails until near the Southwest Spit, the *Magic* keeping the lead, and rolling off knot after knot with a bone in her teeth and a furrow of foam astern, and standing up to her work under lower sails and all three jibs. Soon after she set her main-gaff-topsail and a staysail, which like a Japanese wrestler, gleamed and tugged on her forecastle, and in a moment, it seemed she wheeled round the Southwest Spit, with the *America* second and only four minutes behind. Nineteen minutes later, and tenth in number, the *Cambria* rounded the Spit; and then with lifted sheets, away they all rushed for the lightship off the Hook.

As the yachts neared this, thousands of waiting spectators gave them a most enthusiastic reception—guns roared, men cheered, bells rang, and bands burst into loud and brazen notes of triumph; and when the *Magic* rounded the lightship, making it almost a certainty that the cup was safe, there arose a shout painful in its intensity of delight. Nor was the *Cambria* forgotten, for although hopelessly behind—or perhaps for that reason—the pluck of her owner was recognized, cheers, steam-whistles and guns drowning the awful accompaniment of vagrant musicians, who struck up, with undoubted vigor and against time, what they politely meant for "God Save the Queen."

In the run from the Southwest Spit to the lightship, the *Idler* passed into second place, the *Dauntless* into third, and the *America* into fourth, while the *Magic* added another five minutes three seconds to her lead upon *Cambria*. In this order they ran for home, the wind blowing so strong and so free that the yachts were fairly flying in widening pools of foam, making 12 knots, and stretching their ropeyarns to the breaking point. Off the turn of the Hook there came a sudden puff, and the fore-topmast of the *Cambria* went over the side—the only accident of the day, and unfortunately, where it was most to be regretted.

The strength and beauty of the struggle was soon consummated by a glorious victory, for as the *Magic* rushed across the line it was in the fastest time ever made over the course. Not that she had much time or distance to spare, however, for the echoes of the welcoming cheers were still lingering in the green hills delineating the bay when the stately *Dauntless* passed by the mark, carrying the reverberations of the nation's delight into a further and a greater echo; and as these cheers roared and rumbled in the distance, the harbor, to its farthest limits, caught up a newer and a greater paean of joy, for the *America*, fourth in the race, flew by the finish line.

The *Cambria* arrived eighth on actual time (beaten all around, with and without handicaps), and tenth in order by time allowance.

Seasoned yachtsmen, while recognizing that the *America* had made a good showing in this first challenge race for her cup, nevertheless contended she would have done even better had she not been handicapped by her "Navy rig" and the "Navy cut" of her sails. It was an opinion naturally not held by the Navy, and for the rest of the time the Navy owned the *America* she participated in no further extracurricular contests.

On August 14, 1870—six days after the race off New York—the Navy's ranking admiral, David Glasgow Farragut, died, and Admiral Porter succeeded to his post. This meant that the nature of Porter's duties changed from the administrative to the operational, and no longer could he keep a protective eye on the doings in the Secretary's office. Indeed, the Secretary was not now the same individual, for a short while back, Adolph Borie had resigned the naval portfolio and President Grant had named in his stead George Maxwell Robeson.

A 40-year-old New Jersey lawyer, Robeson had for more than ten years subsisted largely on the fruits of three previous political jobs. A critic of Robeson laughingly suggested that since the gentleman from New Jersey had a reputation for being a first-rate judge of wines, a second-rate trout fisherman, and a third-rate attorney, he might very well prove to be a fourth-rate Secretary of the Navy. Ben Butler, however, appears to have held a more charitable view, for he took the trouble to cultivate

Robeson, and gradually the new Secretary came to look upon the Congressman from Massachusetts as his friend.

By the spring of 1873 the alliance had so ripened that Butler felt he could ask of Robeson almost any favor, including that of selling the *America.* Luckily, at just this time Butler had his client Gazaway Bugg Lamar beholden to him, for he was then handling Lamar's suits for cotton seizures against the Treasury totaling more than a million dollars. Luckily, too, Lamar was a resident of Savannah, Georgia, from which port the *America* was known to have run the blockade, and in addition, as head of the Importing & Exporting Company of Georgia, Lamar, during the war, had owned blockade-runners. It therefore followed, by Butler's logic, that Lamar had owned the *America*—and indeed still owned her, unless the Navy could prove otherwise.

Such proof, while Robeson was in charge, the Navy either could not (by reason of the missing prize-court papers) or did not care to produce. So Robeson fell in with Butler's wishes and ordered the *America* sold. According to law, such a sale had to be at public auction, advertised a month in advance. Consequently this notice was placed in a select and limited number of newspapers:

Navy Department
Bureau of Construction and Repair
Washington, May 20, 1873

The Navy Department will offer for sale at public auction at the United States Naval Academy, Annapolis, on Friday, the 20th day of June next, at 12 o'clock noon, the United States Schooner *America,* with masts, spars, sails, rigging, &c., as she now lies.

An inventory of the articles to be sold with her may be seen on application to the superintendent of the Naval Academy at Annapolis.

The government reserves the right to withdraw the vessel from sale at any time, and to reject any bid or offer which may be considered inadequate.

In addition, at around the same time, there was a brief story in the weekly *Army and Navy Journal* about the forthcoming sale, which gave something of the *America*'s history. It told of her triumphs in England in 1851, touched upon her Civil War experiences, and then said, "She has been somewhat altered and is not so fast now, though she is still a very rapid sailer." The story is notable for its failure to question the Navy's motives in disposing of the historic yacht.

To a certain extent the omission was compensated for by a letter published May 31, 1873, in the New York *Herald* signed "A Voice of the Navy." It may have been written by Commander J. D. Jerrold Kelley, for he possessed both an intimate connection with the *Herald* and what proved to be prophetic knowledge of Washington politics. The letter is here given in full:

> I notice by the papers that the yacht *America* is advertised to be sold. We may next expect to see the old *Constitution* so advertised. No vessel of the Navy has a more national reputation than the *America*. No one can forget the exultation over the country when the news came that she had won the cup against England's swiftest yachts. The Navy is disgusted with the intended sale of this vessel, which is dear to every officer and midshipman who served at the Academy since 1863. Is nothing in the Navy to be held sacred under the ruling that has governed the service for the past four years? The attempt to sell this vessel is a dishonest one and some favorite of the Navy Department will buy her for a mere song. Let the naval officers rise up in protest.

No uprising occurred, and plans for the sale went on apace. Isaiah Hanscom, the Navy's Chief of the Bureau of Construction and Repair (whose rank corresponded with that of a commodore), ordered one of his subordinates, Theodore Delavan Wilson, a professor of Ship Construction at the Naval Academy, to head a two-man board charged with the duty of appraising the "probable value" of the *America* and the articles belonging to her. While such an order was routine as a means of determining what price a vessel sold at auction should fetch, the concluding sentence in Hanscom's instructions to Wilson seemed strange. For that sentence read: "As it is important that your estimate should be strictly private, you will be careful that it be made with no one present but yourselves, and that no copy be kept, and that the original be handed to the Honorable Secretary of the Navy by the senior member of the board in person."

Hanscom gave no reason for super-secrecy. If it was to insure fair, competitive bidding for benefit to the government's pocketbook, its purpose was laudable. But if it was to provide the Secretary of the Navy with a figure in dollars that he might alter as he saw fit and then pass along to some favored bidder, its purpose was disgraceful.

As the date of the sale approached, William Voorhis, owner of the yacht *Tidal Wave*, announced to his fellow members in the New York Yacht Club that he planned to visit Annapolis and buy the *America*. Voorhis made the trip, only to return empty-handed. On reaching the Naval Academy, he later explained, he had been informed that the Government could not guarantee title. What was being sold had amounted merely to whatever rights and interest the Government possessed in the yacht, and those had seemed so nebulous to Voorhis that he had not risked his money.

Other potential bidders met with the same frustrating situation. One, however, did not permit the conditions of the sale to disturb him. This individual, John Cassels, bore a name hitherto unknown in the world of yachting. Cassels bid $5,000 and after an absurdly few moments had rushed by and there was no other bid, the *America* was knocked down to him.

The New York Times, in its issue for Sunday, June 22, 1873, ran a front-page account of the sale, but devoted to it only a single paragraph containing less than a hundred words. The story, dated at Washington on June 21, made no mention whatever of John Cassels, probably for the reason that the *Times* reporter had picked up no biographical data concerning him. Following is what the account said:

> The United States yacht *America* was sold at the Naval Academy yesterday for $5,000. The Secretary of the Navy has to ratify the sale to make it valid. The Government guarantees no title. It is supposed the reason for this is that there may be some who never gave up their right to prize-money from her when she was presented to the Government by a part, at least, of her captors. There was only one bid.

Among those who could have disputed the "prize-money" feature of this news item were Admiral Du Pont and Thomas Holdup Stevens, for both had known the exact circumstances under which the *America*'s salvors turned her over to the Navy for prize-court adjudication, with no strings attached. But by June 1873, Du Pont had been long dead, and Stevens, after 35 years in the Navy, had been promoted from captain to commodore only a few months before and rewarded by assignment from the European Squadron to the Naval Station at Norfolk, with the first shore duty he had enjoyed in quite a while. Thus it might have been not only insubordinate, but certainly impolitic and perhaps destructive of his career for Stevens to have opened his mouth now. Stevens probably felt that if Secretary Robeson wanted it thought that the Navy was without clear title to the *America,* so be it. And Stevens probably also felt that if by fostering such a story the Secretary accommodated some friend, so be that as well.

Such long-ago attitudes, however, should not alter history. Recently, in reply to a pertinent inquiry concerning the *America* made for the purposes of this book, a great-grandson of Stevens wrote, "It has always been gospel in the family that our forebear not only declined his personal share in an award, but was sufficiently endowed in forensics to persuade his crew to forego theirs—a not inconsiderable feat."

A week after the auction, information concerning John Cassels became public knowledge. During the Civil War, as a lieutenant colonel in the Union Army, he had been provost marshal of a military sector in Virginia for a time occupied by the troops of General Butler, and ever since, he and Butler had been thick.

In buying the *America,* Cassels had merely fronted for Butler, and once the Navy signed the yacht over to him, he in turn transferred title to his crony.

Thus Butler got the *America* through a number of intricate, if not devious, devices. Via a dummy bidder. Via the circulation of a story that the salving crew might claim her. And via the circulation of yet another story that the yacht had belonged—and still belonged—to Gazaway Bugg Lamar, of Savannah, who would seek to regain possession.

Information regarding these various gambits emerged during an investigation of possible frauds in the Navy while the Department was administered by Secretary George Maxwell Robeson. A House committee of the 44th Congress, 1st Session, conducted hearings, which went on during the late spring and early summer of 1876. The principal witness called to provide evidence concerning the sale of the *America* was Isaiah Hanscom, chief of the Navy's Bureau of Construction and Repair, and his testimony taken on June 23, was subsequently published by the Government in a *House Miscellaneous Document.*

After being sworn as a witness, Hanscom was first questioned by a Mr. Hill, appearing for the committee, and the exchange between them went in part thus:

> Q. Do you know anything about the yacht *America,* its purchase or sale?
>
> A. Yes; I know something about it.
>
> Q. When was that yacht purchased?
>
> A. There was one sold to General Butler; that is the one I am speaking about now. The old yacht *America* had been sunk in trying to run the blockade, but was taken up by the Government officers and crew. It was never passed through a prize court, I believe, but was taken by the Government for its own use.
>
> Q. What was that yacht worth?
>
> A. I cannot tell you.
>
> Q. Was she condemned by a board?
>
> A. No, sir.

Q. She was ordered to be sold, was she?

A. She was ordered to be sold; that is, the right the Government had in her was ordered to be sold. That right was appraised before the sale.

Q. What did she bring?

A. $5,000.

Q. How many bidders were at the sale?

A. I do not know.

Q. I understand there was but one. How is that?

A. I do not know.

Q. Was there not a protest made against that sale?

A. Not to my knowledge.

Q. Who was the purchaser?

A. That I cannot tell you, but it will appear from the papers.

By his last question, Mr. Hill meant the purchaser of record, and Chief Constructor Hanscom understood it as such. One of the exhibits at the hearing, produced at this point, showed that John Cassels had made the lone, successful bid.

Q. Did you authorize the sale of vessels without their being condemned by a board of officers?

A. This was appraised by a board of officers.

Q. But not condemned to be sold?

A. I do not know whether condemned to be sold or not. She was of no use to the Government.

Q. That is the very object of a board, is it not, to see whether she is of any use to the Government?

A. Yes, but everybody knew she was of no use.

Q. Who objected to the confirmation of her sale when she was sold?

A. I do not know. Some officer sent a protest against her being sold, or a letter or statement about it.

Q. If the yacht *America* was repaired by order of any officer of the Navy, state the facts concerning it.

A. She was repaired at a cost of a little over $19,000.

Q. On whose order?

A. Admiral Porter's.

Apparently Hanscom suffered from nervousness while testifying, for he contradicted himself on first denying there had been no protest against the sale and then admitting as much. Also, he erred in overstating by nearly $6,000 the amount the Navy had spent on repairing the *America* during her Academy service. When Mr. Hill was done with Hanscom, Secretary of the Navy Robeson, in a friendlier manner, asked questions seemingly more to the Chief Constructor's liking.

Q. As to the yacht *America,* what was she good for?
A. She would do very well to go out on a pleasure excursion.
Q. What was she ever used for in the Navy?
A. For a pleasure boat.
Q. Did she ever go to New York?
A. Yes, she went to New York and sailed in the yacht race.
Q. Did she ever do any other duty in the Navy?
A. Not that I know of.
Q. She was advertised for sale at the Naval Academy?
A. Yes, sir.
Q. Do you know that the Government had really any title to her except that of possession?
A. That was all.
Q. Had she ever been condemned by a prize court?
A. We never had any information of it.
Q. Had not her former owner instituted, or was he not about instituting proceedings to get her back—Mr. Lamar, of Savannah?
A. I was told so.
Q. What did we advertise to sell?
A. All the right and title which the Government had in her.

Had he been available, Gazaway Bugg Lamar would have made an interesting witness to affirm or deny his alleged ownership of the *America* and his reputed threat to regain possession of her. But Lamar, as Ben Butler and Secretary Robeson very well knew, was not available and never would be, for he had died more than a year and a half before, on October 5, 1874, at the home of his married daughter in New York. Lamar's last will and testament revealed anew a redeeming aspect of his character. For all his faults, he had never approved the noxious activities of his son, the late Charles A. L. Lamar, as a slave runner, and two of the bequests he made so indicate. By one, he left $100,000 to a home in Savannah for aged Negroes, and by the other an identical amount to such a home in Macon, Georgia.

The crafty moves on the chessboard of politics by which Ben Butler got possession of the *America* served as only a minor feature of the revelations resulting from the House committee's investigation of the Navy Department while Butler's pal, George Robeson, held sway as Secretary. Other evidence disclosed that for a contractor to sell the Navy supplies or materials there were palms to be crossed. While on taking office Robeson had been able to show a net worth of but $20,000, during his incumbency as Secretary he deposited, in his personal accounts in three separate banks, close to $320,000, and in addition permitted a member of one contracting firm to buy for him a piece of expensive property at Long Branch, New Jersey.

Even so, the committee's hearing room constituted no courtroom, and there was no sworn jury to bring in a verdict. Although various minor functionaries in the Navy Department suffered suspension or dismissal, Robeson and his upper-echelon aides got off with only implied and not formal censure. However, following the end of Grant's administration, and hard on the coming of President Rutherford B. Hayes and his new Secretary of the Navy, Chief Naval Constructor Isaiah Hanscom, after 21 years of service, handed in his resignation.

It has been written that Ben Butler, later in life and when among his intimates, often laughed and joked over his tactics in scaring off competition and snapping up the *America* dirt cheap. In addition to creating the illusory Lamar claim, he had (so the story goes) instructed John Cassels to threaten a lawsuit should anyone else put in a bid at the auction.

While this story may be true, it is quite definitely true that Butler was publicly sensitive regarding the matter. His sensitivity increased, the older he grew, with the decline of his political fortunes. In 1884, as candidate of the off-beat Greenback Party, he ran for the Presidency and was overwhelmingly whipped by Grover Cleveland. Soon after Cleveland's inauguration, Butler wrote an article (or had it done for him by James Parton, his ghost writer) entitled "The Story of the 'America'," which appeared in the July, 1885, issue of *Harper's New Monthly Magazine* and is so shot through with errors as to constitute a classic of the genre.

The Butler piece starts off by committing the usual sin of calling the trophy won by the *America* in her 1851 race around the Isle of Wight the "Queen's Cup," and then goes on to repeat as fact the fiction of the Signal Master's lament to Victoria, "Ah, Your Majesty, there is no second!"

Ten years later, according to the Butler article, the yacht, on being seen by "an American gentleman, who was then living in the South, and who has every qualification now to represent his country abroad, purchased her as a Confederate cruiser, put on her a heavy gun, and named her the *Memphis*."

The two errors in the above quotation were doubtless intentional. The first, a crack at President Cleveland, took him to task for appointing to diplomatic posts in foreign lands a number of former Confederates who had campaigned for his election. And yet, in making the statement, Butler, perhaps without realizing it, contradicted his earlier contention that it had been the late Gazaway Bugg Lamar who bought the *America* for use in the Southern cause.

As for error number two, it helped to substantiate a bit of fiction Butler had for long spread among guests sailing with him aboard the *America*. Often such guests admired a handsome ship's bell adorning the yacht, and to explain the inscription on the bell—"*Memphis*, 1862"—Butler was accustomed to say she had borne that name while under the flag of the Confederacy. Actually, the Southern Government had never owned a sailing vessel called *Memphis*. But in 1862, when Farragut took New Orleans, the *Memphis*, an 18-gun Confederate floating battery

—a large, barge-like affair towed by a tug—fell victim to the assault. Butler and his troops entered New Orleans shortly thereafter. Conceivably, considering Butler's penchant for grabbing up all the bells he could find in the occupied city and shipping them home to Massachusetts, he appropriated the bell from the floating battery. If so, this would account for the nativity of the bell that wound up on the yacht.

Next, Butler's article damned Admiral Porter for the money he had caused to be spent on the *America* during her service at the Naval Academy after the war. While the record showed $13,400-odd and Isaiah Hanscom's testimony before the House committee had inflated the sum to $19,000, now Butler jumped it to an alleged $25,000. Porter had wasted this Government money, wrote Butler (or his ghost), so that the *America* might sail in a race "against the *Livonia,* an English yacht which came over here." Actually, never in her entire career did the *America* race *Livonia.*

Indeed, Butler (or his ghost) got so fouled up in the writing of the *Harper's* article that he misstated the year during which he had acquired the *America,* calling it 1871, instead of 1873. Also, the article made a revelation, hitherto unpublicized, that Butler had had a partner in buying the yacht, Colonel Jonas H. French, of Boston. During the war, Colonel French had been Butler's provost marshal during the occupation of New Orleans, and after Butler (accused of fiscal irregularities and maltreatment of the citizenry) had been recalled from New Orleans, Colonel French stayed on as provost marshal general to the military governor of Louisiana. For a time after the war, Butler and Colonel French were co-investors in a quarrying enterprise that sold granite to the Government for the construction of public buildings in the District of Columbia.

If, in fact, Colonel French did put money in the *America,* he wasted it, for he never had use of her. Throughout nearly twenty years, in appropriate seasons, Butler raced the *America* and cruised in her, and after his death she was sailed by his heirs. As for the physical good of the yacht, she could not have fallen into hands more considerate than Butler's, for regardless of expense, he lavished upon her the tenderest care. To sail her, he employed skilled captains and crews—smartly uniformed and highly paid—and whenever she was in need of refitting or repair, the best diagnosticians and surgeons specializing in yachts had her as their patient.

Butler, who delighted in the backstairs areas of politics and in tricky courtroom maneuvers, showed the more gentlemanly side of his nature to his fellow yachtsmen. Most regattas accepted him as an entrant, although from a few he was barred. Often, however, he failed to receive invitations to social functions held in the clubhouses of the more exclusive yachting organizations. Such omissions were due not alone to his reputation, but to his manner and appearance. Robert Schenck, a Congressman from Ohio, once said of Butler, "I always think of old Ben as a cross-eyed cuttlefish swimming about in waters of his own muddying." And David Miller Dewitt, a journalist of Butler's time, described him as possessing "a face, once seen, not to be forgotten. The broad forehead shelving up to the top of the bald crown, the fringe of thin hair encircling the lower head, the eyes asquint and half-hidden by pointed lids, the sharp nose with its nervous sniff, the spasmodic puffing out of the cheeks, the turned-down collar exposing the wide throat, and the right hand uplifted in the attitude of affirming without a book—these striking peculiarities betokened the appearance of Benjamin F. Butler."

At 25, Butler had married Sarah Hildreth, an actress of great beauty. During the Civil War, she was with him for much of the time that he occupied New Orleans, and later, when his forces threatened Richmond, only to be driven back and "bottled up" elsewhere in Virginia, she wrote him, "I actually have bought a carriage hat of straw, white velvet and a long white feather. I thought it would but barely answer to grace the taking of Richmond. I will instantly send it home and order it put in the darkest closet in the attic."

At that time the Butlers could boast but a single home, in

Lowell. After the war they built on their plot of land (eventually extended to 47 acres) on the shores of Ipswich Bay, Cape Ann, a large summer showplace near Bay View. In addition, as Butler's income increased, he maintained in New York a permanent suite of rooms in the Fifth Avenue Hotel (then at 23rd Street); and in Washington, at 220 New Jersey Avenue SE, he built a fabulous mansion of granite which was eventually sold to the Government for $277,000.

Sarah Butler bore four children, three of whom lived to adulthood—a daughter, Blanche, born in 1847, and two sons, Paul and Ben Israel, born respectively in 1852 and 1854. In 1870, Blanche married a man twelve years her senior, Major General Adelbert Ames, who during the Civil War had been awarded the Congressional Medal of Honor and afterwards became the Reconstruction Governor of Mississippi.

As a youth, Paul Butler met with an accident which so injured his legs that for the balance of his life he could walk only with difficulty. Even so, he became a strong swimmer, a champion oarsman, and a yachting and iceboat enthusiast. For the sailing iceboat he invented a sliding seat that permitted the ready shifting of weight. While Ben Butler damned Harvard College for what he claimed were its cultural pretensions, he nevertheless had his son Paul educated there, in order to procure for him what he called "a patent of Massachusetts nobility." After graduation, Paul became an executive of one of the several business enterprises in which his father had financial interest, the U.S. Cartridge Company. General Butler also owned part of a gold mine; shares in a Colorado ranch spread over 100,000 acres; a factory turning out flags and bunting for the G.A.R. and various patriotic and political organizations; and stock in the Middlesex Company, a Lowell textile mill which in one year alone paid him dividends of more than $100,000.

While a Congressman, Butler appointed his younger son, Ben Israel, to West Point. His dislike for the Military Academy exceeded even his enmity for Harvard, for he attributed all of his tactical troubles during the Civil War to the stupidities and cupidities of officers of the regular army. He felt that West Pointers operated as a clique and that they always stood ready to cover up the errors of one another and saddle blame on the shoulders of volunteer officers. In the event of another war, Butler wanted Ben Israel eligible for membership in the elite group. After graduation from the Military Academy, Ben Israel served for a time as a lieutenant assigned to a regiment on the Western plains and then resigned his commission in order to study law at Columbia, preparatory to entering practice with his father.

Following the auction of June 20, 1873, Ben Butler sent to Annapolis a party of men to take possession of his purchase, the yacht *America.* His son Paul, then 21 years of age, led the group, which included a Gloucester sea captain and a half-dozen of his sailors. The contingent reached Annapolis on June 26 and on inspecting the yacht found her riding high at her anchorage for lack of ballast. During the preceding several days, more than 25 tons of lead had been removed from the *America,* and it was the contention of Naval Academy authorities that this valuable metal had not been included in the sale.

Paul Butler found it impossible to reach Secretary of the Navy Robeson, who was absent from Washington seeing to the outfitting of the *Tigress,* a vessel recently purchased by the Navy for an Arctic rescue expedition. Young Paul bargained as best he could with the Academy people and ended up accepting some 20 tons of iron shot as substitute ballast. With the *America* thus weighted—but insufficiently so—the Gloucestermen sailed her down the Severn River, then farther south down Chesapeake Bay, and at the Virginia capes anchored in the lee of Fortress Monroe to await the cessation of a storm raging out in the Atlantic.

By July 5, weather reports indicated that a safe passage north could be anticipated. Consequently the yacht ran through the capes and began her long offshore trek for Massachusetts. The weather reports, no more accurate in 1873 than they are today, proved wrong, and for two weeks the *America,* tied to the surface of an angry sea by bonds of ballast improperly placed and too light for the job, pitched and yawed as she beat toward the harbor of her new owner.

On July 20, wonder of wonders, she made it. Along the way she had lost only a fore-topmast, if the linings of the stomachs of some of those aboard her were not taken into account. Coincident with the dropping of her anchor in General Butler's harbor at Bay View, word of her arrival spread throughout the countryside, and several hundred Cape Ann residents, driven by curiosity, came trekking to the scene. Butler, ever the politician, took advantage of the opportunity to make a speech and rewarded the crowd with a generous number of patriotic sentiments, as always.

In August, the *America* sailed on business to the Charlestown Navy Yard. Aboard she carried a retired naval officer, who was both a friend of Butler's and a friend of a Yard executive. The officer announced at the Yard that he wished to make a trade: So many tons of iron shot for a larger quantity of pigs of lead cast especially for use as ballast. The Yard executive nodded his understanding and the deal went through, with the *America* the gainer and only the American taxpayer the loser.

Owning the *America* so inflated Butler's already inflated ego that, although he was still a Congressman, he felt he should seek the Republican nomination for Governor of Massachusetts. Failing to get it, he massaged his injured pride by joining the Boston Yacht Club and ordering from his tailor a nautical costume worthy of a Gilbert and Sullivan operetta. During the yachting season of 1873, Butler entered his *America* in no race, but she did serve as a judges' boat during a regatta staged by the Boston Yacht Club.

During 1874, Butler broadened his yachting activities. In June, the captain he employed for the *America* succeeded in grounding her on Ram's Horn Shoal, Salem Bay, and by so doing ushered himself out of a job. His successor, Captain James H. Reid, a veteran Boston Harbor pilot, worked for Butler for the next fourteen years, and the two got along beautifully together, for both possessed fluent vocabularies of invective and each refused to take any guff from the other. In August, in a regatta open to all comers staged by the proprietor of a popular Isles of Shoals hotel, Captain Reid brought the *America* first across the finish line in a field of eleven topnotch yachts—a feat that permitted Butler to crow with delight. For years afterward, in his frequent tellings and retellings of the story, he usually neglected to say that the *America*, technically speaking, had not actually won the race. On the basis of time allowance, she lost narrowly to *Vindex*.

In the spring of 1875, Butler had the *America* completely overhauled in the East Boston yard of the famous shipbuilder Donald McKay. She received new masts stepped at a rake not so pronounced as formerly, a new main-topmast, a foreboom, a new jib boom, and new sails. Moreover, she was refurbished below and her staterooms made more comfortable. Lastly, the means by which she had been steered for 24 years—a tiller—was done away with in favor of a spoked wheel. While these alterations could have cost a lot of money, it is doubtful that Butler coughed up the full price. In 1873 he had secured for McKay a Navy Department contract to build the two sloops-of-war *Adams* and *Essex*, for which the Government paid nearly $800,000. McKay's work on the *America* was just about his last, for even then he was suffering from tuberculosis. He soon closed his business and bought the farm on which he died in 1880.

On July 24, 1875, Butler entered the *America* in a second open regatta sponsored by the Isles of Shoals hotel proprietor so eager thus to publicize his establishment. The race, run over a triangular course, resulted in a fiasco, for while it was in progress the judges transferred from one boat to another, thereby changing the finish line, without informing each of the several contestants of their intention. Rather than argue over the prize, a silver punch bowl, all of the yachtsmen except two sailed away. The two were Ben Butler and "Uncle" Rufus Hatch, the famous broker who at one point in his career had become so angry with the New York Stock Exchange that he opened a rival trading mart, which he subsequently sold to the older exchange at a profit.

In a manner redolent with some of the features of this fiscal transaction, Butler and Hatch (owner of the *Resolute*) sailed a private race for the punch bowl, which the *America* won. Then Hatch challenged Butler to six races, one a day for six days, with wagers of $1,000 a side on each match. But Butler, whose gambler's instinct told him that the time to quit was when he was ahead of the game, claimed his silver punch bowl and with it secure in his grasp sailed home to Bay View.

The year 1876 proved to be the most disturbing of Butler's career. It saw the end of his fifth term in Congress, to which body he had not been re-elected, and of the investigation by Congress of the Navy Department, disclosing the corrupt practices of Secretary Robeson, a feature of those revelations being the noxious aura surrounding the sale of the *America.*

In March 1876, there came to Butler a cry for help from General Adelbert Ames, his son-in-law in Mississippi. Ames, charged with accepting bribes as Reconstruction Governor of the state, admitted to Butler that his conviction was a virtual certainty should he stand trial. Needing a mediator, Butler cannily chose Roger Pryor of Virginia, a former Confederate general admired throughout the South, who had not long since begun practicing law in New York City. Pryor hurried to Mississippi and on April 3 wrote Butler, "I opened negotiations with the leading men against us, with many of whom I had old and intimate associations, and, after a strenuous struggle, it was arranged that they should dismiss the charges, and then the Governor should resign."

Although Butler thus saved his son-in-law, he knew of no strings to pull that would spare him his wife. For years she had suffered from a thyroid tumor eventually diagnosed as malignant. While a patient in Massachusetts General Hospital, Sarah Butler died of cancer on April 8, only a few days after receiving the good news from Mississippi that her daughter's husband would not be publicly branded a felon.

Perhaps to get his mind off his family troubles Butler sailed the *America* almost constantly throughout the summer. In June, in an ocean race from Sandy Hook to Five Fathom lightship—a course out and back measuring over 250 miles—he pitted his yacht against the *Alarm*, owned by George L. Kingsland, then serving his last year as Commodore of the New York Yacht Club. There was almost no wind. It took the *America* nearly 44 hours to cover the course. Even so, she came in first—by a wide margin—for it took the *Alarm* 10 hours longer.

That summer saw the centennial of the founding of the Republic, an event celebrated by an International Exposition properly held at Philadelphia. Impelled by both patriotic and political motives, Butler, in early July, set sail for the Exposition, only to come a cropper off the New Jersey coast. The *America* struck a sunken wreck, tore her bottom, and began leaking badly. Luckily a passing tug noted her distress and gave her a tow to a Stapleton, Staten Island, shipyard where she was laid up for two weeks undergoing repairs. No doubt the job would have taken longer had not Butler supplemented the pay of the yard's workmen with as much beer as they could drink.

In late July, Butler entered the *America* in a race for the Brenton's Reef Cup, a trophy offered by James Gordon Bennett, Jr., son of the founder of the New York *Herald* and a former commodore of the New York Yacht Club. The race was from Sandy Hook lightship to Brenton's Reef lightship off Newport, and return. In a field of five starters, the *America* came in last. Butler, in his article appearing in *Harper's New Monthly Magazine* nine years later, attributed the *America*'s defeat to her bobstay's breaking at a critical juncture in the race. It was a new bobstay, he declared, but made from a defective piece of iron and installed at the prow of the *America* by a New York mechanic shortly before the race, as a replacement for the yacht's original bobstay put on her back in 1851.

Butler, ever the realist in law and in politics, often regarded the *America* through eyes so misty with idealism that the boasts he made concerning her, and the excuses he gave to explain away her occasional failures, are not always to be believed. In the *Harper's* article, for instance, he mysteriously erred by two years in placing the date of the Brenton's Reef Cup race (calling it 1878 instead of 1876), and in addition he overlooked the fact—if he knew of it—that the America had given her bob-stay a wrenching fracture at least once before. That fracture had occurred back in June 1863, while the yacht, sailed by Lieutenant Theodore Kane and a crew of midshipmen, had been sent off to search for the marauding Confederate will-o'-the-wisp, Charlie Read.

In August 1876 occurred another challenge match for the America's Cup. This time the challenger, *Countess of Dufferin,* a large centerboard schooner, represented the Royal Canadian Yacht Club, of Toronto, and the Cup was defended by the *Madeline,* another large centerboard schooner, owned by John S. Dickerson. It was a best-two-out-of-three series, and the *Madeline* won easily the first race, run over the New York Yacht Club's inside course.

The second race, held the next day, did not begin until noon, for lack of a breeze all morning. The course lay SSE from a mark-boat in New York Harbor, 20 miles out to sea and back, and soon after the start the two contenders mysteriously materialized into three. Seemingly out of nowhere, the *America* appeared and ran with the racers, but at a sufficient distance from them so as not to interfere with their maneuvers. General Butler steered the old yacht himself, and it was noted that he had aboard a large and gay party of guests, including several ladies. The *Madeline* won the race, and thus the series, beating the *Countess of Dufferin* (and making safe the Cup) by nearly a half-hour. But the judges, for the sake of sentiment, also timed the *America,* and she lost to the *Madeline* by only 7 minutes and 4 seconds. With some justification, Butler, for the balance of his days, claimed he had outsailed both yachts, for in keeping wide of the course he had covered a considerably greater distance than either.

For the next eight years, Butler, busy with his law practice, his diversified business interests, and above all with politics, indulged in no formal yacht races. During this period, however, he used the *America* extensively for both short and long vacation cruises, and no yachting season passed in which she was not in commission, manned by Captain Reid and a full crew. Also during this period, Butler acquired a brass cannon three feet in length which fired round shot about the size of a baseball. Butler christened the gun "Lady Pummel," possibly for the reason that with a projectile propelled by a heavy charge of black powder she could deliver a terrific blow. Normally, however, Butler fired the cannon blank—signaling other yachts and announcing his entrance to and departure from various ports—and took boyish delight in doing so.

In 1877, Butler's son Paul, crippled though he was, made use of some of the tenacity and foresight he had inherited from his father by undertaking a long trip to Russia. He traveled as representative of a family business, the U.S. Cartridge Company, with the purpose of selling the Czar a huge supply of ammunition for Russia's war with Turkey. The journey, precisely timed, resulted successfully. Delay would have spelled failure, for the Russo-Turkish conflict ended in 1878.

Also in 1878—on September 24—James Alexander Hamilton, a member of the original syndicate responsible for the building of the *America,* died at the age of 90. A few years before, he had published his own *Reminiscences* and another volume vindicating the fiscal policies of his famous father, and so his life's work was done.

Two months later in 1878, Ben Butler scattered his political shots by running both for Congress and for the Massachusetts gubernatorial chair. While in the former race he once again hit the target, he missed in the latter by a deflection in aim that infuriated him. He could not understand (nor has history been able precisely to explain) why the electorate of his home commonwealth, several times willing that he should represent them in Washington, remained so hesitant about making him their chief domestic executive.

During the summer of 1879, Butler, his son Paul, and a party of friends enjoyed a cruise of several weeks aboard the *America* to Nova Scotia and the Gulf of St. Lawrence. In inviting one guest, Butler wrote a letter that thoroughly disputed the claim of his enemies that he could not be warm, charming, and amusing (without resorting to vituperation) when he tried.

> I suppose you know the qualifications of a yachtsman [the letter said] . . . to wit, to be able to eat and drink unlimitedly, not to be seasick more than one-half the time and keep good-natured under difficulties if any occur, especially in drizzly weather, and to be able to play any ordinary game of cards except Kino, which is strictly forbidden on the ground that it requires so much mathematics as to be inadmissible. The outfit will need to be the thickest possible clothing and roughest clothing, a rubber overcoat and cap if you desire to be on deck when it rains and a reasonable supply of the latest novels in case the yacht library should not be sufficient.

In Butler's time, the term of a Massachusetts governor ran for one year only, from January to January. In the fall of 1879, after returning from the cruise to Nova Scotia, Butler again sought the office. To finance his campaign he reputedly laid out more than $200,000, but the expenditure availed him nothing.

In 1880, Butler had the *America*'s hull rebuilt in the East Boston shipyard of Daniel D. Kelley. While heretofore her deck beyond the stern had protruded but little, she was now given a much more pronounced overhang, which increased her total length to a bit more than 107 feet. The eagle on her transom, a substitute for the original purloined in England, received fresh coats of gilt; her bow was sharpened and her interior modernized; and the break in her deck forward of the mainmast underwent elimination in favor of a flush deck. All these alterations, structural and otherwise—plus the replacement of rotted timbers wherever found—ran up a Kelley bill for Butler of $15,000, which Butler refused to pay. The two argued and wrangled; Butler finally settled for $12,000; and he and Kelley, both of whom apparently throve on bickering, parted even better friends than before.

In early 1881, Butler planned a cruise aboard the *America* to Mexico and the West Indies. Even then, he contemplated writing his memoirs (with professional help), for rarely was there a surviving Civil War general of stature who did not sooner or later do so. Butler invited James Parton to sail with him. Parton, the author of several biographies, had already published a book about the Federal occupation of New Orleans favorable to Butler. Also, Butler felt that such a cruise would benefit the health of his sons. He was worried particularly about Ben Israel. Of late, this younger boy had been sick a great deal.

On Washington's Birthday, the *America,* sailed by Captain Reid, cleared Boston for Fortress Monroe, where she was scheduled to pick up Butler, Parton, and the others of the party. However, while passing through Nantucket Sound, the yacht went aground on a shoal and hung there. The steamer *Hunter* came along and hauled her off, and the only damage she suffered was that contained in a demand from Captain Davis, of the *Hunter.* He wanted a salvage fee of $400.

Captain Reid thought this exorbitant, offered $100, and when that was rejected, sailed away. Davis, telling something other than the truth of the incident, complained to the Coast Guard, and the cutter *Dexter* set off in pursuit of the yacht. She was halted by a shot across her bows, but when the officer commanding the *Dexter* had heard Reid's story of Davis's greed, he expressed his disgust and permitted the *America* to continue on her way.

On March 2 the yacht entered Hampton Roads, tied up at Fortress Monroe, and Butler, his sons, Parton, and other guests came aboard. Without further mishap, the *America* cruised in Southern waters for more than two months, and ever afterward Butler enjoyed telling the story of the 400-mile run she had made from Nassau to Havana in 40 hours.

In May, while at Bay View, Butler received frantic word from his daughter, Blanche Ames, that her eldest child, Butler —named for his grandfather—was ill of diphtheria in New York City. Blanche wished to bring the boy to Massachusetts, but could not by train because of the infectious character of his disease. Whereupon Butler sailed the yacht to New York as fast as she would go, fetched his daughter and grandson back to Bay View with him, and there the youngster quickly recovered.

Sadly, Butler could do nothing toward assisting Ben Israel in regaining his health. While at West Point, or serving in the army, or studying law at Columbia—somewhere along the line —this younger son of Butler's had fallen victim to a malady eventually diagnosed as Bright's disease, and at that stage of efficacy in the art of medicine the disease had a high rate of mortality. On September 1, 1881, the day appointed for Ben Israel to enter his father's office and become his law associate, the young man died.

During the summer of 1882, Butler and his *America* received nationwide attention as the result of a race in which the yacht was pitted against a full-rigged 1,700-ton ship capable of setting sails containing 7,000 square yards of canvas. The ship, the *North American,* out of Boston, had recently made a record run between Liverpool and San Francisco.

Colonel Henry Hastings, owner of the *North American,* was a close friend of Butler's. During the race, which began off Boston on August 1, Hastings sailed aboard his vesel; Butler commanded the *America;* and distributed between the ship and the yacht were numerous passengers—among them young Paul Butler; Prentiss Webster, a law partner of Butler's; Thomas E. Major and E. C. Carrigan, Butler's secretaries; Frederick Smyth, a former Governor of New Hampshire; William Eaton Chandler, also of New Hampshire, currently Secretary of the Navy in the Cabinet of President Arthur; and James Parton, who from now on, as Butler's close confidant, helped him wield his pen.

The ship and the yacht ran out into the Atlantic for 300 miles. The winds were wholly favorable to the *America,* and she literally sailed circles around the *North American,* a vessel almost exactly ten times her size. Then the two parted, with the yacht returning all passengers to Boston and the *North American* continuing on her way overseas laden with cargo. This cargo consisted of an enormous quantity of railroad iron which, causing the ship to lie deep in the water, had interfered with her speed—an impediment omitted by Butler in his boastful accounts to the press of how his midget yacht had beaten the giantess.

The news stories emerging from this race served as openers in a poker game of publicity played by Butler in his attempt, once again, to get himself elected Governor of Massachusetts. The other cards he held bore the spots of determination and persistence, qualities a substantial portion of the Bay State voters could not help admiring.

In the past, Butler had been defeated partly through the efforts of two brothers, Ebenezer and George Hoar, both of whom had attended Harvard as undergraduates and later as law students. For nearly thirty years, George Hoar served as U.S. Senator from Massachusetts, and Ebenezer, long an Associate Justice of the Massachusetts Supreme Judicial Court, later became a U.S. Attorney General.

The Hoar-Butler feud had started long ago at a political meeting during which some speaker made mention of the practice at Harvard of naming new buildings—called "houses"—after prominent college benefactors. Butler, amused by a pun that had occurred to him, got to his feet and asked: "Sir, do you suppose Harvard will ever have a Hoar House?"

In spite of Hoar opposition, Butler won the election of November 8, 1882, and was sworn in as Governor on January 4 of the year following. However, all of the honors of the office did not accrue to him. While for more than a century it had been traditional for each new Governor of Massachusetts to attend the June graduation ceremonies at Harvard and have conferred upon him an LL.D., Harvard's Board of Overseers, headed by Judge Ebenezer Hoar, refused to sanction awarding the degree to Butler.

Nevertheless, Charles W. Eliot, the President of Harvard, invited Butler to the graduation ceremonies and to the alumni dinner following—a move that caused Senator George Hoar, president of the Alumni Association, to declare that he would not attend if Butler accepted the invitation.

In the face of that, nothing could have kept Butler away. Moreover, having determined to go, he went in great style. Clad in a silk topper, frock coat, and striped trousers, he rode in an open barouche drawn by six high-stepping horses and accompanied by an honor guard of mounted militiamen uniformed as lancers. In the end, Butler got an LL.D.; in 1888 the degree was awarded him by a Harvard rival—Dartmouth.

While Governor of Massachusetts, Butler did no sailing. The *America* lay off Boston and was occasionally used by his friends and employees. Also, Butler sailed only rarely in 1884, for it was during that year that he ran for President on the Greenback Party ticket and received less than one vote for every fifty cast for his opponents—Blaine, the Republican candidate, and Cleveland, the winning Democrat. The crushing experience taught Butler a lesson. Never again did he seek public office.

In 1886, Butler had the *America*'s bottom recoppered and a torpedo-shaped lead keel bolted to a portion of her old keel of wood. This work, together with the installation of a new rig and a new suit of sails, was carried out in accordance with the dictates of Edward Burgess, who had lately come into prominence as the designer of the sloop *Puritan,* which had successfully defended the America's Cup. Earlier, Burgess had been more interested in insects than in yachts, and from 1879 until 1883 he taught entomology at Harvard. It seems doubtful that Butler knew of this. For feeling as he did, the likelihood is that he would not have permitted a former Harvard faculty member to instruct him concerning the size or set of the *America*'s masts, booms, gaffs, or bowsprit, or how her bottom should be coated or her ballast carried. In which event, the yacht probably would have fared just as well. Indeed, as matters stood, she could not have fared much worse. After receiving her Burgess-inspired alterations, she came in first in only one race of the remaining ten she ran during Butler's lifetime.

This race took place toward the end of the yachting season, on September 17, 1887, in Massachusetts Bay. The *America*'s lone adversary, the *Gitana,* owned by William Weld of the Boston shipping family, was a handsome schooner of such superior size that Butler could have demanded a substantial time allowance had he not been too vain to do so. The race was for $500 a side, over a triangular course measuring 30 miles, and turned out to be thoroughly exciting. At the end of the first leg, the *Gitana* ran better than 6 minutes ahead, and by the end of the second the *America* had made this up and stepped out front by more than a mile. Then, on the third, the *Gitana* again caught up, and as the flying vessels neared the finish line, rare was the spectator unwilling to call the race a draw. The judges, however, saw it otherwise. They pronounced the *America* winner by 20 seconds.

Later in 1887, Butler tripped and suffered a serious fall—not aboard his or any other yacht, but in a Philadelphia railroad station—and he was hospitalized with a dislocated shoulder. At around the same time, his sight began failing, and henceforth, wherever he traveled, he was accompanied by one or another of his male secretaries to take dictation, and by Albert West, his valet. In spite of his impediments, Butler cruised aboard the *America* briefly during the summers of 1888 and 1889, and in 1890 he went off on a long cruise that lasted from mid-July until the end of August.

On July 30, 1890, George L. Schuyler came up from New York to New London, Connecticut, by train for a visit to the fleet of the New York Yacht Club lying at anchor there. Since the death in 1878 of James A. Hamilton, his father-in-law, Schuyler was the sole surviving member of the syndicate responsible for ordering the yacht *America* built forty years before.

At New London, Schuyler went aboard Commodore Elbridge T. Gerry's huge steam yacht *Electra,* the flagship of the fleet, where he dined and retired for the night. The next morning he was found dead in his cabin, and the fleet surgeon attributed his death to a heart attack. In Schuyler's obituaries no mention was made of the merciless bargain he had driven with the *America*'s designer and builder. Certain of the obituaries did state, however, that Schuyler's daughter Louisa had been for over twenty years New York City's most dedicated volunteer social worker.

During 1891, Ben Butler used the *America* for cruising, but not for racing. On October 17, James Parton died after an illness of a few weeks at his home in Newburyport, Massachusetts. But by this time the writing of Butler's memoirs was done, the manuscript had been delivered to the publisher, and the book —called simply *Butler's Book*—appeared early in 1892.

The book runs to nearly twelve hundred pages. Page 869 is occupied by a pen-and-ink drawing of the *America* captioned: GENERAL BUTLER'S YACHT AMERICA—ORIGINAL WINNER OF THE AMERICA'S CUP AND BLOCKADE RUNNER DURING THE WAR. But beyond this there is no mention whatsoever of the vessel in the book, nor of Butler's interest in yachting. Perhaps the author felt that if he spoke at all of the *America* in the text, his readers would expect him to tell how he got her. And perhaps he also felt that even after the passage of nearly twenty years it would be better not to relate in print the details of that unorthodox transaction.

Butler cruised aboard the *America* during the summer of 1892. However, he ventured no farther than the waters off New England, and often he was accompanied by a physician. In September, on taking leave of the yacht for the season, Butler was heard to say, "Goodby, old girl. God only knows whether I shall ever set foot on your deck again."

In early January 1893, Butler traveled to Washington, and

on the ninth of the month he argued a case before the U.S. Supreme Court. The next day, in spite of the bitterly cold weather, he visited numerous Government offices and that evening arrived for dinner at his New Jersey Avenue home exhausted. He retired early, but was awakened an hour after midnight by a violent fit of coughing. His valet summoned a doctor, who found him suffering from a bronchial hemorrhage that could not be stanched. He died at 1:30 A.M. on January 11.

At Lowell, Massachusetts, Butler's home town, his body lay in state for several days. Thousands of mourners, many of them veterans of the Union Army, filed past the casket; the city's fire bells tolled 74 times, a stroke for each year of Butler's age; and floral tributes arrived from many areas of the country, including one from the Massachusetts State Penitentiary sent by its inmates.

The *New York Tribune* estimated Butler's wealth at $7,000,000; *The Times* said, "For twenty years he was the leading low comedian of American politics"; and the *Boston Evening Post* declared, "If his morals and political character had been equal to his intellectual versatility, he might have been one of the great historical figures of the period."

Judge Ebenezer Hoar, when asked whether he would attend Butler's funeral, replied, "No, but I approve of it."

EIGHT

"Proceeded Proudly to Her Final Berth"

After the death of Ben Butler, the *America* went into mourning for him, and the period during which she displayed her sorrow, by means of respectful inactivity, lasted for roughly four years. With her deck swathed over by canvas coverings and with a peripatetic watchman keeping an eye on her, she lay dolefully anchored near the bridge connecting the Chelsea and Charlestown areas of Greater Boston. Not much more than a half-mile away she had an acquaintance only four years her junior, but many times her size. This was the 3,274-ton U.S. steam frigate *Wabash,* a creature with a hull of wood, launched back in 1855. Supplanted by steel-sided vessels, the *Wabash,* while no longer of value to the Navy as a cruiser, served very well in her present capacity as a receiving ship for recruits at the Charlestown Navy Yard. Had they possessed tongues and the power of recollection, the *America* and the *Wabash* would have had a lot to talk over, like garrulous old Civil War veterans throughout the land. There were those brave and stirring times, for instance, when the *Wabash* had been the flagship of Admiral Du Pont's South Atlantic Blockading Squadron and the *America* had served in that squadron as a blockading vessel off the coast of South Carolina.

As one of his father's principal heirs, Paul Butler now owned the *America.* However, his widespread business activities kept him so occupied that he eventually faced up to the fact that he would rarely, if ever, find time to make use of her. Consequently, in the spring of 1897, he turned her over to his nephew, Butler Ames (the son of General Adelbert Ames and the former Blanche Butler), who had first graduated from West Point and then taken an advanced degree in engineering from the Massachusetts Institute of Technology.

Butler Ames had the *America* refitted, and to sail her he employed an experienced captain and crew. As a tribute to his late grandfather, he took her first to Bay View, where the populace of the area came aboard in large numbers and picnicked on her deck. Then the *America* visited New York City and cruised up the Hudson. At Poughkeepsie she laid over for a few days, and Ames witnessed nautical contests considerably removed from yacht racing—the annual intercollegiate rowing regatta. That year, over the 4-mile Poughkeepsie course, the eight stalwart oarsmen manning the shell entered by Cornell defeated their opponents from Columbia and Pennsylvania.

Early in his yachting career, Butler Ames became a member of the Boston Yacht Club, the Massachusetts Yacht Club, and the Corinthian Yacht Club of Marblehead. In September 1897, he entered the *America* in a series of races for schooners of her class staged by the Corinthian, for a prize of a silver cup offered by Nathaniel Nash, the Commodore of the Club, and consequently called the "Nash Cup." The series consisted of three runs, one on each of three successive days, the first from Marblehead to Gloucester, the next from Gloucester to Hull, and the last from Hull back to Marblehead.

Five schooners participated. The *America* won the first race, but lost the second to *Adrienne* and the third to *Puritan*, the Burgess-designed yacht which had successfully defended the America's Cup against the British challenger *Genesta* in 1885. With a three-cornered tie on its hands, the Corinthian Club scheduled a run-off race, amid much bewilderment. The fact that the *America*, nearly a half-century old, had so far held her own against craft of comparatively recent conception and build caused gambling yachtsmen throughout New England to wonder now whether to bet with her or against her and how to figure the odds.

Those who bet with her proved themselves blessed by the sea gods, although for a time it looked as though the *America* had been shorn of her chance of winning. Well along in the race, a malevolent gust of wind snapped her fore-topmast, and when the wreckage came crashing down, fouling her rigging, many of her backers among the spectators gave up hope. Her crew, however, showed themselves not so fainthearted, and almost as quickly as the accident occurred, got the debris cleared away. The *America* crossed the finish line 2 minutes ahead of the *Adrienne* and a comfortable 5 minutes ahead of the *Puritan*.

The story made headlines throughout the nation, for a rare thing is it for a superannuated yacht to show such agile rejuvenation. But had the incident occurred a few months later —in late February 1898—few newspapers would have found space to tell of it. The story of another American vessel, the battleship *Maine*, occupied front pages all across the land.

On February 15, while on a "visitation of peace" to Cuba, the *Maine* struck a "Spanish implanted mine" in the harbor of Havana and blew up, with a loss of life to the U.S. Navy of two officers and 264 enlisted men. The ghastly incident brought to a head the long-festering enmities between the United States and Spain, and in April resulted in official pronouncements of war.

As inactive but regularly commissioned officers in the U.S. Army, both Adelbert Ames and his son Butler hustled into uniform, reported for duty, and were sent off to Cuba. In their absence, Blanche Ames and her brother Paul Butler got the yacht *America* into shape for use by the Navy in Spanish-American waters if needed. However, the active phase of the war ended before the Navy could make up its mind whether to accept or reject the patriotic offer.

Even so, the *America* saw useful service in an aftermath of the war. While victory for the United States had been gained with but few of her combatants killed or wounded in the fighting, many returned suffering from malaria and other tropical fevers, and the Government set up huge camps for these invalids far out on the eastern end of Long Island. General Adelbert Ames, with headquarters at Montauk, on one arm of Gardiner's Bay, took charge of the recreational activities of ambulatory convalescents, and was joined there by his wife, son, and brother-in-law—and the fully-manned yacht *America.*

This was not the first time the *America* had entered the waters of Gardiner's Bay on war-connected duty. Indeed, she had been there 34 years before, during the last summer of the Civil War, and had kept a vain watch for Confederate raiders thought to be headed (in imitation of Charlie Read's earlier exploits) for the New England coast.

But now the *America's* work was not that of a sentinel. Unarmed, she made short cruises in fair weather over the waters of the Bay and Long Island Sound, and lolling on her deck enjoying the healthful sea air were those veterans of Santiago, Guantanamo, Siboney, and Daiquiri deemed well enough by their doctors to go for a sail.

With the coming of fall, the *America* returned to Boston and was laid up for the winter at her old anchorage near Chelsea Bridge. In early 1899, Butler Ames received an accolade never awarded his grandfather. He was elected a member of the New York Yacht Club. And his election, of course, affected the status of the yacht *America.* Now, after an intermission of nearly half a century, she was entitled to fly the pennant she had flown at the start of her long career.

In 1899 the Club had as its headquarters a three-story brick house, once a private residence, at 67 Madison Avenue, in the heart of New York City. But this house, purchased fifteen years before, had already proved too small for the Club's burgeoning membership. The building of a much larger and grander clubhouse on West 44th Street between Fifth and Sixth Avenues was already under way. Commodore J. Pierpont Morgan, the international banker, had donated the land (in itself worth a fortune), and on January 19, 1901, the Club moved into its new home, which it continues to occupy today.

In 1899 (as at present) the Club also maintained a number of subsidiary clubhouses (or "stations," as they are termed) close to the water in various yachting areas. These were located on Long Island, at Newport, Rhode Island, at New London, Connecticut, and elsewhere. Thus in the summer of 1899, after Butler Ames had put the *America* in commission for the season, he sailed for New London to join the New York Yacht Club fleet.

On the way, a storm sprang up, and in riding it out the *America* again had trouble with her fore-topmast. When a gust of wind hit, the sturdy spar snapped as though made of an elongated matchstick. Had he been superstitious, Butler Ames might have read into the accident a foreboding that the *America*'s days as a trophy-winning yacht were over—and it so happened that just such an eventuality proved to be the case.

On August 9 the *America* ran with the Club yachts from New London to Newport and finished sixth among the seven schooners in her class. Later in August, she lost two other intramural Club contests, and then forsook racing for the season in favor of a cruise to New York.

On September 26, while anchored in New York Harbor, the *America*—with red, white, and blue bunting strung from her spars and with her "Lady Pummel" cannon firing successive rounds of blanks—paid tribute to a naval officer, now a national hero, who had not seen her since sailing her at the Naval Academy some thirty years before. The officer was Admiral George Dewey. After bringing to its knees the Spanish fleet in Manila Bay, Dewey had modestly remained in the Orient for over a year, and now, on his return home, faced the tortures to which America invariably subjects her foremost heroes: interminable parades, bilious banquets, and equally indigestible orations of welcome in city after city throughout the land.

On October 5, while still at New York, Butler Ames had aboard the *America*, as his guest, Sir Thomas Lipton. This canny Glasgow merchant of Irish parentage had been knighted the year before by Queen Victoria following his contribution of £20,000 to the "Diamond Jubilee" celebration commemorating the fiftieth year of Her Majesty's reign. Lipton's visit to the United States in 1899, at the age of 49, was not his first. He had come long ago as an immigrant youth, had labored at such jobs as driver of a horse-drawn streetcar in New Orleans and as a grocer's clerk in other cities, and had returned to Britain with his scant savings and a headful of valuable knowledge. The latter included a big parcel of awareness that in virtually any enterprise astute advertising pays off, and that if such advertising can be obtained free—or by means of a discount facsimile known as publicity—so much the better.

Perhaps from the start Sir Thomas had a genuine interest in yacht racing, perhaps not. In any event, he saw in the sport a means of getting his name before the public, and since the Lipton name was synonymous with the brands of tea, coffee, gin, whiskey, and canned meats he purveyed internationally, he expanded his nautical activities beyond the British Isles to the more populous United States.

Lipton came to New York in 1899 in the role of challenger for the America's Cup, bringing with him his yacht *Shamrock* as the challenging vessel. To race the *Shamrock,* in a best two-out-of-three match, the New York Yacht Club appointed as Cup defender the *Columbia.* The first race was scheduled for October 16, and on the fifth of the month, when Butler Ames had Sir Thomas aboard the *America,* it was to show him the waters off Sandy Hook over which the series of races would soon be sailed.

Lipton lost the match, much to his public disgust, but perhaps to his greater private pleasure. For had he won, formality would have demanded that he claim the Cup and take it back to Britain. In that event, he could not have challenged for it again, thus terminating an immensely valuable publicity campaign. As matters stood, however, he *was* able to challenge again—in 1901 with *Shamrock II,* in 1903 with *Shamrock III,* in 1920 with *Shamrock IV*, and finally in 1930 with *Shamrock V*. By this time, Sir Thomas was not merely a knight, but had been long since created a baronet. Moreover, he was 80, tired of sailing, and no doubt equally tired of piling up millions.

Butler Ames did not put the *America* in commission during the yachting season of 1900. The following year, however, she was readied in July and joined the New York Yacht Club squadron at its Glen Cove, Long Island, station. In July, she entered and lost three Club races—the third by 20 minutes to the schooner *Corona* over a course of 37 miles.

This was the *America*'s swan song as a racing yacht. She sang it a month shy of a half-century after winning her Cup at Cowes back in 1851. The wonder is not that the old girl's voice was cracked, but that considering her age she could sing at all.

Like his famous maternal grandfather, Butler Ames soon displayed political ambitions. He joined the Massachusetts State Militia and as a West Point graduate rapidly advanced to a generalship. His rank assured him, should he run for some civilian office, of a substantial vote, and he consequently announced himself a candidate for Congress. Elected, he served his constituents so well that he was re-elected over and over again.

Butler Ames's dedication to his Congressional duties and his family's widespread business interests left him no time for yachting. From 1901 until 1912 the *America* lay unused off Chelsea Bridge, Boston, and then for five additional years she suffered a period of similar inactivity at another anchorage—in Fort Point Channel, near a bridge connecting South Boston with the central part of the city.

This 1912 shift occurred virtually coincident with the arrival in New York of a decorative artifact from the *America* lost in England many years before. The artifact was the original gilded eagle, with wings spread and claws clutching a shield, arrows, and a furled banner of Stars and Stripes, which had graced the *America*'s stern from the time of her launching until shortly before 1858, when Henry Sotheby Pitcher, of Northfleet, bought the yacht from Viscount Templetown.

The eagle disappeared while the *America* lay unused at the Isle of Wight and years later turned up hanging as a sign near the entrance of a hotel called "The Eagle" at Ryde. Eventually, with a view toward presenting the decorative carving to the New York Yacht Club, the Royal Yacht Squadron challenged the right of the hotel proprietor to possess it and somehow (through purchase, persuasion, or threat of court action) wrested it from him.

But once the Squadron got the eagle, its members proved dilatory about packing it up and shipping it to New York—and many more years passed. Then finally, in 1912, when a Squadron member, Cromartie Leveson-Gower, the 4th Duke of Sutherland (who had been born, incidentally, in 1851, the year the *America* won her Cup) announced his plans for a trip to New York, his fellow Squadronites prevailed upon him to take the bird along.

So he did—and in an appropriate ceremony presented the eagle to the Club, and received in return a lavish dinner and an official letter of thanks. Today the eagle, mounted on a plaque and still proudly clutching shield, arrows, and furled banner, hangs prominently placed in the West 44th Street clubhouse of the New York Yacht Club, on the east wall near the main stairway.

Eventually the members of the Ames and Butler families grew tired of maintaining the *America* unused. Also, they had been mentioned in news stories deploring the possibility that the yacht, lying where she lay, might fall victim to rot. In time, a representative of the families announced that they would be willing to sell the *America,* provided they received a satisfactory offer.

But meanwhile the United States had become embroiled in the World War—"Mr. Wilson's World War"—which began officially for this country on April 6, 1917, and along with the disruption of other pleasurable pursuits put an end to salt-water yachting all along the Atlantic Coast. There were consequently no bids for the *America* from sportsmen, and so a representative of the Butler and Ames families placed the yacht in the hands of a broker.

He soon received not a high, but a reasonable, offer that when passed along to the owners proved acceptable, and a small sum of money binding the deal changed hands. The prospective purchasers were a group of Cape Verde Islanders who planned to use the yacht as a trading vessel, sailing her back and forth between New England and their home waters loaded with all manner of commercial products.

News of the impending sale reached the ears of Charles Henry Wheelwright Foster (A.B. *cum laude,* Harvard '81) and he was shocked. One of the more proper of "Proper Bostonians," Foster had founded and served as president of the Brookline National Bank; he sat on the directorial boards of various railroads and manufacturing enterprises throughout New England; and in company with his sons he was an enthusiastic yachtsman and a member of the Eastern Yacht Club and the New York Yacht Club.

To Foster's way of thinking, it was nothing short of sacrilege for the *America* of hallowed memory to wind up her days as a drudge in lowly trade. He had seen the Cup defender *Puritan* go that way and had ever since regretted not having heard of the transfer in time to halt it. But now in the case of the *America* he believed that should he act quickly and diplomatically he stood a fair chance of saving the day.

Foster and his representatives scouted around and found for sale a commercial schooner newer, larger, sounder, and in all other respects more suitable as an ocean-going cargo carrier than the *America.* Foster took an option on her, got on the right side of the broker acting as go-between with the Cape Verde Islanders, and rose from the bargaining table victorious, with all concerned satisfied.

Now owner of the *America,* Foster moved her to the basin of George Lawley & Son, the Boston shipbuilders. He had never thought well of the torpedo-shaped bulb of lead bolted to her keel back in 1886 when Ben Butler caused her to be refitted, and consequently had it removed. Later, as the involvement of the United States in the World War deepened, these twenty or more tons of lead found their way to a munitions factory and from there, in the form of bullets, to such areas of conflict as Chateau Thierry, Belleau Woods, St. Mihiel, and Meuse-Argonne.

After World War I, the *America* continued lying in the Lawley basin, with Foster uncertain as to just what to do with her. He did not believe that regardless of how much money might be spent on her, she could ever again be put in condition as a first-class racing yacht. While the thought occurred to him that surely it would be fitting for the *America* to go on permanent display, perhaps at some nautical museum, he received no overtures to his liking from any such nonprofit institution.

Foster's problem was resolved for him in the spring of 1921, as the result of a conversation between William U. Swan, a Boston-based writer on yachting for the Associated Press, and Elmer Jared Bliss, founder and president of the Regal Shoe Company chain, whose yacht *Verona* had not long since won a race to Bermuda. These two, talking one night over after-dinner coffee and cigars, concluded that the Naval Academy was the proper place for the *America* to be enshrined, since it afforded facilities for her maintenance and public display, and since, too, she legally belonged there and would, indeed, still be there but for the machinations of Ben Butler and Secretary Robeson back in 1873.

Swan, soon after his exchange of views with Bliss, approached Foster and found him more than willing to contribute the yacht, provided the Navy agreed to accept her and arrangements could be made to put her in shape for a safe voyage to Annapolis. Swan knew just the man capable of pulling all the right strings—Robert Means Thompson, who had graduated from the Naval Academy and Harvard Law School, had served on the

Boston Common Council and as president of the Naval Academy Alumni Association, had been chairman of the American Olympic Association and donor of the Thompson Cup played for annually by the West Point and Annapolis football teams.

Although past 70, Thompson welcomed the proposed project as grist for his still-energetic mill. He quickly secured the necessary permissions and assurances of acceptance from the Navy Department and the Naval Academy. Then since Foster, a man of modesty, did not wish to appear as sole donor of the yacht, Thompson arranged with Herbert Mason Sears (A.B., Harvard '89), a member of the New York Yacht Club and Commodore of the Eastern Yacht Club, for the *America* to be registered as nominally the property of the Eastern. Lastly, Thompson formed an "*America* Restoration Fund Committee" to receive contributions needed to put the yacht in good enough shape for her trip from Boston to Annapolis and to pay her expenses en route.

Swan, of the Associated Press, served as secretary of the Committee, and Charles Francis Adams (A.B. *cum laude*, Harvard '88) was its chairman. The year before, Adams, the great-great-great-grandson of President John Adams, had been helmsman aboard the *Resolute* in defending the America's Cup against the challenger *Shamrock IV*, and a few years hence he would become Secretary of the Navy in the Cabinet of President Hoover. Adams loved yachting, not for its fancy social side, but for the opportunity it gave him to get outdoors and pit his wits against his fellow yachtsmen and the sea. His nephew, George Homans, sailed with him as a boy and in the July 1965 *Atlantic Monthly* contributed a delightful recollection of his disgust with the frivolities and frills adorning many yachts, of which the following is but a brief quotation:

> His method was characteristically elimination rather than addition. He was above all death on superfluous weights. When he bought a boat secondhand he went over her with a screwdriver taking off useless gadgets and dumping them unceremoniously overboard.... All cushions and mattresses went the

same way: should anyone want to lie down, there were always the sail bags, which were in fact much more comfortable. He would have been glad to get rid of the heads, and the boats he had built for himself never had one. Even for crowded waters, a canvas bucket was just as good. In brief, he was, in his care for speed the supreme rationalist, the supreme functionalist.

Others who, following the lead of Adams, contributed to the *America* Restoration Fund included:

Willard Herbert Brownson, mentioned previously in this narrative as the Naval Academy first classman who had sailed the *America* back to Annapolis from Newport during the summer following the close of the Civil War. Brownson, made a Rear Admiral in 1905, had subsequently served as Commander-in-Chief of the Asiatic Squadron, and then after nearly fifty years in the Navy had resigned to act as a director of the International Nickel Company.

Louis Adams Frothingham, a Boston lawyer related to Charles Francis Adams.

Arthur Curtiss James (M.A., Amherst '89), Chairman of the Board of the Western Pacific Railroad and a Vice-President of the Phelps Dodge Corporation. He was a member of the Atlantic Yacht Club, the New York Yacht Club, and the Seawanhaka Corinthian Yacht Club. From 1902 until 1907 he had been Commodore of the Seawanhaka and during 1909 and 1910 he was Commodore of the New York Yacht Club.

Demarest Lloyd (A.B., Harvard '04; Harvard Law '07), for many years diplomatic correspondent of *The Christian Science Monitor,* based formerly in London and presently in Washington. He was a member of the Eastern Yacht Club and the New York Yacht Club.

Edgar Palmer (B.S., Princeton '03). He was Chairman of the Board of the New Jersey Zinc Company and a director of six railroads, five public utilities, and three banks. His ten clubs included the American Yacht, the Eastern Yacht, the Larchmont Yacht, and the New York Yacht.

Thomas Nelson Perkins (A.B., Harvard '91; Harvard Law '94). He was Chairman of the Executive Committee of the Boston & Maine Railroad and a director of the American Telephone & Telegraph Co., of General Foods, and of several banks. Although a member of numerous clubs, he belonged to no yacht clubs.

Herbert Mason Sears (A.B., Harvard '89). He was First Vice-President of the Suffolk Savings Bank of Boston, a director of the Northeastern Trust Company of Boston, and a director of the Boston & Albany Railroad. For his distinguished service in World War I the French Government awarded him the *Croix de Guerre.* His clubs included the Eastern Yacht and the New York Yacht.

Henry Walters (Harvard '73). A man so reticent as to appear shy, and yet possessed of enormous wealth. He maintained offices in Baltimore and New York and residences in these cities and elsewhere. He was Chairman of the Board of the Atlantic Coast Line Railroad and of the Louisville & Nashville Railroad, and held controlling stock in both systems and in other rail complexes throughout the South. He served as a trustee of the New York Public Library and of the Metropolitan Museum of Art, and owned a huge collection of paintings and sculpture, which he continually added to while traveling in Europe three months each year. He also owned the steam yacht *Narada,* and, although a close friend of Sir Thomas Lipton, he regularly gave financial support to the syndicates building America's Cup defenders.

Along with contributions from individuals, the *America* Restoration Fund received gifts from the Newport Chamber of Commerce, from the New London Chamber of Commerce, and from fourteen yacht clubs based in Pennsylvania, New York, and New England. With all this heavy, dedicated backing, the Fund was soon oversubscribed, for the amount needed to put the *America* in good enough shape to make the trip of but a few hundred miles was by no means staggering. Although she received a requisite number of coats of paint and caulking for her seams, she was not given a new keel or inside ballast of such weight as to supplant the loss of her outside bulb keel of lead contributed to the 1917–18 war effort. Without such ballast, her sails could not be set or even her masts stepped, lest her delicate balance be so disturbed as to cause her to capsize. Consequently, when she was finally ready for her journey south, she was towed by a vessel supplied by the Navy—the submarine chaser *408,* commanded by Ensign Donald M. Weaver, of Portland, Maine.

In a story dated Boston, September 10, *The New York Times* for the following day—Sunday, September 11, 1921—told of the *America's* activities on the front page of its sports section, saying in part:

> The schooner yacht *America* set out on her last voyage today. The boat which went to England seventy years ago and brought back the Cup that has since become the classic trophy of yachting competition the world over is bound for Annapolis, there to be turned over to the Government for preservation at the Naval Academy.
>
> The *America's* sailing days are over and it was with masts lashed to her deck and sails stowed away that she started on her final cruise . . . the itinerary of which includes stops at many ports between here and Annapolis in the next twenty days. . . .
>
> Arrived at Annapolis, the *America* will be delivered to Secretary [of the Navy Edwin] Denby by Charles Francis Adams, skipper of the *Resolute* in the latest defense of America's Cup. Mr. Adams, as Chairman of the *America* Restoration Fund . . . will receive in return $1, the Government's nominal purchase price.
>
> As the *America* came up the harbor to a wharf here, boys at the Farm and Trade School at Thompson's Island lined the shore, and, with their band playing, sang "America." The passage through harbor shipping was accompanied by a nautical ovation. At the dock, "America" was again sung and sounded by bugle; yachting enthusiasts at this, the *America's*, home port for nearly half a century had a last look at her; the homeward-bound pennant was raised and she was given over to the boys of the Pleon Yacht Club, junior yachting champions of Massachusetts Bay, to command. The old yacht then was taken in tow by the sub-chaser and started for her first port of call, Marblehead.

The Pleon Yacht Club youngsters remained aboard the *America,* playing tag on her deck, until she put in at Marblehead, to the sound of ringing church bells and booming cannon. She lay there overnight and by the next night had reached the eastern entrance of the Cape Cod Canal. The following day, while crossing Narragansett Bay, the *America* was met and greeted by a powerboat at the helm of which stood Jesse H. Metcalf, a member of the New York Yacht Club and a trustee of Brown University, who would soon become a United States Senator from Rhode Island.

On September 16, off Newport, the yacht was overhauled by the destroyer *Rodgers,* bearing Rear Admiral Ashley Herman Robertson, who during the World War had commanded the battleship *New Mexico* and was presently stationed at Newport as Chief of Staff of the Naval War College. Admiral Robertson came aboard the *America* and, just to get the feel of her, took her wheel for a short time.

At Newport the yacht was the official guest of the Chamber of Commerce and had a luncheon given in her honor. Among those who attended were Admiral William Sowden Sims and members of his staff. During the World War, Admiral Sims had commanded U.S. naval forces operating in European waters, and now, a year before his retirement, he served as President of the War College.

On September 17, at New London, the *America* was visited by Mr. and Mrs. George E. Tilford. Mrs. Tilford had as much right as anyone to come aboard, and more right than most. Before her marriage, Mrs. Tilford had been Julia Finlay, and her father, J. Beekman Finlay, as a member of the syndicate responsible for ordering the *America* built seventy years before, had shared in her initial cost.

The next day, while traversing the rough waters of Long Island Sound between New London and New Haven, the *America* came near foundering when the towline connecting her with sub chaser *408* snapped. However, quick action on the part of Ensign Weaver and his crew aboard the *408* prevented disaster. They rigged a new line, hauled in the ends of the broken hawser, and within an hour were on their way. With the weather stormy, they put in for one night at Saybrook, Connecticut, for another at New Haven, for still another at Stamford, and then crossed the Sound to the station of the Seawanhaka Corinthian Yacht Club at Oyster Bay, Long Island, where Vice-Commodore Junius Spencer Morgan (A.B., Harvard '14), a partner in J. P. Morgan & Company, gave a big dinner to celebrate the *America*'s visit.

The next day—September 22—the sub chaser *408* towed the yacht back across the western end of the Sound to Larchmont, New York, where cannon of the Larchmont Yacht Club fired a greeting, and where that evening the Club's members, with Commodore James B. Ford serving as toastmaster, held another dinner in honor of the veteran vessel. Then, on the morning of the 23rd, the *America* left Larchmont for New York City, and during this leg of her journey passed through the waters she had first known—those into which she had been launched on May 3, 1851. In telling the story, *The New York Times* for September 24 said:

> Delayed by an adverse tide, the yacht *America*, in tow of Submarine Chaser *408*, passed through Hell Gate [where nearly a century before the father of George Steers had attempted to find British gold aboard the sunken *Hussar*] and the East River early yesterday afternoon to anchor in Gravesend Bay, off the Marine and Field Club, Brooklyn. The old schooner carried on her last voyage neither masts nor standing rigging. But stepped amidships was a short jury mast, and from the truck streamed out the fifty-foot homeward-bound pennant presented to the yacht by the boys and girls of Marblehead, Massachusetts.
>
> As the *America*, lashed close beside her guardian, passed the foot of East Twelfth Street, the spot on which she was built, and from which she took the water, this pennant was dipped in salute. Old salts, who had often seen the fleet schooner in her prosperous days, took off their hats to the shorn vessel proceeding slowly, but proudly to her final berth.

The Marine and Field Club, which had secured the honor of entertaining the distinguished guest in the metropolitan district, had its launches kept busy conveying visitors to and from the *America's* gangway. William U. Swan of Boston, who was instrumental in saving the famous craft from the junk dealer and the flames [?], and who has been honorary Captain of *America* on this voyage, showed the throng of guests about the deck and narrated again and again the thrilling history of the schooner.

The *America* will start tomorrow on the last leg of her voyage to Annapolis. It had been planned to take her through the Raritan Canal and the "inside" route, but her draught, even with her lead removed, proved to be too great. Hence Sub Chaser *408* and her charge will pass out through the Narrows and make their way carefully down the coast to the mouth of the Delaware before they turn inland.

The *America* will touch at Philadelphia, to be entertained by the yachtsmen of the Quaker City, and will thence proceed to Annapolis, where she will be received by Secretary Denby in the name of the Government.

The populace of Philadelphia, treasuring as always relics of past glory, kept the *America* there for two days so that the Philadelphia Corinthian Yacht Club might have an opportunity to throw a banquet marking her visit. The delay proved fortunate, for during the course of it William U. Swan found a means of getting rid of Ben Butler's private flag—a long streamer bearing the initials "B. F. B." in white against a blue ground—which had turned up in one of the yacht's lockers. It was given to an old sailor who came aboard claiming he had been a member of the *America's* crew when Butler raced her more than thirty-five years before, and he went away happily clutching the big bundle of bunting.

To pass from the Delaware River into the upper waters of Chesapeake Bay, the *America* and the sub chaser *408* made use, on September 28, of the Chesapeake Canal, near the western end of which the yacht went hard aground. Not until after nightfall was she worked free, and on the following day she traveled serenely southward down the Bay and entered the Severn River in the early afternoon. At this point two Navy seaplanes dipped down toward her in maneuvers of welcome, and a few minutes later a flotilla of launches escorted her to her appointed moorings in Dewey Basin within the Naval Academy's precincts.

On this same day, September 29, *The New York Times* announced a change in plan for the ceremony at which the *America* would be received back into the Navy after an absence from its Ship Roster of 48 years. While Charles Francis Adams would remain as representative of the "sellers"—the Eastern Yacht Club and the *America* Restoration Fund Committee—Secretary of the Navy Edwin Denby had found his duties in Washington so pressing he would not be able to visit Annapolis on the day scheduled for the event, Saturday, October 1, and had delegated Admiral Henry Braid Wilson, Superintendent of the Naval Academy, to act in his stead.

No one who knew both Secretary Denby and Admiral Wilson lodged any complaint about the change. Wilson, who had graduated from the Naval Academy in 1881, had since seen forty years of active and honorable service in the Navy—lastly as Commander-in-Chief of the Atlantic Fleet—before his recent return to the Academy as its head. Denby, on the other hand, was a Harding appointee who many years before had become famous as a football player at the University of Michigan, and who would soon suffer senatorial accusation of having listened to the signals called by Edward L. Doheny, Albert B. Fall, and Harry Sinclair in the games they were playing with naval oil reserves at Elk Hills and Teapot Dome. However, there was nothing to indicate that Denby profited from the alleged frauds. On February 12, 1924, the *New York Tribune* said as much, with this statement: "Stupidity is the high crime and misdemeanor of which the Senate accuses Mr. Denby, and the only one."

At 10:30 on the morning of Saturday, October 1, 1921, the more than two thousand members of the Naval Academy's corps of midshipmen and their officers formed ranks along the sides of Dewey Basin. Aboard the *America*, just forward of her skylight, Charles Francis Adams stood bareheaded, with his derby in his left hand, facing Admiral Henry Braid Wilson. Nearby stood the members of Admiral Wilson's staff and William U. Swan of the Associated Press.

In but a few words typical of his Back Bay Boston reserve, Adams, as representative of the Eastern Yacht Club and of the *America* Restoration Fund Committee, presented the *America* to the Navy. Then Swan read a letter of acceptance from Secretary Denby. Next, Admiral Wilson handed Adams a one-dollar bill. Enlisted men, pulling the lanyards of the yacht's stern staff and jury mast, hauled down her club ensign from one and ran up the Stars and Stripes on the other. Finally, the Academy's band played "The Star-Spangled Banner," and that marked the end of a ceremony which had lasted for only a few minutes.

Throughout its history the U.S. Navy has had various rules concerning what it may or may not receive in the way of gifts. Ships, for instance, are not ordinarily permitted to be donated, but are acquired only through capture or purchase, except in rare circumstances. Consequently, in taking title to the *America*, it was necessary for the Naval Academy to enact the farce of "buying" her for one dollar.

The *America* Restoration Fund Committee had raised through contributions a sum of money far larger than the amount needed merely to put the yacht in good enough shape to withstand the trip from Boston to Annapolis. The excess, it was hoped, could be used to pay for a complete and thorough overhauling and refitting of the *America* after the Academy had taken possession of her. She was, in other words, not unlike a bride who enters wedlock bearing a substantial dowry.

But in this case the rich bride found her groom unable or

unwilling to accept the marriage portion she had brought. If and when money was to be spent on the *America,* it would have to be the Navy's money. Such a ruling from Navy Department higher-ups tied the hands of the Restoration Committee representatives, and they returned to Boston with their pocketbooks as bulging as when they had journeyed to Annapolis. Today there is no information extant as to what became of this excess; it probably was returned *pro rata* to contributors or spent in fostering some other worthy nautical endeavor approved by all concerned.

As a result of the Navy Department's ruling—an absurd ruling, in the view of many yachting enthusiasts—the *America* suffered. She lay in Dewey Basin with virtually nothing done to preserve her, although her masts were stepped and secured upright by guys; below deck various bulkheads separating cabins were dispensed with so that visitors aboard her might have more freedom to roam around; the installation of a permanent gangplank, railed on either side, allowed such visitors safe and easy access to her; and a brass tablet prominently affixed told of her restoration to the Naval Academy on October 1, 1921, "After 48 Years of Private Ownership."

Around 1924, a boy living near Annapolis was taken by his father to see the *America,* and he later wrote that he had found her "a sad sight," with the paint "peeling from her topsides," her "brightwork . . . badly in need of varnish, and her bilges . . . full of stagnant water." In 1930, soon after Charles Francis Adams became Secretary of the Navy in the Cabinet of President Hoover, he ordered the *America* sent to the Norfolk Navy Yard for an inspection to be followed by the submission of an estimate of what it would cost to put the yacht in a state of complete repair. The estimate rendered named a figure close to $80,000—four times as much as George Steers and William H. Brown had been paid to build the *America* back in 1851—and in that Depression year of 1930, Adams, as much as he regretted doing so, was forced to turn thumbs down on the contemplated project, on the grounds of both its economic infeasibility and its political inexpediency.

Amazingly, an article about the *America* appearing two years after this, in the May 1932 issue of *U.S. Naval Institute Proceedings*—a journal published at Annapolis and circulated among many thousands of Naval Academy alumni—made no mention whatsoever of the yacht's sadly deteriorated condition. On the contrary, a reader gathers from the general tone of the article that all was well with the *America,* and the piece ends with a sentence which, while curiously constructed, augments such an impression. The sentence reads: "So the gallant old cup winner now rides peacefully at her moorings but her decks are daily trod by admiring visitors who revere her as a cherished shrine."

In early 1941, lest the *America* keel over and sink where she lay, the Navy made a move, albeit a tardy one, to award the yacht a basic amount of repair. But many of her timbers, when dug into, were found to be as deteriorated from rot as were portions of her metal fittings from rust, and the officers in charge of the survey had to face up to the fact that the facilities of the Naval Academy were insufficient to cope with the situation.

Somehow money was wangled, either by means of a frank appeal to Washington or shaved off appropriations already received by the Academy for other purposes. Luckily, just across Spa Creek from where the *America* lay in Dewey Basin stood the Annapolis Yacht Yard, a private concern bearing a fine reputation for its skill in the building and repair of boats. The Academy contracted with this yard to tow the *America* over, haul her out, and do what could be done to repair and refit her within the limits of an agreed-upon sum.

The yacht withstood the towing complacently enough, but when introduced to the marine railway and made aware of the fact that she would soon be required to forsake her watery cloak and immodestly show her bottom, she complained bitterly. Indeed, on being hauled out, the end of her stern dropped several inches. This was the overhang part added by order of Ben

Butler. The timbers of her original stern proved sound, as did her oaken keel and the teak planking in those areas of her hull which had not been disturbed since leaving the hands of George Steers ninety years before.

The yard in which the *America* found herself was a busy one, for war raged in Europe and in the Orient, and the United States had need of the sort of torpedo boats the yard had geared itself to produce, against the probability that Hitler and Tojo would soon strike in the direction of the North American continent. As a result, the workmen in the yard applied themselves to the *America* only occasionally, tearing out those areas of her deck, hull, and ribs found to be unsound, when not called upon to perform duties of a more urgent nature.

In the yard, supported in an upright position by scaffolding, the yacht occupied a piece of ground near the main shop. As winter closed in, the yard's workmen, in their off hours, built over the *America* a tall and heavy shed that had a double purpose. It protected from the elements both the yacht and the artisans occasionally engaged in attempting to make her whole and sound again. Meanwhile certain artifacts of a valuable and/or fragile nature had been removed from the *America* and stored away. These included her wheel, binnacle, skylight, companionway hatch, circular cockpit seat, decorative trailboards, and items of hardware from her rigging such as pulleys and deadeyes.

Following that fateful day, December 7, 1941, all work on the *America* came to an immediate halt. On December 8, in wake of the attack on Pearl Harbor, the United States declared war on Japan, and three days later Germany and Italy declared war on the United States. In the rush to get out more and more torpedo boats at the Annapolis yard, the *America* was all but forgotten.

Indeed, not until nearly four months later was the yacht given any consideration whatsoever. That came about on Sunday, March 29, 1942—Palm Sunday.

Annapolis, situated as far south as it is, rarely gets a really big fall of snow. However, in the early morning of Saturday, March 28, 1942, a blizzard hit the area, and the snow kept coming down throughout Saturday, Saturday night, and most of Sunday. Estimates of its depth ranged anywhere from 24 to 36 inches; tree branches split off and utility lines snapped; and the Weather Bureau chalked up the snowstorm as the heaviest ever to hit the area since the bureau had begun keeping records.

At that stage of the war, the Annapolis Yacht Yard worked seven days a week. But on Palm Sunday morning, out of a normal force of several dozen men, only fourteen were able to make it in. At around 9:30, while in a shop fitting a depth finder far forward on a torpedo boat, Captain Joe Dawson, the yard foreman, heard a crash so frightening that it sent him scurrying outside.

Where the *America* and her shed had been Dawson saw only a mountain of snow and sticks. His great fear was that some workman had been beneath the snow-laden shed when it fell, smashing the brittle skeleton of the yacht to bits. So Dawson hurried to the time clock, pulled all the cards of the men who had punched in, and then rushed around counting noses until he was able to assure himself that no one had been trapped.

This was the end of the *America*. Born on land, she died on land close to ninety-one years following her birth. A model of her, carved from one of her timbers, is today on display at the Naval Academy, as are her wheel and binnacle. Other of her artifacts of historical interest may be studied at The Mariners Museum, Newport News, Virginia, and at Mystic Seaport Museum, Mystic, Connecticut.

Portions of the *America*'s spars are included in these exhibits. Other portions came into the possession of an Annapolis antique dealer who cut them into sections and made from them the bases of handsome lamps. However, all of the bits of wood circulating around Annapolis and represented as having once been a part of the famous yacht *America* are not authentic, and one of the town's residents has warned, "If every piece of that wood had really come from the *America,* she would have been as big as the *Great Eastern.*"

The *Great Eastern,* launched in 1858, was an early ocean liner famous for her size—32,160 tons. The yacht *America,* launched in 1851 and of even greater fame as a racer, could boast but 170 tons, plus a fraction.

Sources

Books

Rear Admiral Daniel Ammen, *The Old Navy and the New* (Philadelphia, 1891).

Park Benjamin, *The U.S. Naval Academy* (New York, 1900).

Claude G. Bowers, *The Tragic Era* (Cambridge, Mass., 1920).

Francis B. C. Bradlee, *Blockade Running During the Civil War* (Salem, Mass., 1925).

Jerome E. Brooks, The $30,000,000 Cup: *The Stormy History of the Winning and Defense of the America's Cup* (New York, 1958).

James D. Bulloch, *Secret Service of the Confederate States in Europe* (New York, 1884), 2 vols.

Benjamin F. Butler, *Butler's Book* (Boston, 1892).

Branch Cabell and A. J. Hanna, *The St. John's—A Parade of Diversities* (New York, 1943).

Edward Channing, *History of the United States* (Boston, 1925), vol. 6.

Howard I. Chapelle, *The History of American Sailing Ships* (New York, 1935).

Mary Boykin Chesnut, *A Diary from Dixie* (New York, 1905), edited by Isabella D. Martin and Myrta Lockett Avary.

Captain Roland F. Coffin, *The America's Cup—How It Was Won by the Yacht America in 1851 and Has Since Been Defended* (New York, 1885).

Charles Cowley, *Industrial History of Lowell* (Boston, 1868).

Charles Cowley, *Leaves from a Lawyer's Life Afloat and Ashore* (Lowell, Mass., 1879).

T. Frederick Davis, *History of Jacksonville, Florida* (Jacksonville, 1925).

William Watson Davis, *The Civil War and Reconstruction in Florida* (New York, 1913).

George Francis Dow, editor, *Slave Ships and Slaving* (Salem, Mass., 1927).

James Alexander Hamilton, *Reminiscences of James A. Hamilton; or Men and Events, at Home and Abroad, during Three Quarters of a Century* (New York, 1869).

John W. Headley, *Confederate Operations in Canada and New York* (New York, 1906).

George F. Hoar, *Autobiography of Seventy Years* (New York, 1905).

Robert S. Holzman, *Stormy Ben Butler* (New York, 1954).

Caleb Huse, *The Supplies for the Confederate Army* (Boston, 1904).

J. D. Jerrold Kelley, *American Yachts* (New York, 1884).

A. J. Kenealy, *Yacht Races for the America's Cup–1851–1893* (New York, 1894).

Jacques and Helen LaGrange, *Clipper Ships* (New York, 1936).

Alexander A. Lawrence, *A Present for Mr. Lincoln–The Story of Savannah from Secession to Sherman* (Macon, Ga., 1961).

Thomas W. Lawson and Winfield M. Thompson, *The Lawson History of the America's Cup–A Record of Fifty Years* (Boston, 1902). Published for private distribution; edition limited to 3,000 copies.

Richard C. McKay, *Some Famous Sailing Ships and Their Builder Donald McKay* (New York, 1928).

Allan Nevins, *Hamilton Fish–The Inner History of the Grant Administration* (New York, 1936).

B. S. Osbon, *Hand Book of the United States Navy* (New York, 1864).

James Parton, *General Butler in New Orleans* (New York, 1864).

Admiral David D. Porter, *Incidents and Anecdotes of the Civil War* (New York, 1885).

Admiral David D. Porter, *Naval History of the Civil War* (New York, 1886).

Rowland H. Rerick, *Memoirs of Florida*, vol. 1, edited by Francis P. Fleming (Atlanta, 1902).

William Morrison Robinson, Jr., *The Confederate Privateers* (New Haven, 1928).

William Howard Russell, *My Diary North and South* (New York, 1863).

J. Thomas Scharf, *History of the Confederate States Navy* (New York, 1887).

General William T. Sherman, *Memoirs of General W. T. Sherman* (New York, 1875), 2 vols.

John R. Spears, *The American Slave Trade* (New York, 1900).

William P. Stephens, *American Yachting* (New York, 1904).

William P. Stephens, William U. Swan, and Winfield M. Thompson, *The Yacht 'America'* (Boston, 1925).

Herbert L. Stone, editor, *The New York Yacht Club Centennial* (New York, 1944). Privately published by the Club from data prepared by Harry L. Maxwell, a member, and with a foreword by George L. Roosevelt, Commodore.

Herbert L. Stone and Alfred F. Loomis, *Millions for Defense—A Pictorial History of the Races for the America's Cup* (New York, 1934). Limited edition of 950 numbered copies.

Herbert L. Stone and William H. Taylor, *The America's Cup Races* (Princeton, 1958).

Lately Thomas, *Sam Ward: "King of the Lobby"* (Boston, 1965).

Robert Werlich, *"Beast" Butler* (Washington, 1962).

Richard S. West, Jr., *Lincoln's Scapegoat General—A Life of Benjamin F. Butler* (Boston, 1965).

Periodicals

W. T. Adams, "*America's* Civil War Career," *The Rudder* (September, 1964).

Margaret Butterfield, "Samuel Ward, Alias Carlos Lopez," *University of Rochester Library Bulletin* (Winter, 1957).

J. B., "The *Wanderer*," *The Aquatic Monthly & Nautical Review* (New York, October, 1872).

J. B., "The *America*," *The Aquatic Monthly & Nautical Review* (New York, October, 1872).

Alexander Crosby Brown, "A Contemporary Half-Model of the Yacht *America*," *American Neptune* (Vol. 11, 1951, pp. 245–50).

Benjamin F. Butler, "The Story of the 'America,'" *Harper's New Monthly Magazine* (July, 1885).

E. B. Coddington, "The Activities and Attitudes of a Confederate Business Man: Gazaway B. Lamar," *Journal of Southern History* (Vol. IX, No. 4, 1943).

Theodore R. Davis, dispatches and drawings appearing in the issues of *Harper's Weekly* for May 4, May 18, June 1, June 8, and June 22, 1861.

Ruby R. Duval, "The Yacht *America* Now Rides Peacefully at Her Moorings," *U.S. Naval Institute Proceedings* (May, 1932).

Carlos C. Hanks, "A 'Blackbirder' That Flew the Burgee of a Famous Yacht Club," *Yachting* (October, 1946).

Thomas Robson Hay, "Gazaway Bugg Lamar, Confederate Banker and Business Man," *The Georgia Historical Quarterly* (June, 1953).

J. R. Hildebrand, "England's Sun Trap Isle of Wight," *The National Geographic Magazine* (January, 1935).

George C. Homans, "Sailing with Uncle Charlie," *Atlantic Monthly* (July, 1965).

Charles H. Jenrich, "The Checkered Career of a Gallant Lady," *Boating* (September, 1962).

J. D. Jerrold Kelley, "The Modern Yacht," *Harper's New Monthly Magazine* (August, 1883).

[Charles A. L. Lamar], "A Slave-Trader's Letter-Book," *North American Review* (November, 1886). *Note:* This album of Lamar's containing his 1856–1860 correspondence was found by one of Sherman's soldiers during the occupation of Savannah and taken North.

Malcolm D. Lamborne, Jr., "A Report on the State of 'America,'" *Yachting* (May, 1942).

Littell's Living Age (October, 1851). *Note:* This issue of the Boston periodical carried reprints of unsigned stories appearing in *The Times* of London and the *Liverpool Journal* about the August 22 Regatta at Cowes and the *America* winning her cup.

Alfred F. Loomis, "'Ah, Your Majesty, There Is No Second,'" *American Heritage* (August, 1958).

Louis Taylor Merrill, "General Butler in Washington," *Columbia Historical Society Records* (Vol. 39, pp. 71–100).

The Nautical Magazine and Naval Chronicle. This London periodical, in its September, 1851, issue, carried an unsigned story of the

America winning her cup at Cowes, and in its October, 1851, issue another unsigned story of her victory over *Titania.*

William Dana Orcutt, "Ben Butler and the Stolen Spoons," *North American Review* (January, 1918).

Marcus W. Price, "Blockade Running as a Business in South Carolina During the War Between the States, 1861–1865," *American Neptune* (January, 1949).

Marcus W. Price, "Ships That Tested the Blockade of the Georgia and East Florida Ports, 1861–1865," *American Neptune* (April, 1955).

H. K. Rigg, "Death of the America," *The Skipper* (January, 1967).

G. W. Sheldon, "The Old Ship-Builders of New York," *Harper's New Monthly Magazine* (July, 1882).

James R. Steers, "The Log of the Yacht 'America,'" *Yachting* (December, 1946, and January, 1947).

William H. Taylor, "The 'America' and Her Cup," *Yachting* (August, 1951).

Winfield M. Thompson, "The Yacht *America* and Her Cup," *The Rudder* (March, 1914).

Manuscripts and Miscellaneous

Edward Clifford Anderson Diary, 1861–1862 (Vol. 5 of *Edward Clifford Anderson Papers*), in the Southern Historical Collection, University of North Carolina Library, Chapel Hill. Entries begin on April 6, 1861; they occupy 190 large, closely written, thoroughly legible pages and conclude on March 13, 1862.

James D. Bulloch, lengthy obituary and portrait of, in *Confederate Veteran* (Vol. 9, pp. 128–130). Bulloch died in Liverpool on January 7, 1901.

Emily Forbes (Mrs. L. Victor) Froment, letters of, in the G. W. Blunt White Library, Marine Historical Association, Inc., Mystic, Conn. During 1930, Mrs. Froment, of Warrenton, Va., corresponded with William P. Stephens, a writer on yachting, concerning the voyage of her Confederate grandfather, James Heyward North, to Britain aboard the *America* (then called *Camilla*) in 1861.

James Alexander Hamilton, "Address Delivered Before the Students of the U.S. Naval Academy," pamphlet (New York, 1865).

Charles C. Hemming, portrait and accounts of the exploits of this young Jacksonville, Fla., soldier, in *Confederate Veteran,* Vol. 7, p. 110; Vol. 14, pp. 124–7; and Vol. 15, p. 457.

Investigation of the Navy Department, 44th Congress, 1st Session. *House Miscellaneous Documents,* Vol. 7, No. 170, Pt. 5, Serial No. 1704, pp. 539, 604, 605, 653 and 660 (Washington, 1876). Concerns Benjamin F. Butler, Gazaway Bugg Lamar, and the sale of the *America* at auction in 1873.

Henry Rootes Jackson, speech of, "The *Wanderer* Case," pamphlet (Atlanta, *circa* 1859).

Ray Knight, "Classic Sailing Ship Closely Linked to City," feature story about the *America* in the *Jacksonville Journal,* April 25, 1962, during the Civil War Centennial.

Gazaway Bugg Lamar, Appellate Court reports and decisions arising from cotton claim litigation, *Lamar vs. A. C. Brown, et al* (92 U.S. 187–202); *Lamar vs. McCulloch* (115 U.S. 164–88), (7 Court of Claims 603); *Lamar vs. McCoy* (115 U.S. 235–38).

James Heyward North Diary (*James Heyward North Diary and Papers*), Southern Historical Collection, University of North Carolina Library, Chapel Hill. The diary begins January 5, 1861, at Norfolk, Va., and concludes November 15 in Paris, with pages for the remainder of the year blank, missing, or occupied by trivia.

Leonard Smith, scrapbooks of. Smith, a master mariner, shipped out of Boston during the last few decades of the 19th century and in two large scrapbooks pasted up a vast number of nautical clippings from Boston papers. Today the scrapbooks are owned by his son, Frank Leon Smith, of New York City, for many years a writer in Hollywood.

James R. Steers, *Log of the Yacht America,* copy made from the original by William P. Stephens. In 1956, Eleanor Stephens, his daughter, gave the copy to the G. W. Blunt White Library, Marine Historical Association, Inc., Mystic, Conn.

Edwin Augustus Stevens, letter to his daugter Mary in Hoboken, written at Cowes on August 29, 1851, a week after the *America* won her cup. Copied from the original at the New York Yacht Club.

Commodore Thomas Holdup Stevens, USN, letter from, in the June 14, 1873, *Army and Navy Journal,* concerning the raising of the scuttled *America* in Florida eleven years before.

William Ross Wallace, speech of, "A Discourse . . . on the Genius of the Late George Steers, the Great American Ship Builder," delivered at the New York Tabernacle, February 12, 1857, and published in a hodgepodge volume, *The Loved and the Lost* (New York, 1860).

U.S. Navy Dept., *Official Records of the Union and Confederate Navies in the War of the Rebellion* (Washington, 1894–1922), 30 vols. Material concerning the *America* (occasionally called *Camilla*) and the men involved with her appears in Series I, Vols. 1, 2, 4, 5, 7–9, 12–16, and 27; and in Series II, Vols. 1–3.

U.S. War Dept., *War of the Rebellion: A Compilation of the Official Records of the Union and Confederate Armies* (Washington, 1880–1901), 128 vols. Material concerning the *America* (occasionally called *Camilla*) and the men involved with her appears in Series I, Vols. 6, 14, 26, 28, 35, 44, 47, 51, and 53; Series II, Vols. 2 and 3; Series III, Vol. 1; and in Series IV, Vols. 1–3.

Contemporary daily newspapers on both sides of the Atlantic provided substantial quantities of material, as did the British weekly magazines *Bell's Life, The Illustrated London News,* and *Punch;* the New York weekly *Spirit of the Times;* the London monthlies *Gentleman's Magazine* and *Hunt's Yachting Magazine;* and the London annual *Hunt's Universal Yacht List.*

For data on various American figures in the saga of the yacht *America,* the several editions of *Who's Who* proved indispensable, as did the twenty volumes and two supplements of the *Dictionary of American Biography.* In a like manner, facts concerning numerous Britishers involved were culled from the *Dictionary of National Biography;* Boase's *Modern English Biography;* Burke's *Landed Gentry; Landed Gentry of Ireland; Peerage, Baronetage and Knightage;* and Cokayne's *The Complete Peerage.*

Index